P9-DVX-760

Canadian Women & the
Struggle for Equality

Canadian Women & the
Struggle for Equality
Lorna R. Marsden

OXFORD
UNIVERSITY PRESS

OXFORD
UNIVERSITY PRESS

Oxford University Press is a department of the University of Oxford.
It furthers the University's objective of excellence in research, scholarship,
and education by publishing worldwide. Oxford is a registered trade mark of
Oxford University Press in the UK and in certain other countries.

Published in Canada by
Oxford University Press
8 Sampson Mews, Suite 204,
Don Mills, Ontario M3C 0H5 Canada

www.oupcanada.com

Library and Archives Canada Cataloguing in Publication

Marsden, Lorna R., 1942–
Canadian women and the struggle for equality since 1867 /
Lorna R. Marsden.

Includes bibliographical references and index.
ISBN 978-0-19-543049-3

1. Women—Canada. 2. Equality—Canada.
3. Women's rights—Canada—History. I. Title.

HQ1453.M37 2012   305.40971   C2011-907086-3

Cover image: Three woman employees arrive for work at the John Inglis plant, Toronto,
May 1941. Credit: National Film Board of Canada. Photothèque / Library and Archives
Canada

Printed and bound in the United States of America
1 2 3 4 — 15 14 13 12

Contents

Foreword

This study about social change in Canada starts with the question "Why were women ignored in the first Constitution Act of 1867?"

Historians might respond that the answer is obvious. In the nineteenth-century Western world, at the time that our constitution was framed, European women in Canada occupied a secondary position in society. Aboriginal women occupied an even lower social position. Historians have contributed greatly to our knowledge of the lives of women in Canada's past. To answer this question, I will draw on their research and, at the same time, question their conclusions.

The full explanation must show how women worked their way out of considerable inequality in just over a century. Having been preoccupied with the study of social change in Canada for many years, I have written this book in an attempt to put the question of why women and their rights were ignored in the Constitution into a different context and also to consider the particular sociological circumstances in which the major improvements in the status of women have occurred.

What has happened to reduce inequality between the sexes has come about in some unexpected ways. Women were not the only agents of change in Canada. They have had allies among men and in some world events that impinged on Canada. Women have recognized and seized opportunities as they have arisen. I cannot do justice to all the important changes that occurred, which have both reduced and perpetuated inequality. However, since that first Constitution Act of 1867, known to most people as the British North America Act, some patterns have emerged that reveal how women's organizations and some individuals have succeeded in creating lasting changes.

The study of women is especially interesting to a sociologist because, unlike other demographic groups described as minorities, women form an important part of all social classes and economic strata. Women have always been essential to the economy, and clearly families cannot be formed or maintained without them. So tracking the changes in the status of women over the decades provides insight into the dynamics of Canadian society. It shows us the profound impact of war, economic downturns, and disease on our society, and in particular, the way these powerful forces created opportunities for changes in the status of women.

The study of particular events in the history of women allows us to explore the methods of social change. There was no year, or even decade, when Canadians took collective action to alter women's secondary status. There was no revolution in thinking or behaviour and no popular revulsion at women's exclusion. Rather the process of social change in Canada is slow and accretive, with unexpected advances and sobering retreats taking place throughout our history.

This book is written primarily for undergraduate students of sociology. I have had the pleasure of working with some superb undergraduates since 1972. So many of the students I have encountered, especially those who have not grown up in a British tradition, are bewildered by Canadian society and history. Perhaps this exploration of social change in our past and present will inspire some of them to do further research on this intriguing subject.

My personal views and experiences are found throughout this book. As a keen supporter of women's equality, rights, and independence, I have been a member of feminist organizations most of my life. Having served in the Canadian Parliament as a senator from 1984 to 1992, I have observed the strengths and frustrations of our Constitution and system of government. John A. Macdonald and George Brown, two of the Fathers of Confederation, thought they were creating a nation with strong central powers. I wish they had built a constitution to achieve that goal, but instead the provinces began Confederation with very significant powers and have fought with determination to protect and expand their powers ever since.

Why would stronger federal powers be desirable? For one thing, greater geographic mobility across provincial borders and more comparable family laws would have eased the lives of women in many ways. There are clear reasons why the founding constitution was developed in the way it was: granting extensive provincial powers was the only way to bring the colonies into Confederation at all. Reading the Quebec Resolutions of 1864 that formed the basis of the constitution, one is struck by the detailed powers and privileges conferred on the former colonies. After nearly 150 years of living with this division of powers, Canadians continue to struggle over our situation.

After this manuscript was submitted to the publisher for review, the third edition of *Canadian Women: A History*[1] was published. Like its two previous editions, it is a truly marvellous work, drawing on several fields of knowledge and evidence, and it is so well-written that it can be read cover-to-cover with pleasure. So why repeat the authors of that book and other scholars, biographers, and

---

1. Gail Cuthbert Brandt, Naomi Black, Paula Bourne, and Magda Fahrni, *Canadian Women: A History*, 3rd ed. (Toronto: Nelson, 2011).

autobiographers? *Canadian Women and the Struggle for Equality* contains no original research and does not test a theory of social change. Rather, by reference to the work of others, I have attempted to expand on an earlier analysis of social change in Canada in which Edward B. Harvey and I put forward a theory of our society.[2]

Others are also attempting to look at the fabric of our society in new ways. In particular, the series of studies titled Extraordinary Canadians (edited by John Ralston Saul) is casting new light on Canada's past leaders and their contributions to how women understand themselves. In contrast to that series, this book does not single out a particular individual as an agent of change. Instead, the focus is on the means through which Canadian women have been able to move their agendas into law or common practice. These dynamics go beyond a particular social movement, such as a women's movement, and they are helped (or hindered) by social structural factors such as demography, global events, the limitations of our economy, and the powerful cultural inheritance of the British and French institutions built into our origins as a country. Given the power of these structures, the improvements in the status of women are amazing accomplishments. The determination and cleverness of so many women in seizing opportunities to change minds makes a fascinating narrative.

Many friends and colleagues have contributed to this work. In particular, my feminist colleagues—both scholars and activists—at York University, at the University of Toronto, and in women's and political organizations to which I have belonged have shaped my thinking. Without naming them individually, I acknowledge their powerful influence on my ideas and the value of their friendship. Some

---

2. Lorna Marsden and Edward Harvey, *The Fragile Federation: Social Change in Canada* (Toronto: McGraw-Hill Ryerson, 1979).

of these feminist colleagues are men, and I note with pleasure that progressive women throughout our history worked with male allies. Members of my family over four generations have caused me to think about the status of women, and studying in the United States during the Vietnam War gave me a great appreciation of the differences between our two societies in methods of social change.

Sarah Martin, Betanya Meru Tefera, and Alexandra Ross, all students at York University, provided important research assistance, and the librarians at the Frost Library and other York libraries have been extraordinary in their helpfulness. The University has provided research funding, and Joshua and Leeza Richman Gould dealt with many technical problems at short notice. I am grateful to them all.

I cannot thank enough my editor at Oxford, Jennie Rubio, whose patience and optimism about this work made it all happen. My husband, Edward Harvey, has been a listener, a constructive critic, and a support through 50 years of partnership, both personal and intellectual, for which I am enduringly grateful.

I am aware that many colleagues will not agree with the ideas in this book. That is why feminism and the women's movement in Canada continue to be so interesting. While my colleagues' many different ideas have helped to shape my ideas about this topic, I bear sole responsibility for the errors and omissions that may be in this book.

Lorna R. Marsden
Toronto, 2011

I

The Setting and the Purpose

These days the equality of women and men is not an uncommon subject of discussion. This is true not only of theorists, philosophers, and activists but ordinary people as well. We all willingly accept gender equality as an important concept in daily life. The fact that it is a widespread subject of discussion, however, does not mean that women and men are equal, or treated equally or even equitably, in our society.[1] But equality is a widespread aspiration for both men and women. We will see below how this aspiration emerged some centuries ago in the writings of British and European thinkers back across the Atlantic. Crucially, however, this aspiration was not widely accepted at the founding of our constitution.

At the time of Confederation, the law and customs of the colonies failed to protect women in many significant ways. When Canada was formed from these established colonies in the late nineteenth century, the concept of equality for women was absent. The consequence of this was that

---

1. Being equal in social status, being treated by law and custom as equal, or being treated differently but in an equitable fashion are all different but important aspects of the development of laws, regulations, and social programs in Canada. They are discussed later in this chapter.

neither laws nor customs favoured women's citizenship; women were secondary in many ways, legally, culturally, and economically.

Constitutionally speaking, equality arrived many decades after 1867. In April 1985, the equality rights sections embedded in the Canadian Constitution Act of 1982 came into effect. At this point, the concepts and aspirations associated with gender equality became an active part of one of our most important institutions—our Constitution. Unlike most parliamentary systems built on the British model of common law, the Canadian Constitution now spells out citizens' rights and freedoms in the Charter. This innovation resonates down through the many levels of government, the courts, and most of the institutions of Canadian society. It affects us all.

Since this change in our Constitution, there have been concerns about the implementation of equality rights in Canadian law and life. Legal theorists and practitioners, sociologists, psychologists, historians, school teachers and trustees, police officers, and above all parents concern themselves with questions about gender equality on a daily basis.[2] This is evidence that the ideas of gender equality have been institutionalized in our thinking.

This change in the popular mind is remarkable. In the 1860s in Canada, the concept of gender equality was confined to a very few minds. Even in the expressions of women's rights in that period, "separate but equal" or "separate spheres" was as far as most enlightened citizens would go.[3] These phrases suggested that women and men occupied entirely different

---

2. See, for example, Fay Faraday, Margaret Denike, and M. Kate Stephenson, eds., *Making Equality Rights Real* (Toronto: Irwin Law, 2009).

3. See, for example, Derrick Thomas, "The Census and the Evolution of Gender Roles in Early Twentieth Century Canada," *Canadian Social Trends*, March (2010): 40–46.

statuses within all social, political, and economic institutions—ranging from the family to Parliament and from the
lowliest occupations to the justices of the Supreme Court.
Most Canadians of any walk of life considered women to be
secondary to men in every way. Those who did not share
such views believed that it was through motherhood that
women achieved a higher moral status. In practice, however, this idea relegated women to a maternal role, denying
them any significant participation in other aspects of society.
Unlike today, only a very small minority of people gave serious consideration to women's independence and equality.

Since then, many aspects of women's lives have changed,
ranging from economic to political status and from demographic to legal conditions. Whether these changes can be
considered improvements depends on the particular issue
and viewpoint. However, over the decades, the efforts of a
number of ambitious reformers and concerned citizens have
transformed many, but not all, institutions. A good example
of this kind of transformation is the case of citizenship. Until
1946, this important legal status was based on a husband's
or father's citizenship—that is, children had the nationality of their father, and a wife was deemed to be of the same
nationality as her husband.[4] If a woman married someone
who was not a British subject, she could lose the right to
vote (along with the other rights of citizenship). It was an
important legal change when the right to vote was no longer
based on sex or marital status. Another example of a transformation is the dramatic change in the labour force. The
proportion of adult women who worked for pay increased,
and changes were made to our laws—including employment

---

4. Caroline Andrew, "Women as Citizens in Canada," in *From Subjects to Citizens:
    A Hundred Years of Citizenship in Australia and Canada*, ed. Pierre Boyer,
    Linda Cardinal, and David Headon (Ottawa: University of Ottawa Press, 2004),
    95–106.

equity and pay equity laws—which the majority of citizens expected to follow and apply. The change is not only in the dramatic increase in the proportion of women with young children in the labour force, but also in the widespread acceptance of this dual status for women.[5]

However, improved status has not come to all Canadian women in equal measure. For example, under the Indian Act, some groups of women are still treated differently by the law. The Indian Act came into effect in 1876 and has imposed limited rights, especially for women. Despite some important changes to the Indian Act since 1985, issues of property rights and family law are still contentious. The list does not end there. Not all groups of Canadians are encompassed by equity rules of behaviour. Women in some groups are caught between their rights as citizens and their cultural practices. Some religious organizations still reject many equality rights and restrict the rights and freedoms of women in Canada. In addition, while most Canadians are law-abiding citizens, not all Canadians believe in equality or practice it in their personal relationships. This clash between value systems may contribute to incidents of domestic violence, workplace problems, and differences in political ideologies. Over time, our history, laws, practices, and notions of acceptable personal behaviour have changed, but the highest of equality ideals have seldom prevailed in daily life.

How might these social changes have played out in the lives of young women at different eras in Canadian history? Let us imagine a young woman in the 1860s, one in the 1960s, and one in the contemporary period. Each of these imaginary women would face a quite different set of horizons. For each woman, life was marked by issues of access to education; to

5. For a discussion of this period of change in the labour force, see Charles Jones, Lorna Marsden, and Lorne Tepperman, *Lives of Their Own: The Individualization of Women's Lives* (Toronto: Oxford University Press, 1990).

health care, including sexual health; and to employment—all topics discussed in different chapters in this book.

In the 1860s, a young woman contemplating her future in Canada would foresee a life of marriage and children, unless she had a religious calling. This young woman might anticipate a life of very hard work as the wife of a farmer or a rancher. If she was an urban woman, she might think of working at home on piecework for the textile industry. If she were an upper-middle-class woman, she might consider how she would manage her future household in order to be a successful hostess in support of her family. Her view of her prospects of old age would be tempered by her knowledge that many women died in childbirth or of a communicable disease, such as tuberculosis. Her children would be her responsibility when they were young; although their father would control their education and other major decisions about their lives as they grew up. This woman would not have the vote for the legislatures even if she was interested in political affairs; nor in most cases would she enjoy property rights. She would be able to engage in community activities and domestic arts if she had the time and resources. In times of ill health or other crises, she would have to rely on her family and friends: maintaining those relationships would be crucial to her well-being. If our imaginary woman were an Aboriginal woman, her life would be totally different from the lives of the non-Aboriginal women of her time, except in unusual cases. Outside her own culture, she would be treated almost as a non-person and her rights would be non-existent in European terms.[6] In the dominant culture,

---

6. Exceptional cases were well known and included Aboriginal women, such as Amelia Douglas in Victoria, who were married to Europeans. Even more in the post-Confederation years than in the earlier years of the fur trade, Aboriginal women were excluded or badly treated. See, for example, Brandt et al., *Canadian Women*, 73–75.

if our imaginary woman had a sexual preference other than heterosexual, she would keep it a secret from her community, where she would attract criticism or worse.[7] If she had cancer, she would not talk about it. In some social classes, she would not talk about pregnancy until close to giving birth.

This context describes the Victorian age. Respectability would be an important personal goal. She would be judged by the values of the period, even if she did not share them. There were many reforms during the period, both in the Canadian colonies and in the mother country. Those reforms, however, did not embrace the idea of women's equality but were concerned with women's protection. So, as Lori Chambers says of the Married Women's Property Act in Ontario in 1884,

> None of the acts was motivated by any desire to emancipate women. Instead the guiding intent of legislation was to "better protect" women from the potential coercion and cruelty of their mates, to allow women to support themselves and their dependent children when husbands were absent, abusive, or economically irresponsible. Reform was popularly justified by the belief that women, being "weak and liable to be imposed upon by their husbands," required special legal protection not equal rights based on their humanity.[8]

Consider Agnes, the new wife of John A. Macdonald. Agnes and John had been married in London days before the British North America Act began its passage through the British Parliament in 1867. Like many other women, upon marriage she became a stepmother, and in her case she also became a helpmate for her husband's political career. (Macdonald's first wife had died some years earlier.) Agnes Bernard had grown

---

7. Close friendships between women, including sexual ones, were by no means unknown. See, for example, Sharon Marcus, *Between Women: Friendship, Desire, and Marriage in Victorian England* (Princeton, NJ: Princeton University Press, 2007).
8. Lori Chambers, *Married Women and Property Law in Victorian Ontario* (Toronto: The Osgoode Society/UTP, 1997), 4.

up in Jamaica and England but also lived with her mother and brother in Barrie, Ontario, so she knew what to expect of life in Canada. Her life story tells us a great deal about the contours of a woman's life in the nineteenth century.

>-⊢-◆>-◦-<◆-⊢-<

One hundred years later, in the 1960s, a young woman contemplating her life in Canada would have seen her future very differently. This young woman was very likely to have been born elsewhere and been part of the postwar immigration. She would have been encouraged in high school to think of a career, but not to the exclusion of marriage and children. Children would be viewed as her main responsibility, as they had historically been, but she and her husband would jointly make decisions about the education of their children. Her anticipation of a long and quite comfortable life—in comparison to the life of a woman living in the nineteenth century—would be justified. However, it is important to note that even in the 1960s, Aboriginal women faced much poorer life chances than other Canadian women.[9]

World War II had ended a decade or so earlier, and (like World War I) had brought a new round of changes to the lives of all women. Women who had been in the armed forces might now be settled into new work or a new life. The war had also left numerous war widows in any town or village.

Women in the 1960s had more years of education than their counterparts of a hundred years earlier, and many became teachers, nurses, or office workers, among other possible

---

9. For a discussion of the life expectancy of Aboriginal women in Canada, see Cleo Big Eagle and Eric Guimond, "Contributions that Count: First Nations Women and Demography," in *Restoring the Balance: First Nations Women, Community, and Culture*, ed. Gail Guthrie Valaskakis, Madeleine Dion Stout, and Eric Guimond (Winnipeg: University of Manitoba Press, 2009), 46–60.

careers. Those careers, however, were still sex-stereotyped and gender segregated.

Other aspects of inequality remained. In the 1960s, women could vote at all levels of government but were only rarely represented by a woman in the legislatures or the courts. Our imaginary woman's doctors would probably be men, and she would give birth to her children in a hospital. In other ways her health care was very different. For example, Canada had suffered a serious outbreak of polio in the 1950s and many people were left partially paralyzed. Tuberculosis was still a common affliction. Reproductive health was also quite different from the Victorian period. Birth control was available for married women, but it was difficult to obtain for young and unmarried women. People had more knowledge about sexual matters, and attitudes about premarital sex had become somewhat more relaxed. The movies, the high school health curriculum, and the experiences of two world wars had changed Canadian attitudes about relationships between men and women. However, if a young woman became pregnant out of marriage, and if her family could afford it, she would "visit an aunt" far away or be sent to a place that cared for "unwed mothers." If the woman's family could not afford to send her away to give birth to the child, her pregnancy would cause community criticism, and the child might be taken away for adoption or be brought up by the young woman's parents.[10] If a young woman were lesbian, she would hide that fact from her employers and most of her family and friends. She might well hide it from herself and would probably not discuss it with others. If she got breast cancer, uterine cancer, or any other cancer, she would find it hard to talk to anyone other than health providers. Any sexually transmitted disease in a

---

10. For a description of attitudes toward women and girls in the late 1960s, see Barbara M. Freeman, *The Satellite Sex: The Media and Women's Issues in English Canada, 1966–1970* (Waterloo: WLU Press, 2001).

woman—although not in a man—would be a "disgrace" even if it were treated successfully.

A married woman would have to get her husband's signature for most property or major financial transactions. She would still be dependent on her husband's income or could expect to live on modest means if single or widowed. She would almost certainly know that her income would be lower than that of her brother, not only in any given year but throughout her lifetime. In particular, in most cases her old age would be very financially constrained.

If she were the wife of the prime minister, she would not have a career but would assert her rights in the marriage and in the society. She would share the responsibility for the children but still have the role of helpmate to her husband's career, for example, appearing with him on political platforms wearing a hat and gloves. She would not be encouraged to have opinions, despite knowing that some political wives, such as Eleanor Roosevelt, wife of an American president, had strong public opinions and made her own life and work.[11] She would be expected to symbolize the values of loyalty, good works, and family commitment.

In the 1960s, women lived in the context of postwar values in which home and family and the acquisition of goods were considered important. If our young woman was following events in the world, she would be aware that the oppression of people on the basis of race was becoming a burning public issue in the United States and elsewhere. But her own rights to equality were still not widely discussed. She was not likely to consider herself the equal of a man. Even if she

---

11. Eleanor Roosevelt, married to US President Franklin D. Roosevelt, was very well known across Canada. There are several biographies about her, but see Jean Edward Smith, *FDR* (New York: Random House, 2007), and Blanche Wiesen Cook's two-volume biography, *Eleanor Roosevelt* (New York: Viking Press, 1992 and 1999).

did believe she was a man's equal, her opportunities to express this belief in the public sphere were limited.[12]

>-+-+>-+-O-+<-+-+-<

A young woman thinking of her future 150 years after Confederation is likely to have a radically different view than other women from any previous time in our history. She would assuredly count on her own abilities and education to make her livelihood, and she would no longer count on a lasting marriage. She would be likely to marry, however. And, like women in the nineteenth century, she would also likely remarry, probably following a divorce rather than the death of her spouse. On divorce, she would expect to be entitled to half the marital property in most jurisdictions, and divorce would not be a matter of social shame. She might plan to have children regardless of marriage or she might become a single mother. She might prefer to have no children at all even if married. Custody of children would probably be shared, and a "combined" family of children from previous partners would not be unusual. She might have a partner of either sex or none at all. Her health care would not rely on family or friends but would be provided by experts in medical settings. She would be vividly aware of preventive health measures such as vaccination, nutrition, not smoking, and weight control. She would be prepared to discuss a full range of diseases, including cancers, sexually transmitted diseases, and mental health, and to read about them in the popular press. She would have access not only to chemical

---

12. The first women's suffrage association in Canada was formed by Dr. Emily Howard Stowe in 1877 and was called the Toronto Women's Literary Club. In the 1960s, there were strong women's organizations and ongoing struggles for improvements such as equal pay and employment opportunities, but women's equality was still not a major public debate. In fact, women's equality was less of a public issue than it had been during the struggle for suffrage a generation earlier.

and other forms of contraceptives, but also, somewhere in the country, to legal abortions. She would have a much expanded range of political and legal rights and would not think it unusual to be represented by women in the legislatures and the courts or to be treated by a woman in medicine.

But still, she would not be facing a perfectly equitable world. Most probably, she would not have equal pay, although she would have the right to demand it in many jurisdictions as well as have the opportunity to apply for almost any job. Without post-secondary education she would be at a disadvantage and might expect to hold down several jobs, with no benefits, and struggle to make ends meet. She would rely heavily on government programs of support. The gap in living standards between the highly educated and those without post-secondary education would be as great as in the nineteenth century. But the idea of equity between the sexes in any living situation would be strong.

Our imaginary woman might be the prime minister, the Governor General, or a military general, or aspire to hold these jobs. If she were the wife of the prime minister, she might keep her own name and have, or have had, an important career. She would be treated as a person with opinions in her own right. The prime minister might never marry, or be divorced, and her or his sexual orientation would not matter much except to a minority of citizens.

The context here is post–Second Wave feminism. Second Wave feminism was a social movement during which many laws and practices changed just as the structure of the economy changed, drawing women into advanced education in increasing numbers and opening up most if not all jobs. Our woman would certainly have had ideas about equality and would manage her own affairs in the context of her independence.

Since the Confederation of Canada in 1867, issues affecting the rights and opportunities for women have been under continued discussion and change. Sometimes the debate has been scarcely audible, and sometimes it has been loud and clear. There has always been pressure for change, and this pressure continues to this day. The struggle over voting rights, marriage, divorce and property laws, custody of children, access to certain occupations, pensions and benefits, alcohol and temperance, and birth control have often been resolved by the legislatures and the courts. Laws concerning these issues change over time but sometimes only over a very long time as laws change province by province. The struggle over ideas about "womanhood," comportment, propriety, the role of the wife, the single woman, and the widow, and over equality and inequality continue and are worked out within a wide variety of cultures and social practices, generations, and philosophies. Some of these ideas are more widespread and acceptable in broad social institutions such as education, religious beliefs and practices, the military, and the arts. Because of the nature of our democratic practices, many ideas survive in minority cultures that are not acceptable to the state or law. Polygamy is one such social practice that is widely condemned in Canada but sometimes practised in subgroups.[13] That is, it is neither institutionalized nor accepted by the society as a whole, but it does still take place, just as violence against women and

---

13. In southeastern British Columbia, the town of Bountiful is renowned for its polygamous colony. See, for example, Daphne Bramham, *The Secret Lives of Saints* (Toronto: Random House, 2009). But note that monogamy was forced onto First Nations cultures, many of which practised a wide range of marriage arrangements. See Sarah Carter, "'Complicated and Clouded': The Federal Administration of Marriage and Divorce among the First Nations of Western Canada, 1887–1906," in *Unsettled Pasts: Reconceiving the West through Women's History*, ed. Sarah Carter, Lesley Erickson, Patricia Roome, and Char Smith (Calgary: University of Calgary Press, 2005), 151–78.

discrimination on the basis of sex continues to be acceptable to some groups and in some contexts. Some of that ebb and flow of mainstream beliefs about women's roles and rights is discussed throughout these pages.

By the turn of the twenty-first century, women in Canada were quite well off in comparison to women in much of the world, and they were certainly better off in comparison to the lives of women at the time of Confederation. In common with women throughout the developed world, life expectancy had extended significantly; health status had improved in many ways, in terms of childbirth, communicable diseases, public health, and the quality of life in old age. Education for women matched that of men, and paid labour-force participation was at an all-time high. Women had citizenship, the vote, personhood, and constitutional protections and held the highest public offices. Furthermore, the idea that women should have equality rights and equity in institutions was held by mainstream thinkers.

To our great benefit, historians of Canadian life and demographers have been researching many aspects of the lives and history of women, immeasurably enriching our understanding of all aspects of women's lives. While by no means a book of history, this book will draw on historical accounts to ask questions about the role of women in changing Canadian society.

Sociologists are interested in the lives of Canadian women, both historically and contemporaneously. They are interested in women as a social category different from the category of men, but they are also interested in women's behaviour as a source of social change. This book examines a very long period to analyze how women, as a type of underclass, have changed ideas, behaviour, and laws in Canadian society. In particular, I consider the ideas and behaviours that lead to greater equality between women and men.

I also describe some areas of life in which the social gap between women and men has narrowed, in some instances considerably. How does this happen? Hundreds of thousands of Canadian women and men have been involved in these changes. Our interest focuses on those who worked on bringing about and institutionalizing that change: labour organizations bringing concepts of equality into labour contracts; lawyers and legislators changing laws; women's groups finding sources of change; journalists covering women's groups and placing new ideas before the public; and people using the privileges of class, occupation, or talents, or their capacity as spouses of powerful leaders, to create change.[14]

There are some elements of any society that affect women regardless of age, ethnicity, social class, or creed. They affect women in every society and at all points in history. Two questions in this book are "How do they affect women in Canada?" and "What is it about Canadian society, history, law, and culture that make life a unique experience for women?" The social dynamics and events in Canada and abroad that changed ideas, or even simply changed life circumstances, have been more powerful than the social movements usually described as the First Wave (suffrage) and Second Wave (charter rights). Transforming a society is a very complex process. A long list of issues could be discussed here; however, this book focuses on only a small number that reveal the process of change. Sometimes change takes place in the life experience of women in Canada, sometimes by the action of women in groups and often by external

---

14. In Canada, so long as women could not hold public office and were barred from the professions, it was helpful when the wives of premiers and prime ministers, or the wife of the Governor General, for example, took an active interest in issues of concern to women. Lady Aberdeen, wife of a Governor General in the nineteenth century, is a very prominent example. See Doris French, *Ishbel and the Empire* (Toronto: Dundurn Press, 1988). (See also pages 146–50.)

circumstances beyond the control of women. But, mostly, these changes take place because of a concatenation of events that have resulted in changes in values, behaviour, laws, and opportunities.

Two key terms underlie this discussion: *Canada* and *equality*.

First, Canada and Canadian society here refer to the state created by Confederation in 1867 and expanded by new provinces and territories since then. A great deal of pre-Confederation history is very important in understanding the lives of women in Canada, both Aboriginal women and women who came to Canada as settlers from Europe and elsewhere. But this book is about the country in which we now live, from the point of Confederation and the debates leading up to that legislative act into the twenty-first century—a period of nearly 150 years. A great period of settlement and immigration from the United Kingdom, France, and other parts of Europe took place before Confederation.[15] While much more settlement was still to come in the West and the North, the colonies of Canada (Upper and Lower), Nova Scotia, New Brunswick, and Prince Edward Island were settled with dominant values and customs built out of their separate histories that continue to be influential to the present day.

The words *equality, equality rights, social equality, equity,* and many others have been used for a long time to examine the relationship between women and men in society, to express an aspiration for the future of women, and to describe inequities in societies and cultures. Delving into the history

---

15. There are many accounts of this settlement, but it is economically described by Marvin McInnis in his chapter "The Population of Canada in the Nineteenth Century," in *A Population History of North America*, ed. Michael Haines and Richard H. Steckel (Cambridge, MA: Cambridge University Press, 2000), Chapter 9.

of Western cultures, historians and sociologists have noted those words and ideas used for a variety of purposes.[16]

But what does equality between women and men mean? In any given relationship the extent of its meaning is important to the individuals involved but not to those studying a society as a whole. It is a term that changes over time in the same society. To many sociologists, equality is operationalized in terms of life expectancy, income, education, or other statuses that are measured by population data or studies of a group, institution, or historical period.[17] For lawyers, the term is fundamental to concepts of justice, although difficult to define, and to political scientists, it is fundamental to democracy.

"Equality is an amorphous concept—slippery, uncertain, flexible, dynamic, by definition comparative, by implication restrained," says Diana Majury, writing about the Canadian Charter of Human Rights and Freedoms. "These attributes are at the same time the potential and the limitations of equality, and the reason equality is controversial, both as a goal and as strategy for women."[18]

We shall see in what follows that women and their allies in Canada have sought equality for generations, often confounded by the need to describe or demonstrate what equality would mean. In fact, almost all aspects of life are conditioned to a greater or lesser extent by differences based on sex (biological) or gender (culture and society),

---

16. See, for example, Lynn McDonald, *Women Founders of the Social Sciences* (Ottawa: Carleton University Press, 1994). Note also that these terms were not used in the Report of the Royal Commission on the Status of Women, 1970, at least not in the same way they are used in the twenty-first century.

17. For a clear discussion of these sociological concepts see Lorne Tepperman, *The Sense of Sociability* (Toronto: Oxford University Press, 2010), Introduction and Bibliographic Essay.

18. Diana Majury, "Women's (In)Equality before and after the *Charter*," in *Women's Legal Strategies in Canada*, ed. Radha Jhappan (Toronto: University of Toronto Press, 1992).

for the most part wrapped around the fact that men do not bear children. The cultural gender differences attributed to all women and all men for generations were built on that distinction.

Throughout the history of the Dominion of Canada, the terms *equality* or *equal* or *equity* have been used to express the relationship, or the desired relationship, between men and women in society. Some scholars would argue that the proper way to analyze that relationship is to examine social class struggle, or language, or power, because they are more profound issues than equality. But even these scholars have some concept in their minds of what is meant by the phrase *equality between the sexes.*

After the Charter, with its sections 15 and 28 dealing with equality rights, was proclaimed, Judge Rosalie Abella was charged with operationalizing the term for labour market purposes. In her seminal report *Equality in Employment*, Abella described what equality would mean in a manner that allowed legislators, lawyers, and others working in the field to use the ideas in establishing laws, programs, sanctions, and study guides. She described the ideas so well that they dominate thinking in the early twenty-first century. It is against the standard that she set in that report that we are thinking about equality in this study.

> Equality is, at the very least, freedom from adverse discrimination. But what constitutes adverse discrimination changes with time, with information, with experience, and with insight. What we tolerated as a society 100, 50, or even 10 years ago is no longer necessarily tolerable. Equality is thus a process—a process of constant and flexible examination, of vigilant introspection, and of aggressive open-mindedness . . .
>
> Equality in employment is not a concept that produces the same results for everyone. It is a concept that seeks to identify and remove, barrier by barrier, discriminatory

disadvantages. Equality in employment is access to the fullest opportunity to exercise individual potential.

Sometimes equality means treating people the same, despite their differences, and sometimes it means treating them as equals by accommodating their differences.[19]

These ideas—and many others in Abella's report—mark a new consciousness in the public sphere about concepts of equality. They have opened up law and judicial decisions in a number of instances. Most importantly, they opened up the thinking of individual Canadians.

I will not attempt to define equality here. Who knows what the women were thinking when they used the word *equality* in their work for suffrage or property rights? Who knows what equality looks like in any given institution—in religions, communities, cultures, occupations, or education— to the women living in them then or now? The point here is not that all women at all times were thinking in terms of the same concepts when they declared their equality-seeking interests, but that they expressed their desires in those types of words. Now the Abella standard is a general measuring stick that allows us to discuss the struggles, victories, and defeats in this complicated country.

Consider this: the vote is the only pure play in equality in Canada. Men and women vote on exactly the same terms at the same time with equal results; that is, their ballots are counted without any awareness of who cast them. All the other issues one can think of are somehow conditioned by gender roles or physical differences in some way. In the courts, physical differences are visible and condition responses, something that has become clear in the debate over the wearing of face coverings. Sex differences are visible in

19. Judge Rosalie Silberman Abella, *Equality in Employment: A Royal Commission Report* (Ottawa: Canadian Government Publishing Centre, 1984), 1, 3.

working life. Even in the biology of birth sex differences appear. We all are born and die, but males are conceived more often than females and their causes of death and the treatments they receive as they approach death are shown to be different. There is no equality in birth or death—except for the reality that they take place.

All this emphasis on gender differences may change. For example, some sociologists now focus on the inequalities caused by group differences of "race" or ethnicity.[20] For many concerned with sex or gender inequalities, this distinction must be studied alongside other attributes. This focus is not new in Canada, as immigrants of many national, cultural, or religious origins; Aboriginal peoples; people with disabilities; and people of various age groups have always been subjects of interest to those concerned with inequalities. Studies about access to education, employment, income, citizenship, services, and treatment under the laws incorporate analyses of group differences. These differences are important to Canadians and remain the site of constant struggle. In confining this book to the female–male inequalities, I remain fully aware of all these other differences. But my goal here is to consider the processes and the barriers—some of them structural—that exist or that have been modified or struggled against in the search for female–male equality in this Confederation.

⊱⊶⊷⊙⊶⊷⊰

---

20. *Race* is a political term as equally impossible to define as *equality*, but its meaning is usually discernible in context. Race is a social perception and changes over time. In the nineteenth century, it might have been used in relation to nationality (e.g., the Irish). Usually—but not always—it refers to skin colour, but sometimes it means self-identification with a group such as Aboriginal or First Nations. There are many forms of inequality in Canada, and sex inequality can be a component of most of them. See, for example, Tepperman, *Sense of Sociability*, Chapter 5.

In the century and a half since Confederation, vast changes in the world have affected Canada. There have also
been extensive changes in Canadian society itself. Events
and turning points of great significance have affected the
lives of women and, from a sociological viewpoint, there is
much to be learned about how these particular events have
changed the lives of women.[21]

What, then, are the issues that provide insight? Each
issue is continuous—that is, it has affected women's lives
throughout our history and continues to do so today, although in different ways. Each issue is also universal. In
other words, women throughout the world and throughout
history have been affected by similar types of events—but
not the same events, not with the same consequences, nor
with the same ingredients. That is why these issues lead us
to a thesis about social change in Canada.

First, we live in a country with rules of conduct set out in
a legal structure. Many of our ways of living and behaving
are not part of the legal structure, but some vital aspects of
women's lives are controlled by law and regulation, and these
affect and have always affected women's lives differently
from the lives of men. Laws regarding marriage and divorce,
property rights, and political rights are examples. Chapter
2 focuses on the conditions surrounding the Confederation
process, asking why women's rights did not receive attention
when they might have otherwise. The succeeding impact of
this on women is considered next, particularly in the period

---

21. In his studies *Social Change in the Twentieth Century* and *Social Change in the
Modern Era*, Daniel Chirot has taken the broad sociological view. In the preface
to the latter book, Chirot writes, "I remained convinced that the study of social
change limited to any single society or time . . . is foolish and misleading. . . .
Furthermore, no change exists outside the history that preceded it. So it is only
by studying social change within a global and historical context that it can be
understood" (iv). While I agree with Chirot, that large task is beyond the scope
of this book.

immediately following Confederation and the conversion of territories into provinces. I look at the peculiarities and difficulties inherent in our constitutional regime and how these shape the lives of women. In particular, I consider the "qualified" personhood that women have inhabited for most of the time since Confederation and which in many ways continues today.

Second, our country, like most others, has been frequently at war. All women are affected by war. They are participants through their work, their families, and now as combatants. We think of our country as a peace-seeking one. Comparatively speaking that may be true, but since well before Confederation and during the Boer War, World Wars I and II, the Korean War, the Afghanistan War, and the campaign in Libya, we have been combatants, and through our peacekeeping missions we have been on the site of many more wars. Our country has flourished through the wars and misery of others—refugees, postwar immigrants, brain drains in our favour, war resisters—as we have gained people from across the globe who have been pushed rather than pulled into Canada. These people have been remarkable contributors to the richness of our society in every sense. During wars, we have been suppliers of goods and services to our allies, and as a consequence, some of our industries have innovated and flourished. Furthermore, engagement in wars forces changes on the lives of a country's citizens. In periods of war, women have seized the day to gain rights with a success they would not ordinarily have had.

Third, like women everywhere, Canadian women have children and, like women everywhere, look after them. The obligations of child-bearing and child rearing may be similar worldwide, but the ages of bearing children and the rates of fertility and mortality have seen some unique Canadian moments. Our currently low rates of fertility and small family size hide some remarkable periods in our history. Child-bearing and child rearing are bound up in all societies with sexuality and the construction of gender and relationships between the sexes. This interrelationship is complex in all cultures and equally but somewhat differently so in Canada. While there are widespread differences across all Canadian cultures, the intersection of law and custom when it comes to raising children is now in a state of flux.

Fourth, politics and social movements have changed our society and the lives of women. There are patterns in the demographic and economic data, but the actual work of change is carried forward largely by organized efforts. Women in feminist and religious associations, unions, and all sorts of other groups—including local, regional, and national organizations—have shaped decisions throughout our history. Individual women have used their networks and access to decision-makers to influence lawmakers. Often men have been deeply involved in these changes both as champions and resisters of the women's ideas and contributions. Women have changed existing institutions, such as the family, education, and the economy, and built new institutions of equality.

All women make their living somehow. Chapter 6 considers this key element in many generations. All women everywhere are involved in the economy through paid and unpaid contributions to their households. As Canadians worked to create a strong economy throughout the economic changes following Confederation, they were challenged by the country's vast geography and the need for large amounts of capital for transportation, manufacturing enterprises, and infrastructure. Governments and public enterprises created grand projects such as the cross-country railways, a military, and a series of national institutions. Around such projects, many towns and small businesses were established.

Many women worked as paid public servants or as employees in private companies, in a wide variety of occupations, and in hospitals, schools, and libraries. Women have earned wages on farms, in factories and offices, in household services, and in a myriad of creative ways. The increasing importance of women and their work in the productive and reproductive economies has led to different expectations of both sexes and of family life. Women who immigrated to Canada brought new and different ideas, and their work has been influential in building the current Canadian economy. Our work, our families, and our communities were strengthened by the vigour of diverse ideas and institutions that new immigrants shared as they created their lives in Canada.

Finally, in Chapter 7, the dynamic elements in Canadian women's lives are examined. Where does change in the status of women come from? There has been no revolution in the cause of women's rights, no overthrow of government or leadership by violent means, little violence at all in public, and not even a lot of shouting. Yet the changed status of women has been revolutionary in its effects on how Canadians live. This chapter includes several examples of how this happened. However, despite these revolutionary changes, I must agree with Alexander Brady that Canada continues to be a country of "slow and secure change."[22]

Canada is an interesting case to examine because of how social change occurs. In a previous study,[23] Edward Harvey and I proposed a theory of social change in Canada. Within the social structure created by both economic relations and demographic patterns, groups of people and some individuals have changed our institutions through unique dynamics. The dynamics can be seen in the actions of elites

---

22. Alexander Brady, "Canada and the Model of Westminster" in *The Transfer of Institutions*, ed. W.B. Hamilton (Durham, NC: Duke University Press, 1964), 69.
23. Marsden and Harvey, *The Fragile Federation*.

in national, regional, and sectoral institutions, and in the push of social movements. Both directions of these dynamic forces create ongoing pressure for change.

All societies have elites, but Canada's are different from those of the "old countries." We have no hereditary aristocracy. Social mobility between socio-economic statuses has been high. No one who achieves leadership in an organization, business, or political party can expect to hand that position on to his or her children. In all periods of our history, women and their allies have never stopped seeking greater rights and improvements in their lives and they have been a major part of the dynamic of change. Equally, in all this time, the state of the economy, the patterns of fertility, life expectancy, and population growth have constrained the choices of organizations and individuals seeking equality. We argued that it is necessary to examine what is different about how Canadians make their living as individuals and as a country, and it is necessary to look at the way in which people organize around their social identities and modes of social action. We argued that social class formation and interests are a powerful dynamic in Canada.

This book includes a different type of analysis of social change, one more closely tied to changes in a segment— albeit the largest segment of our society: it analyzes the impact of our institutions on women and women's impact on our institutions. This approach considers women less in social class terms—given that women share in the formation and change of all social classes—and is more an examination of women's relationships to our major institutions. In particular, I focus on the way in which some significant events, such as suffrage, war, the constitution, and the evolution of the labour force, have been formed from the determined efforts of women for change in their lives and status.

II

Women Struggle with the Law: The Law Struggles with Women

A woman in Canada today reading the accounts of the agitation for women's rights at the end of the nineteenth century must wonder why in 1867 women had so few rights. Thereby hangs a tale . . . But the woman of 1867, should she return to life now, might wonder not only why women have not achieved equality, but also how their rights could be so entangled. In other words, the tale's final chapter has yet to be written.

For women in all societies, the laws of the jurisdiction in which they live play a crucial role in the conduct of their affairs. Whether in informal and popular understanding of the laws and their application, or in a more formal knowledge of the law, people's awareness of their freedoms and restrictions influences their behaviour. Major events such as births, deaths, and marriages—all of which have important cultural properties—have attached legal requirements as well. These events must be registered, and they set up legal relationships. These relationships must be honoured. Economic matters such as property ownership, control over children, wills, trespass, speed limits, and now intellectual property affect the behaviour of everyone, but there are particular ways in which they affect the lives of women.

In all the former colonies, Canadian laws are based largely on those of Great Britain. The exception is Quebec. At the federal level, all provinces live under the laws of Canada. Provincially the Quebec regime evolved from eighteenth-century French law to the Civil Code adopted in 1865 and amended almost continuously up to the present time. Quebec civil law is an exception, but all provinces have rather different laws in their areas of jurisdiction.

At Confederation, those existing laws and their underlying ideas were structured into our first Canadian constitution in the creation of the British North America Act (BNA Act), promulgated by Britain in 1867.[1] That Act is marked by several features that have created problems for Canadians—and in particular for women—ever since.[2]

With the constitution they created in 1867, the Fathers of Confederation incorporated some of the leading ideas of their period. However, it should not be thought of as necessarily an improvement for the rights of the citizens, either as individuals or as groups. Rather, the BNA Act was shaped through negotiations driven both by ideals and pragmatic necessities.

By the middle of the nineteenth century, vigorous debate about the joining of the provinces, colonies, and territories was underway. Leaders in politics, law, the church, and other interested citizens were concerned about the future of

---

1.   While it is correct to call it the Constitution Act, 1867, for the sake of clarity, this book will refer to it as the BNA Act to distinguish it from the events of 1982.

2.   For example, the division of assets upon the death of a partner or the dissolution of a "common-law relationship" is somewhat different in each province. While marriage used to be the norm, it no longer is. In Quebec, where nearly half of all parents are not married, the laws governing assets and alimony are still based on marriage contracts and are currently being challenged. In 2011, a case before the Supreme Court of Canada may cause Quebec to change its laws. See *Eric v. Lola.*

the colonies. For some leaders of the day, the ideas for a new Canadian nation were born of the debates in Europe and in the United States over liberty and individual freedoms, the rights of minorities, and ideal forms of responsible governments. To some leaders it was becoming apparent that considerable danger lurked in their independent colony statuses, despite the historical and cultural differences among them. The dangers came from a variety of sources but most urgently from US expansion. In particular, those of French language and descent in Lower Canada looked at the absorption of the Louisiana colony by the United States with concern about the preservation of their rights and customs. If Quebec was invaded by the United States, could it encounter the same result? Many doubted their capacity to raise funds for the building of the badly needed infrastructure of transportation and urban centres. Others held strong views about the type of society they wished to live in. The last half of the nineteenth century was a time of nation-building in many parts of Europe, and there was considerable ferment on key questions: the separation of church and state, the forms of government, federal and unitary systems, and responsible government. It was the time of the reforms following the American and French Revolutions of the eighteenth century and the suffrage expansion of the British Reform Act of 1832. It was the time of civil war in the United States, a battle of ideas as well as military prowess. The ideas were studied and debated in the colonies of British North America.[3]

---

3. For a description of all these issues, see Janet Ajzenstat et al., eds., *Canada's Founding Debates* (Toronto: University of Toronto Press, 2003). See also Ajzenstat, *The Once and Future Canadian Democracy: An Essay in Political Thought* (Montreal and Kingston: McGill-Queen's University Press, 2003) in which she contends that the knowledge and thinking of the Fathers of Confederation was well informed; it was not "from Hicksville" (53).

As the leaders of the colonies—who later became and remain famous as the Fathers of Confederation—debated these issues in the 1860s, it became apparent that if their best interests lay in forming a tight relationship among the colonies of British North America, a very practical approach was required to bring together the various parts. In the reforms of the mid-nineteenth century, responsible government had been achieved in the Province of Canada (created out of Upper and Lower Canada in 1840), so the power of the elected members of Parliament increased. However, as the population of Upper Canada grew relative to that of Lower Canada, a stalemate blocked the governance of the Province of Canada. When the conservative and liberal groups came together in a "grand coalition" led by John A. Macdonald, joining the various colonies and territories in some sort of constitutional structure began to be seen as a solution to many of the problems faced by all sides.

The four provinces that finally joined together in 1867—Ontario, Quebec, New Brunswick, and Nova Scotia—were already well settled. Altogether they comprised a population of about three and a half million people, three million of whom were spread nearly equally between Quebec and Ontario.[4] For generations they had operated their own jurisdictions with laws and legislative processes that were different from each other, modified versions of British or French law that had evolved in each colony. These laws applied to women in relation to families, property, marriage, and the custody and treatment of children, and were well embedded in each colony. While these laws affecting women were different from colony to colony, it does not appear that there

---

4. McInnis, "The Population of Canada," 373. These numbers account for Europeans only because estimates of Aboriginal populations were removed from these estimates. However, for a discussion of the Aboriginal population then and now, see Big Eagle and Guimond, "Contributions that Count," 35–68. See also Ajzenstat et al., *Canada's Founding Debates*, 114–15n.

was any movement to change them or to coordinate them in the process of Confederation. They were accepted as given, and while a clause was included to harmonize laws across the country, standardization was not the outcome (see page 38). This has left a legacy that women have worked hard to overcome ever since—with mixed success.

The desire and need to produce some form of larger state led to the constitutional debates of 1864 in Charlottetown and Quebec City. While the Charlottetown debates resulted in agreement in principle, the Quebec Conference negotiations produced 72 resolutions. These and debates in the legislatures of the colonies led the Fathers to London, England, in 1866, where the proposal for Confederation was finally agreed on. It was taken through the Parliament of Britain and passed as the British North America Act of 1867. The Act came into effect on 1 July 1867, forming the nation of Canada. This process has been described and analyzed in great detail through some official records, diaries by observers, newspaper accounts, notes by participants, and autobiography and biography.[5]

The pragmatism revealed in the Confederation debates and in the final agreement was the foundation of the success of the project. Indeed, that pragmatic approach has become the hallmark of subsequent constitutional conferences and amendments in Canada. Some of that pragmatism took the form of ambiguity in certain issues. While matters were highly specified in the division of powers between two levels of government, and the composition of the Upper Chamber, other matters were not discussed. Both

---

5. Among the most interesting accounts is Richard Gwyn's biography of John A. Macdonald, *The Man Who Made Us*, vol. 1; Donald Creighton's biography of Macdonald, *John A. Macdonald: The Young Politician. The Old Chieftain*; Peter Waite's *Life and Times of Confederation*; and Louise Reynolds's book *Agnes: The Biography of Lady Macdonald*. (See Bibliography for complete publication information.) But countless other articles and histories enrich the story.

pragmatism and ambiguity are part of the culture of "slow and secure" change that characterizes Canadian culture.[6] Each party to the agreement gave up certain goals and compromised on some ideas to achieve the whole, while maintaining their diversity and some of the idealism that infused the confederation project. Confederation achieved all this in the aftermath of the American Civil War and the Fenian raids, in the midst of British indifference to the maintenance of the colonies, and in the determination of a few Canadian leaders to remain loyal to Britain or at least to stay out of the clutches of the United States.

However, the agreement also contained two major decisions—flaws in my view—that have complicated the lives of Canadians ever since. One could argue that women started their lives under Confederation with their hands tied behind their backs. One hand was tied by the lack of citizenship rights and by the necessity to conduct their lives through their fathers, brothers, and husbands. The other hand was tied by the division of powers between the federal and provincial governments that complicated much of daily life. Did it need to be this way?

The Great Flaws of Confederation

The first major flaw was the complete omission of rights or recognition of women. Women neither participated directly in nor were mentioned as a group in the debates that led to the BNA Act. It is not that the leaders were unfamiliar with the limitations on the lives and rights of women. In fact, they were familiar with the philosophy and arguments for expanded voting rights in the

---

6. See Brady, "Canada and the Model of Westminster." See also John Ralston Saul, *Louis-Hippolyte LaFontaine and Robert Baldwin* (Toronto: Penguin, 2010) for a viewpoint on the Canadian style of government, especially its ambiguity.

ideas of John Locke,[7] John Stuart Mill, and the struggle for women's suffrage. These political theory ideas were widely debated. Some of the views of Mill were referenced during the debates. In the Atlantic colonies and other settled regions, newspaper editors were keen exponents of new ideas from Britain and the United States. Many Canadians had been educated abroad and returned with ideas about reform of many kinds.[8] Despite a great deal of discussion on individual liberties and how to guarantee them and on who should have the right to vote in federal elections—a debate that continued as other colonies joined each other and then Confederation—ideas concerning women's equality, let alone suffrage, were never topics on the agenda. This occurred despite the fact that women had voted in some colonies previously. For example, historians have told us that between 1791 (when the first Legislative Assembly was created in Lower Canada) and 1834, women who met the age and property qualifications could—and did—vote.[9] Some women voted in Upper Canada. There was a similar practice in New Brunswick and Nova Scotia.[10] But by the time the idea of a confederation was approached, the values and practices had changed.[11]

Given the patriarchal values of the times and in the European founding cultures, the failure to enfranchise

7. John Locke may not have argued for women as lawmakers, but he did consider them free and equal citizens. See his First Treatise.
8. See, for example, Margaret R. Conrad and James K. Hiller, *Atlantic Canada: A History*, 2nd ed. (Toronto: Oxford University Press, 2010), 116–21.
9. Bettina Bradbury, "Women at the Hustings: Gender, Citizenship, and the Montreal By-Elections of 1832," in *Rethinking Canada: The Promise of Women's History*, 5th ed., eds. Mona Gleason and Adele Perry (Toronto: Oxford University Press, 2006), 73–94. See also John Garner, *The Franchise and Politics in British North America, 1755–1867* (Toronto: University of Toronto Press, 1969), Chapter 12.
10. See the discussion in Brandt et al., *Canadian Women*, 113–15.
11. See Saul, *Louis-Hippolyte*, 207ff. Also Ajzenstat et al., *Canada's Founding Debates*, 114–15n.

women is not surprising; but it is most unfortunate.[12] The dominant role of men in all the major institutions of the society, including the household and the custody of children, was unquestioned in public debate and rarely discussed in private life.[13] Individual women, of course, had frequently questioned the power of individual men over their lives.[14] Cases of delinquent, drunken, and violent husbands and fathers had been dealt with by the Canadian courts in several of the pre-Confederation provinces and territories, and justice was dealt out to benefit particular women. But the idea that men as a class should not have dominance over women was not a public debate until much later.

As the Fathers carried the BNA Act through the British Parliament in 1866–67, the focus of the British Parliament was not on Canada and its constitution. Rather, the British were intensely focused on their own Reform Acts, intended to widen suffrage to men outside the aristocracy and landowners. When Benjamin Disraeli, leading the Conservatives on this file, saw that he must accept this expansion of

---

12. It is impossible to know from the available records what was in the minds of the Fathers of Confederation. We do know that the secondary status of women assumed at that time in Britain was not true of all Aboriginal cultures, however. Aboriginal people were not considered in nor party to these discussions, and the results of that were deleterious for subsequent generations. For a fuller discussion, see J.R. Miller, *Skyscrapers Hide the Heavens*, rev. ed. (Toronto: University of Toronto Press, 1989).

13. John Ralston Saul in his fascinating account of Baldwin and LaFontaine and their struggle for responsible government in the Province of Canada says with respect to suffrage that in the 1930s "Canada already had as full an expression of that as the nineteenth century could imagine. We had virtually universal male suffrage because most males were land-owning farmers and so met the property requirements of the day" (54). But Saul then goes on to discuss women voting before 1850 (*Louis-Hippolyte*, 207ff) and ascribes the rise of the women's movement to the groundwork laid by Baldwin and LaFontaine (*Louis-Hippolyte*, 220).

14. There was a vigorous suffrage debate in Canada before and after Confederation. When Prime Minister John A. Macdonald introduced the Franchise Bill in 1885, eventually proposing male-only suffrage, there was "limited agitation from some Canadian women seeking political equality" (Reynolds, *Agnes*, 101). It is argued that Macdonald would have included female suffrage if he had thought

suffrage (over the staunch objections of many of his Tory members), he became interested in women's suffrage as a possible means of expanding the Tory vote, at least for property owners. He overrode objections in the Cabinet, leading to several resignations, and went on to accept all of the proposed amendments to his Reform Bill of 1867—with the sole exception of Mill's proposal of suffrage for women.[15]

From this we can deduce that the idea of women's suffrage had support in Britain—enough to have it placed firmly in front of their Parliament at the precise time the BNA Act was being drafted. Given the indifference of the British parliamentarians to the Canadian legislation, the Canadians might have included it in the BNA Act had the will existed to do so. But by then it was too late.

Some of the Canadian leaders, including John A. Macdonald and George Brown, appreciated the intelligence and minds of women and drew on their advice. Macdonald had admired his first wife, Isabella, as well as his mother and sisters. He had supported them, consulted them, and protected them. In his later 1885 Franchise Bill debate, he expressed clear

---

it had a chance of passing. Instead, he proposed suffrage for widows and unmarried women. In response to an amendment to strike out women suffrage, Macdonald said, "I had hoped that we in Canada would have had the great honour of leading in the cause of securing the complete emancipation of women, of completely establishing her equality as a human being and a member of society with man . . . I believe a majority of this House is opposed to female suffrage" (Canada, *Official Report of the Debates of the House of Commons of the Dominion of Canada*, 27 April 1885: *The Electoral Franchise*, Sir John A. Macdonald, 1388). In fairness, however, the main purpose of Macdonald's Bill was to create a federal definition of the electorate, which, at Confederation, had remained with the provinces, creating great inequities in who could vote across the country. Macdonald had trouble getting even this Bill passed, and it was reversed some years later. See also Veronica Strong-Boag, "'The Citizenship Debates': The 1885 Franchise Act," in *Contesting Canadian Citizenship*, eds. Robert Adamoski, Dorothy E. Chunn, and Robert Menzies (Peterborough, ON: Broadview Press, 2002).

15. See Anne Stott, "The Second Reform Act, 1867", October 2010, http://nine-teenthcenturybritain.blogspot.com/2009/10/second-reform-act.html (accessed November 11, 2011). Note also that John Stuart Mill had published his *Thoughts on Parliamentary Reform* in 1859, including proposals for woman suffrage.

support for women's equality with men, including suffrage. It seems reasonable to ask why Macdonald—a thoughtful leader, a coalition builder, a pioneer in Confederation, a sophisticated thinker, and a persuasive debater who was *not* an exploiter of women—could not argue for some moves toward recognizing women's rights in our founding document. Of course changes in voting rights were not addressed in the Quebec resolutions or the Constitution of Canada at the time, although language rights and special interests were addressed.[16]

As the Bill was prepared, John A. Macdonald married his second wife, Agnes, who was an exceptionally well-read and intelligent woman of strong opinions. When they married, they signed a contract for Agnes's financial protection—revealing Macdonald's full awareness of the dearth of women's property rights. Macdonald was not alone in his respect for women. Another of the Fathers, Liberal leader George Brown, had such a close and consultative relationship with his wife, Anne, that she was unofficially known as "the mother of confederation." His letters to her show him seeking her opinions and, as Careless tells us, Anne had studied in Germany and was described as "strong minded, intelligent and cultivated."[17] But this respect did not lead to the protection of women constitutionally. Even if suffrage for women was not to be included, the rights of women in other areas could have been improved in the BNA Act. They were not.

Indeed, as other colonies debated joining Confederation, suffrage issues arose. For example, during the 1870 Convention of Forty at Fort Garry, during discussions of

---

16. See resolutions 43.6, and resolutions 56 to 69, which deal with the particular needs of particular provinces.
17. J.M.S. Careless, *George Brown and the Mother of Confederation, 1864* (Ottawa: Canadian Historical Association, 1960).

property qualifications for voting, Alfred H. Scott, a delegate from Winnipeg, asked, "Is it the intention of the convention to allow women to vote? No doubt many such will come in and be householders. (Laughter)."[18] Aware of all these ideas and proposals, even prior to 1866 and certainly in the subsequent concerns about voting qualifications, the Fathers of Confederation nonetheless created the BNA Act without the right of women to vote or be elected, whether they were property owners and taxpayers or not. No other specific rights for women were contemplated. It appears to have been assumed without question that women would occupy the same status in Canada as did women in Britain, as translated in each of the colonies. It is clear in Quebec Resolution 26, which refers to the qualifications of the electors and the elected, that no effort was made to include women. By the time the Fathers arrived in England to get an act of the British Parliament, it was too late, and sections 41 and 84 of the BNA Act simply repeated the outcome of the Quebec resolution. This is surprising given that the Fathers defied convention in other ways. For example, they were the first colonials remaining within the British Empire to write their own constitution and we are told they were conscious of the significance of this. It was a bold and innovative move. Yet given the opportunity to be progressive for women, these men did not even officially discuss such matters before this first constitution was promulgated by Britain. Thus, they embedded in the founding document

18. See Ajzenstat, *The Once and Future*, 118, and the footnote of Ian Gentles (ed.) therein. It is not surprising that the idea of allowing women to vote should provoke laughter, since very few people at the time—male or female—supported it. Scott was a delegate with the support of the American population of Winnipeg, and perhaps the debate of women's suffrage in the United States led to his question. The American suffrage associations were active before and after the Civil War. The American Equal Rights Association was founded in 1866. The carefully disguised suffrage seeking group the Toronto Women's Literary Club was founded in 1877.

of primary importance the inequalities that the women of Canada have been correcting ever since.

In the debates, the "rights of minorities" referred to the French minority in Ontario and the English minority in Quebec, as well as their respective rights to education in their language and religion. Because of the religious background of political parties in the Maritimes and Newfoundland, "minorities" also referred to religious minorities. Memories of the religious wars of earlier times in Europe, combined with the importance of the separation of church and state as the means of allowing religious liberties, was the background to strongly held views about the rights of religious minorities. In addition, in the Red River Colony of the West, Louis Riel was determined to protect the status of the Métis. There were debates about the addition of this western territory to Confederation in 1870. On the subject of who might vote, Riel argued vigorously for property qualifications to protect the rights of all (including Métis) property holders who had a minimum of three years of residence in the country. Women's status was never questioned in those debates. The idea of women as a separate "minority or class" became part of the public debate only many years later.

The Fathers did not deny women's personhood—that came later[19]—but seem to have thought of women as a group almost exclusively in terms of their family status as daughters,

---

19. The now famous Persons Case of 1929 concerned the right of women to sit in the Senate of Canada; the Courts in England stated in a case at common law in 1876 women were persons in matters of "pains and penalties but not privileges"—in short, women were not "persons." But the Fathers of Confederation were familiar with the ideas of John Locke who thought of women as individuals, equal in intelligence to men if not in physical strength. See Chris Nyland, "John Locke and the Social Position of Women," *History of Political Economy* 25, no. 1 (1993): 39–63. Nonetheless, Locke thought that in marriage the husband would prevail. In the founding of the country of Canada, therefore, a hierarchical series of human groups was assumed, with European males in the dominant position. Their values, laws, and customs were to prevail, but in the Enlightenment, not the Absolutist, sense.

wives, or mothers, or even as taxpayers, as derivatives of men rather than as independent persons. Meanwhile the debate over women's rights was underway in the former colonies and was even more loudly expressed in the United States in the same period. Furthermore, since the relationship between paying tax, owning property, and voting was not at all new in Britain, France, or, indeed, Canada, the failure to give even women property owners the vote is retrograde.[20]

The second great flaw in the BNA Act arises from another pragmatic solution to the question of whose laws and customs would prevail in civil society. The provinces, colonies, and territories had adopted laws from Britain at various times in their development. Colonial governments then adapted the laws to the needs of their population. At Confederation, there was a patchwork of laws regarding most aspects of daily life. Quebec, for example, had institutionalized civil rather than common law, especially after the Union of 1840. Rather than contend with the problem of legal diversity among all the provinces considering joining in Confederation, the Fathers struck a pragmatic bargain. They created a division of powers that leaves to each individual province and territory most laws that affect family life, children, property, labour and working conditions, education, health, and a wide variety of other matters. Those new provinces, in their former condition as colonies, had built up a body of law over the years, depending on the time they were adopted and how they were translated and interpreted by judges and courts in the colonial regimes. No two colonies were the same. Therefore, each new province carried forward its previous laws subject only to the division of

---

20. John Ralston Saul argues that allowing women property owners to vote embedded class distinctions and that the women tended to be Tory voters, and thus not in the interest of the Reformers. He also argues that the rise of industrialism led men to assert their maleness as "the great protectors." See Saul, *Louis-Hippolyte*, 206–7.

federal/provincial powers, and whatever urgently required change. Both the Quebec Resolutions (resolution 33) and the BNA Act (section 94) provide for the federal government to harmonize the laws among the provinces. Resolution 33 talks about the central government "rendering uniform all or any of the laws relative to property and civil rights . . . but any statute for this purpose shall have no force or authority in any province until sanctioned by the legislature thereof."[21] Section 94 says much the same except that "rendering uniform" has become making "Provision for the Uniformity of all or any of the Laws relative to Property and Civil Rights."[22]

Civil society and its institutions define the ways in which we live. These civil institutions are created by developments in family, community, and national relationships over long histories. Beliefs found in religious values and practices often are embedded in the customs that govern daily life. For example, it was ecclesiastical courts that had first dealt with divorce. Customs and beliefs are institutionalized by laws that are enforced by the state, such as marriage and the obligations of support between spouses. The idea that upon marriage man and woman are one—and that one is the man—had religious origins. Its interpretation into law prevailed for a long time, even among most secular lawyers, courts, and petitioners.[23] The Christian origins were buried in layers of local law and custom created by decades of decisions made on those assumptions.

So in leaving each colony with its existing laws and customs in respect of the division of powers between the

---

21. See Ajzenstat et al., *Canada's Founding Debates*, Appendix A.
22. The BNA Act, 1967 – Enactment no. 1 can be found at http://www.laws-lois.justice.gc.ca/Eng/Const/Print.E.pdf.
23. See, for example, Mary Beard, *Women as a Force in History* (New York, Macmillan, 1946); Chambers, *Married Women and Property Law*; Constance Backhouse, *Petticoats and Prejudice: Women and Law in Nineteenth-Century Canada* (Toronto: Women's Press, 1991).

provinces and the central government, the Fathers avoided fighting over deep-seated convictions and practices in each colony that would have delayed Confederation. These convictions and practices arose because of the differences from the French and British traditions, but also because of the beliefs brought by others such as the United Empire Loyalists in the Maritimes, southern Ontario, and along the St. Lawrence, and the Acadians. Accounts of the debates in years leading up to the BNA Act seem to indicate that the problems of nation-building when leaving such powers to the provinces were not deeply considered. At the Charlottetown Conference in September 1864, George Brown gave a long speech on the federal proposals, including the division of powers. He argued that every power not explicitly given to the provinces—the residual powers—should remain at the federal level. The focus at the Quebec Conference later in the year was also the residual powers. E.B. Chandler of New Brunswick challenged the central government's control of the residual powers, and a debate ensued about where these powers should lie—with the national or the local governments. After two days, it was resolved in favour of the national government, although the Ottawa legislature would require the use of French as well as English in an agreement with Quebec. From accounts of those debates, it seems that the matters of health, family law, and welfare were not debated, and no one foresaw the long-term consequences of allowing local governments to keep many powers.[24] Education in terms of religion and languages was debated and agreed on. No one appears to have asked what would happen as families moved across provincial boundaries. It served the interests of both the French in Quebec and everyone else

---

24. See the account of all the conferences in Donald Creighton, *The Road to Confederation: The Emergence of Canada, 1863–1867* (Toronto: Macmillan, 1964).

to avoid dwelling on what might have become an issue so divisive it would end the confederation project. In the final London talks before the BNA Act was passed, all focus was on the retention of the powers of the central government rather than on the powers of local governments.

There is a great deal of evidence that key leaders such as John A. Macdonald, Charles Tupper, and George Brown strongly hoped for a unitary state, having witnessed the terrible problems that emerged from decentralized power in the United States (in particular the tragedy of the Civil War). Macdonald was determined to have strong central powers and, furthermore, thought he had achieved them with, among other things, the residual powers residing in Ottawa.[25] Both before and after Confederation, he, Brown, and others thought that the provinces might wither into powers comparable to municipalities. Then, as now, finances were a key issue, and grants to the provinces persuaded more than one Maritime leader that federalism was a good thing. As Gwyn points out,

> that unnervingly perceptive critic Christopher Dunkin [predicted]: the "cry of the provinces will be found to be pretty often and pretty successfully—'Give, give, give.'"[26]

But while the provinces needed debt and financing provisions in 1864, as most do at the present time, conceding any of their powers was not on the agenda.

---

25. When Canada's situation is compared to that of the United States, Macdonald had achieved something. For example, for women to gain suffrage in the United States, they were required to win the right in a majority of the states first and then fight for the federal vote after ratification. See Mary Walton, *A Woman's Crusade: Alice Paul and the Battle for the Ballot* (New York: Palgrave Macmillan, 2010) for a recent account of that process. It should be noted that the Equal Rights Amendment was never ratified in the United States, largely as a result of the States' rights process.

26. See Gwyn, *The Man Who Made Us*, 332 and 353. In *Nation Maker* Gwyn expands on the use of the Judicial Committee of the Privy Council in Westminster by premiers to expand their powers and by others to amend the BNA Act.

The debate over the division of powers has never truly ended. It has become a tussle over what "belongs" to the federal government and what "belongs" to the provinces: which level of government pays for what and whether or not the two levels of government co-operate.[27] As Jennifer Smith has pointed out in her study titled *Federalism*, citizen participation in the federal system is complicated by jurisdictional issues.[28] These issues have bedeviled attempts to improve the status of women. Problems concerning women involve all jurisdictions and must be approached at so many levels that it is difficult to mobilize interested people and make changes that provide equality across the country (some examples will be explored later in this book).[29] It is even more central to the situation of Aboriginal peoples in Canada, who, with their lands, were put under the federal Parliament, which, very shortly afterwards, enacted the Indian Act of 1876.

For the general population, marriage and divorce were given to the federal level of government, while the solemnization of marriage and family law was given to provinces. So the division of property on marriage breakdown, the custody of children, domestic disputes, and laws in inheritance

---

27. In his second volume of the John A. Macdonald biography, Richard Gwyn describes at length the struggle over the division of powers as Oliver Mowat gained provincial powers for Ontario through use of appeals to the Judicial Committee of the Privy Council of Great Britain. This eroded the powers of the federal government to Macdonald's dismay. Richard Gwyn, *Nation Maker, Sir John A. Macdonald: His Life, Our Times, Volume Two: 1867–1891* (Toronto: Random House, 2011), 373–82. "The most pressing constitutional issue of the 1920's was not the protection of equality rights but rather the division of powers and the scope of Parliament's residuary power under the Peace, Order and Good Government clause of section 91 of the BNA Act," say Robert Sharpe and Patricia McMahon in their absorbing study *The Persons Case: The Origins and Legacy of the Fight for Legal Personhood* (Toronto: University of Toronto Press / Osgoode Society for Canadian Legal History, 2007), 5.

28. Jennifer Smith, *Federalism* (Vancouver: UBC Press, 2004), 96–97.

29. For example, see Mary Eberts, "Women and Constitutional Renewal," in *Women and the Constitution in Canada*, eds. Audrey Doerr and Micheline Carrier (Ottawa: Canadian Advisory Council on the Status of Women, 1980).

vary across the provinces. As Owen and Bumsted say in their study of divorce on Prince Edward Island,

> Despite the granting of jurisdiction over divorce to the Dominion in . . . the British North America Act, . . . the provinces retained a substantial say on the subject. Sections 129 and 146 provided that all laws in force and all courts to enforce them—including divorce courts—in the provinces entering union would be allowed to continue. . . . Provincial variation . . . was a way of life before the federal divorce reform of 1968, and, since that legislation operated through provincially administered courts and did not deal with many questions integral to divorce proceedings still in provincial jurisdiction (such as property rights and family law) the role of the provinces has remained crucial—and distinctive.[30]

The results of the 1867 BNA Act were that women were *ignored* in public life. Only males who met age and property qualification were eligible to vote or stand as candidates in federal elections. Women, registered Indians, and some religious denominations were excluded. Women were *suppressed* in private life. The control of fathers and husbands over women extended to their real property, their children, and any activities outside the household. Since that time, both public and private institutions have been changed considerably and the struggle of women has been to a very large extent to change the culture of patriarchy in Canada and to institutionalize such changes.[31]

The model of our confederation, with its deep attention to local issues and its need for powerful national voices, also

---

30. Wendy Owen and J.M. Bumsted, "Divorce in a Small Province: A History of Divorce on Prince Edward Island from 1833," *Acadiensis* XX, no. 2 (Spring, 1991): 86–104.

31. It must be pointed out that the federal voting rights of registered Indians and people of Asian origin were delayed much longer than the suffrage of women. Asian Canadians won suffrage in 1948, and registered Indians living on reserves got the vote only in 1960.

became the model for some civil organizations. As we shall see in Chapter 5, it is a testimony to the astute women who founded the National Council of Women in Canada in 1893 that their structure so carefully shadowed the structure of Confederation in this way.[32]

The story of how women won suffrage, the right to sit as senators, the right to higher education, the right to the ownership of property and a share in marital property, custody of their children, rights in the labour force and the economy, and how the ideas and interpretation of equality came into being more recently constitute the body of this book. From the sociologist's viewpoint, the dynamics of social change are a key to understanding the workings of our society.

First, we look at an example of the extraordinarily long time that passed before the change came into effect. Just as many women were agitating for the vote in the 1890s,[33] decades before suffrage was won, women were arguing for their share of the household assets and resources a hundred years before the law in Canada was changed.

The Case of Marital Property

In 1973, Canadians interested in equality issues were stunned to read the verdict in the case of Alberta ranch wife

---

32. There are several histories of the organization, but two stress the structural elements: Veronica Strong-Boag, *The Parliament of Women: The National Council of Women of Canada, 1891–1929* (Ottawa: National Museums of Canada, 1976) and N.E.S. Griffiths, *The Splendid Vision: Centennial History of the National Council of Women of Canada, 1893–1993* (Ottawa: Carleton University Press, 1993).

33. For example, in 1894, there was a motion for the vote for women in the New Brunswick Legislature but it was defeated. Attempts to gain suffrage for women in the Maritimes and elsewhere were widespread, if unsuccessful, and were supported in the women's movement of the time, which was dominated by the Women's Christian Temperance Union (see, for example, Sylvie McClean, *A Woman of Influence: Evlyn Fenwick Farris* [Victoria: Sono Nis Press, 1997], Chapter 1, 24ff).

Irene Murdoch. What happened to Murdoch illustrates both of the great flaws identified in the decisions of 1864–67; that is, the underlying view of equality had not taken root in property issues, and the provincial legal history made the situation worse.

In 1968, as a result of domestic violence, the Murdoch marriage of 25 years had come apart. Having moved away from the farm to avoid the violence, Irene Murdoch asked for a share in the property that she and her husband had built up together over many years. As she testified in her trial, her work included haying; raking; swathing; moving; driving trucks, tractors, and teams; quieting horses; taking cattle back and forth to the reservoir; and dehorning, vaccinating, and branding the animals. She testified she did anything that had to be done. She was also asked if her husband was ever away from the 480-acre properties. She testified that he was gone five months of the year. To the utter surprise of most married women, the Alberta courts decided that what Mrs. Murdoch had done was what any other ranch wife would have done and so did not entitle her to an interest in the lands. She appealed all the way to the Supreme Court and lost. In 1973, the Supreme Court of Canada ruled to uphold the decision of the lower court with respect to ownership of the property. This decision marked a turning point in Canadian history and in attitudes to this aspect of family law.[34]

Most reasonable people in Canada thought that the work Irene Murdoch had done for all those years *was* considerably more than the "normal work of a wife." Indeed, most thought it looked more like a partnership in the family business. On marriage breakdown, most people believed that the wife was

---

34. M. Elizabeth Atcheson, Mary A. Eberts, and Beth Symes, *Women and Legal Action: Precedents, Resources and Strategies for the Future* (Ottawa: Canadian Advisory Council on the Status of Women, 1984); Mysty S. Clapton, "Murdoch vs. Murdoch: The Organizing Narrative of Matrimonial Property Law Reform," *Canadian Journal of Women and the Law* 20 no. 2 (2008): 197–230.

entitled to some form of support from the marriage. Irene Murdoch did receive an order for monthly spousal support in the final court decision but received no entitlement to a share of the property—the remedy she had sought.

The Canadian courts did not agree on her right to property based on the existing law and it is law that frames the lives of every woman in Canada. For example, while owning property is no longer the basis for enfranchisement, Canadian law does protect property holders from theft and trespass on their property. For Canadians, from the largest business owners to the ordinary mortgage-paying citizen, property holds a key place in their thinking about economic security, social status, and economic opportunity. It is part of the Enlightenment tradition that ordinary citizens can hold and protect their property and that their citizenship is tied to this. For example, holding real property remains a qualification, among others, for appointment to the Senate of Canada. Property ownership was part of the struggle that women had taken up in suffrage: as property owners, many women could vote in municipal elections and in their own right they were citizens. In 1973, people found it outrageous that decades after suffrage, Irene Murdoch, having invested 25 years in building up an asset, was unable to enjoy any benefit from it and was denied her citizenship even apart from equality rights.

Several issues confronted women in that 1973 decision of the Supreme Court, such as property and support rights for wives, widows, and separated or deserted women from a family business. While they recognized that the law varied by province, most women had not had the occasion to examine closely the particular issues faced by Murdoch. Murdoch's case concerned her rights as a substantial contributor to how the family made its living. As such, her situation was different from that of a divorced woman who had been a homemaker or who had worked in the waged economy. The shock this case created encouraged women in any situation to ask about their rights to property or support in the case of marriage breakdown. Only a few years later, all provinces had reviewed issues of the division of property after divorce or separation and had updated or revised their laws, as shown in the table on page 51.

The widespread shock at the final Murdoch decision occurred because public opinion had moved well ahead of the law and the courts in terms of the relations between spouses—so far ahead that women across the country were aghast at the outcome of the Murdoch case, as were many men.[35]

The judges who ruled in Murdoch's case were required to use existing law and precedent. That is, for generations men and women saw farm property as somehow intrinsically the property of men. Christine Georgina Bye's description of several generations of farm women and of her own life in Saskatchewan illustrates the point vividly. She points out how the tradition of men dominating farm life was passed down through her great-grandmother to her own generation not only in the division of labour on the farm, but also in property inheritance:

> Sadly, Kate's [her grandmother] commitment to dominant notions of masculinity and femininity did not serve her or future generations of prairie farm women very well. It meant that women in her family and rural society in general would continue to shoulder heavy workloads, to see themselves as "farmers' wives" rather than as farmers, and to enjoy far less power than men.[36]

---

35. Owen and Bumsted also note that before Confederation Prince Edward Island had a divorce court but it was "dormant" until after World War II. In 1945, it was "resurrected." This is a particularly fascinating instance of the complexities of the federal–provincial jurisdiction in matters concerning the family.

36. Christine Georgina Bye, "'I Like to Hoe My Own Row': A Saskatchewan Farm Woman's Notions about Work and Womanhood during the Great Depression," *Frontiers* 26, no. 3 (2005): 154. This vivid description of life in prairie farming shows how little change occurred until generations later, well after the Murdoch case.

This belief included accepting the idea that farm property belonged to men and that, despite the gruelling work that women contributed to the farm without wages, they had no rights in inheritance of the property. The Murdoch case raised the question of other similar situations in which couples had invested in businesses together and worked in them together.

So as the women of Canada mulled over the Murdoch decision, it became clear that women had not yet struggled sufficiently with many aspects of family law since Confederation.

In the early years of the twentieth century, women's groups had come to grips with the inadequacies of the law with respect to marriage, marital property, child custody, and other family-based issues. Many agitated for change, with some effect.

In British Columbia, for example, the Local Council of Women and the University Women's Club both worked on issues of family law and its reform.[37] British Columbia was formed by the union of two colonies, the colony of Vancouver Island and the colony of the Mainland. They joined in 1866, and in 1871 they joined Confederation as the Province of British Columbia. Each of the former colonies had adopted laws from Britain and adjusted them prior to their union. It took generations for those differences to be reconciled. In Vancouver, it was Helen Gregory MacGill and Evlyn Farris who led the University Women's Club to take up many issues of unfair and sexist family law. While other aspects of law, mostly related to economic matters such as commercial and labour laws, had been updated earlier in British Columbia, as late as 1917 family law and other laws related to women's lives remained resolutely patriarchal. Women in Vancouver had been shocked at that

---

37. For excellent descriptions of this work, see Elsie Gregory MacGill, *My Mother the Judge* (Toronto: Ryerson Press, 1955), reprinted 1981 with new introduction by PMA Books, especially Chapter 7; and McClean, *A Woman of Influence*, especially Chapters 2 and 3.

time and set out to make reforms. In other provinces, women were leading the debate on family law reform. Even so, and after all the reforms in the provinces, the Murdoch decision still came as a shock to many Canadian women.

We might ask why the tradition of husbands' ownership of the family property in the western world was carried on to the frontier society of Alberta, a province of new ideas where Nellie McClung had lobbied for suffrage, and the Famous Five had launched the Persons Case decades earlier. And how was it that the people of Alberta in the 1970s, when beliefs about the rights of women and traditions of married women's economic activity had changed so much, could still have in their laws the customs and beliefs of remote generations? This occurred because under our system of government laws are changed only when legislatures or courts and judges change them. Legislators are motivated to change laws only when social, economic, or legal situations are urgent or legislators are under pressure from citizens or expert groups. Laws related to employment and industrial practices had changed greatly since 1867 in every province and territory, for example, but laws related to family property and family business had not changed satisfactorily for wives throughout the generations.[38] In the Murdoch case, the majority of judges felt compelled to uphold the law that reflected old patriarchal values. Judges interpret laws, but they do not make them.

The case of divorce law is equally difficult. The Murdoch case was not in the first instance about divorce. The history of divorce in the first 40 years of the twentieth century, analyzed by James Snell, makes abundantly clear the underlying sentiments.[39]

---

38. See Constance B. Backhouse, "Married Women's Property Law in Nineteenth-Century Canada," *Law and History Review* 6, no. 2 (1988): 211–57.

39. James Snell, *In the Shadow of the Law: Divorce in Canada, 1900–1939* (Toronto: University of Toronto Press, 1991), 9.

A study of divorce reveals both women's systematic inequality in marriage and their continuing struggles to alter that situation. At common law it was well established
that at marriage the two parties were united into one
entity with a single domicile, and that domicile was the
husband's. Upon her marriage the wife lost her status as
femme sole, and her independent rights at law were quite
limited. For both women and men, marriage was an institution that fundamentally established their relative power
and status. Any attack on marriage, either individually or
generally, could be perceived as an attack on the distribution of power between the sexes or within the couple.

Murdoch's claim to property formed a clear-cut case of an
"attack on the distribution of power . . . within the couple."
Separation and maintenance agreements were very common
in Canada, in every province, and the courts by and large
worked to ensure that wives who were the victims of domestic violence were not destitute on leaving the family home.[40]
As much of the history of the provinces up to that time shows,
most laws had changed to entitle wives to some form of economic support on marriage breakdown, not equitable support but enough to ward off destitution. But claiming support
on the basis of contribution to the household economy was
not usual, and this applied most obviously to family businesses such as farms, ranching, and small businesses in which
family members worked without shares or wages.

One of the concepts of property rights for married women
carried out to the colonies was dower. The concept then became embedded in laws in the colonies. This concept is an-
cient in British law, antedating the Norman Conquest there.
It gave a widow the right to a third of her husband's real
property during her lifetime. Under this concept, a wife had

---

40. See Judith Fingard, "The Prevention of Cruelty, Marriage Breakdown and the
    Rights of Wives in Nova Scotia, 1880–1900," *Acadiensis* XXII, no. 2 (1993):
    84–101.

to give her consent when her husband sold property or put aside her dower rights. Dower rights remain a rather uncertain concept in many Canadian provinces, but in 1886, when Alberta was still a territory, dower rights were abolished. It was only in 1905 that Alberta joined Confederation; so, unlike wives in the older eastern provinces, wives in the western provinces had no protection. Through the agitation of women and their male supporters, Alberta brought in the Home Protection Act of 1916. This Act gave women the right to own property and gave widows some rights. But, as in the colonial regimes, the Act still assumed the primacy of the husband in property ownership and prevented only the destitution of a widow. The new law had not gone to the question of family asset ownership raised by the Murdoch case.

In short, as millions of Canadian women realized in 1973, one might work to build the family business and yet receive no benefit for all those years of labour. A woman in the paid labour force would be entitled to a pension and other benefits, but a wife working in the family business would not. A wave of reform swept across the country, led by women's groups and others concerned about these issues. But, again, the reforms that occurred between 1974 and 1981 were different in every province and territory.

So it was after the fury caused by the Murdoch case, and in a much changed Canada where women lawyers and judges were active in all provinces, that the laws regarding marital property and women's rights to a return on their investment of labour were revised.

Each of the acts listed in the table on page 51 improved the situation concerning marital property after divorce, but each was somewhat different and remains so. Family business assets are still complex. Canadians now accept the fact that most of the issues that affect their daily lives vary from province to province. Barriers to interprovincial trade

Reforms to Marital Property Following the Murdoch Case

Province/ Territory	Title of Act	Date of Proclamation
British Columbia	Family Relations Act (R.S.B.C. 1979, c. 121)	March 31, 1979
Alberta	The Matrimonial Property Act (R.S.A. 1980, c. M-9)	January 1, 1979
Saskatchewan	The Matrimonial Property Act (S.S. 1979, c. M-6.1)	January 1, 1980
Manitoba	The Marital Property Act (S.M. 1978, c. 24 [M-45])	October 15, 1978
Ontario	Family Law Reform Act (R.S.O. 1980, c. 152)	March 31, 1978
New Brunswick	Marital Property Act (S.N.B. 1980, c. M-1.1)	Jamuary 1, 1981
Nova Scotia	Matrimonial Property Act (S.N.S. 1980, c. 9)	October 1, 1980
Prince Edward Island	Family Law Reform Act (S.P.E.I. 1978, c. 6)	December 31, 1978
Newfoundland	The Matrimonial Property Act (S.N. 1979, c. 32)	July 1, 1980
Northwest Territories	Matrimonial Property Ordinances (sections 1, 2, 27, 28) (R.O.N.W.T. 1974, c. M-7)	July 1, 1974
Yukon	Matrimonial Property and Family Support Ordinances (O.Y.T. 1979 [2nd], c. 11)	January 1, 1980
Quebec	Revision of the family law provisions of the Civil Code of Quebec had been undertaken earlier; family law and matrimonial regimes were reformed in 1969, partnership of acquests was introduced in 1970, paternal authority was abolished in 1977. In 1980, a major reform of family law established the principle of spousal equality in marriage and within the family unit.	

Source: Adapted from "Murdoch v. Murdoch and Family Property Law in Canada." Section15.ca. http://section15.ca/features/reviews/2006/07/07/murdoch.

are raised at almost all the meetings of the premiers, as are other issues on which some provinces would seek harmonization. Child custody, for example, is the subject of attempted harmonization. Despite Charter equality rights, and despite the work of many, the primacy of the provinces in so many aspects of women's lives means the barriers across the country are still in place.

Women faced with problems of desertion, separation or divorce, property, taxation, credit, child custody, or the citizenship of their children, or a myriad of other issues, must consider the relevant rules of the province in which they live, or other provinces in which a spouse might live, before they take an action. They will need expert advice. Guidebooks for women and the law list these differences and, of course, have to take into account the constant changes as the laws are amended.[41] Lawyers must keep up with these changes for their clients, and as Canadians became more mobile for work or other reasons the bureaucratic, legal, and personal burdens have grown. Many constitutional amendments have been made since Confederation.[42] However, these amendments have not resolved many of the problems that were

---

41. There are many such popular guidebooks but the series by Linda Silver Dranoff, *Every Woman's Guide to the Law* (Markham, ON: Fitzhenry and Whiteside, 1985), and the series by Marvin Zuker and June Callwood, *The Law Is Not for Women* (Toronto: Pitmans, 1976), are two examples that list the provincial differences relevant to the period in which they were written. Books on family law such as the following also elaborate on these issues: Julian D. Payne and Marilyn A Payne, *Canadian Family Law* (Toronto: Irwin Law, 2006).

42. For lists of changes and amendments go to Canadiana.org, 1931–1982: Toward Renewal and Patriation, http://www.canadiana.ca/citm/themes/constitution/con stitution15_e.html (accessed December 15, 2011), and Parliament of Canada, The Constitution since Patriation: Chronology, November, 19, 2010, http://www.parl. gc.ca/Parlinfo/Compilations/Constitution/ConstitutionSincePatriation.aspx (accessed November 22, 2011). These sources list a large number of federal–provincial constitutional conferences since 1867, most involving constitutional amendments. The latter website lists events "with constitutional significance" since 17 April 1982. It is a very long list.

unforeseen by all those intelligent and committed men—the Fathers—who worked to create our federation.

While there have been improvements, even if not definitive ones from the woman's point of view, the structural situation of women is the same as it was before these improvements took place. That is, the province in which one lives determines the applicable civil law and almost all aspects of marital law. This explains why where one lives is such an important and defining factor in analyzing what it means to be a woman in Canada. The laws changed, but they changed within the context of the underlying values and assumptions of 1864–67: that is, the provinces are both separate from the central government and also separate from one another. In addition to this jurisdictional problem, as Snell pointed out, whereas in the late nineteenth and early twentieth centuries there had been many "informal marital" relationships, increasingly the state was a player in family law. For example, law now regulated the economic aspects of the dissolution of a common-law relationship, including same-sex relationships.[43]

One might argue that the United States is also a federation with many different laws in each state. The United States, however, has developed circuit courts that work toward the harmonization of law and the creation of a more common standard. No such courts exist in Canada, and nothing of the sort seems to be under consideration.

There have been many attempts to harmonize or coordinate laws in Canada and countless proposals over the years by commissions and by governments to change the division of powers. "The need to re-evaluate the distribution of

---

43. See Nick Bala, *Family Law in Canada and the United States: Different Views of Similar Realities* (Toronto: Oxford University Press, 1987); and Jason Wang, "Property Rights of Common-Law Spouses in Canadian Provinces," *Money and Family Law* 21, no. 4 (2006): 30–32.

legislative power in light of temporary problems and responsibilities is stressed again and again by governments" said
constitutional expert Mary Eberts in 1980. For example, the
issue of marriage has been a difficult one in terms of the division of powers ever since Confederation. Marriage is largely
within the federal jurisdiction but the provinces have power
for the solemnization of marriages and set requirements for
marriage licenses. There are many differences among the
provinces in these matters. Divorce was gradually ceded to
the federal domain although the related issues of custody
and property remain provincial matters. It is still the case
that some couples "shop around" for the best province in
which the division of property suits their circumstances.

The Murdoch case was a spur to the Second Wave women's
movement. This movement took on the federal and provincial governments when, in 1978, a constitutional conference
proposed to move divorce to the level of the provinces, re-
taining sufficient power at the federal level only to ensure
that divorce from one jurisdiction was recognized by the
other jurisdictions. This change would have destroyed the
gains women had made in 1968 under the divorce law, which
made it impossible for a husband to avoid divorce by moving
to a different province; the law also made the grounds for
divorce more equitable for both parties. This 1968 change
had been sought for many years and was brought before the
government of Canada by the National Council of Women,
the Canadian Federation of University Women, and allied
groups. The federal government retreated from its proposal after the 1978 protestations ("a storm of reaction") from
women's groups.[44]

The Murdoch decision came more than a century after
Confederation and after waves and waves of legislative

---

44. See Eberts, *Women and Constitutional Renewal*, for a discussion of this and
    many other similar issues concerning jurisdiction.

change brought about by reformers, activists, and external pressures; after suffrage was won; after divorce reforms; after the Canadian Bill of Rights; and after the Report of the Royal Commission on the Status of Women in 1970. After all of this, we found buried in our laws and in our thinking this extraordinary inequality. Change takes a long time in Canada, and the institutionalization of change is not simple.

>−+◆>−○−<◆−+−<

The Constitution and Parliament
A Chronology

1864   Confederation debates in Charlottetown. Debates continue in Quebec City leading to 72 resolutions that form the basis of the British North America Act.

1865   Quebec (Lower Canada) adopts French Civil Law.

1866   Fathers of Confederation go to London to gain Confederation legislation.

1867   Passage of the British North America Act, which comes into effect 1 July with the provinces of Ontario, Quebec, Nova Scotia, and New Brunswick.

Gradually the colonies and then the territories join Confederation as provinces.

1870   Fort Gary Convention – The Manitoba Act passed by Parliament.

1870   The Hudson's Bay Company transfers Rupert's Land and the North-Western Territories to Canada in June.

1871   British Columbia joins Confederation.

1873   Prince Edward Island enters Confederation.

1898   The Yukon becomes a separate territory.

1901	Saskatchewan and Alberta created as provinces.
1949	Newfoundland, a separate Dominion, joins Canadian Confederation, the tenth province.
1999	Nunavut is formed from Northwest Territories.

1876   The Indian Act passed by Parliament.

1885   Franchise bill before Parliament, during which Sir John A. Macdonald expresses his views on women's equality.

1929   Decision in the Person's Case by the Judicial Committee of the British Privy Council: women are "persons" and eligible for appointment to the Senate.

1930   Carine Wilson appointed first woman senator by Mackenzie King.

1931   Statute of Westminster; allows Dominions in the Commonwealth independence from decisions of the British Government making Dominions independent under "the Crown," raising many issues in our constitution including citizenship and an amending formula to our Constitution. The 1947 Citizenship Act allows women control of their own citizenship and Canadians are no longer "British subjects." In 1949 no further appeals from the Supreme Court of Canada to the Judicial Committee of the British Privy Council are permitted; in 1952 Canada has its first Canadian Governor General.

1960   The Canadian Bill of Rights is passed by the Diefenbaker Government.

1961–63   Presidential Commission on the Status of Women in the US.

1967–70   Prime Minister Pearson's Government establishes the Royal Commission on the Status of Women (RCSW) under pressure from organized women. It is chaired by Florence Bird (later Senator Bird) and the Executive Secretary is Monique Bégin (later minister in the Trudeau governments and famously Minister of Health when the Canada Health Act was passed). The Commission reports in December 1970, setting off a wave of social pressure for implementation of the recommendations.

1968–69   As Minister of Justice, Pierre Trudeau brings in Criminal Law Amendment Act in December 1967 to make birth control legal, ease the inequalities of divorce, and make therapeutic abortion legal under restrictive conditions and other measures to get the state out of "the bedrooms of the nation." It passes only in 1969.

1969–70   The Abortion Caravan moves slowly across the country from Vancouver to Ottawa raising consciousness and support for further reform of abortion law.

1973   The Murdoch decision of the Supreme Court shocks the nation. The Lavell Case exposes the weakness of the Bill of Rights to change the situation of Indian women who marry non-Indian men.

1982   The Constitution Act patriates the former British North America Act and all its subsequent amendments and adds a reworded Charter of Human Rights and Freedoms on the insistence of women and other equality seekers. Jurisdictions are given three years to amend their legislation to conform with the new Constitution and particularly the Charter.

1984   Based on the work of the Abella Commission, employment equity takes both legislative and regularity form at the federal level of government, and many provinces adopt employment equity laws. Judge Rosalie Silberman Abella is appointed to the Supreme Court of Canada in 2004.

1985   The Equality Provisions of the Charter come into effect (sections 15 and 28).

III

Women, War, and
Social Change in Canada

Since Confederation in 1867, Canada has been involved in wars directly several times and indirectly many times as peacekeepers, observers, and suppliers. There is a long pre-Confederation history of wars, riots, and uprisings in what is now Canada. There were raids and war on Canadian territory, most notably the War of 1812. Women in Canada, although only recently participating as combatants, have played many important roles in wars and the military. Women have always had views about, and have organized in support of, both war and peace. In their capacity as mothers, wives, and daughters—as well as voters and politicians—and as workers in the paid and volunteer economies, women have always been deeply involved with every war and every peacekeeping operation in which Canada has been involved.

The issues that confront us here are several: Did these roles in wars help to spur change in the structure or the culture of Canada, either to improve the rights of women or to keep women from gaining rights and status? How did the involvement of women directly and indirectly change the opportunity structure in economic life? Wars changed the nature of economic, social, and political life for all Canadians, of course, but was it also war that led to increased political rights for women during World War I? Was it their war work or the suffrage movement that put pressure on provincial governments to give women the vote? Did the need for labour lead to new opportunities for women, which in turn created new forms of equality? Or did women only temporarily occupy those roles? Did the roles that women played, both in war and in the home front during war, when wives and mothers managed the households for absent husbands for years at a time, change the nature of patriarchy? If so, did that lead to increased status and power for women and increased postwar equality?[1]

From Confederation and up until the Statute of Westminster in 1931,[2] Canada's role in any international affairs, including participation in wars, was directed by British policy and from London. However, as the experience of women nurses in the South African War shows, not all policy was directed by London.[3] From the start, Canada established differences from the colonial centre. Talent unique to Canada was mobilized in wartime.

---

1. Ruth Roach Pierson asked similar questions in her *Canadian Women and the Second World War*, Booklet No 37 (Ottawa: Canadian Historical Association, 1983), now sadly out of print. "It is often assumed that war accelerates social change. This may be true of the wars that have taken place in this century, and particularly of World War II, which saw the introduction of social welfare policies as well as of increased employment for women in Canada. What of the social position and role of women in Canada? Did World War II greatly or permanently alter the place of women in the labour market, corridors of power, and homes of the country?" Pierson's detailed article is most valuable but our interest is more general in terms of the impact of war on Canadian women. There is a growing literature on these issues: see Margaret Randolph Higonnet et al., eds., *Behind the Lines: Gender and the Two World Wars* (New Haven, CT: Yale University Press, 1987), which looks at many issues and several countries, although not Canada.
2. The 1931 Statute of Westminster made many changes in the status of the British colonies, including permitting Canada a largely independent foreign policy. For one description, read Andrew Cohen, *Lester B. Pearson*, Extraordinary Canadians (Toronto: Penguin Books, 2008).
3. Susan Mann, *Margaret Macdonald: Imperial Daughter* (Montreal and Kingston: McGill-Queen's University Press, 2005).

Soon after Confederation, in 1884, and at the request of Britain, Canada sent 389 men, including Ojibwa and Mohawk boatmen as well as lumbermen and voyageurs, up the Nile to relieve the siege of British General Charles Gordon at Khartoum. The Canadians were too late for the relief: Gordon was dead when they arrived. However, the involvement of Canadian voyageurs, with their experience at scaling rapids, was an indication of the specialized skills that Britain saw in Canadians. Sixteen of the voyageurs lost their lives in the course of this expedition. None of these was a woman, but Canadians and especially the families of those involved were highly conscious of this very first involvement of the Canadian nation in war overseas. It is important to note that Aboriginal peoples were involved in overseas wars at this early point. Armed forces were also deployed in the Canadian West both in the Northwest Rebellion of 1885 and in the gold rush in the Yukon in 1898. In both these actions, volunteer nurses had accompanied and cared for the sick and wounded.

Accounts of these events reveal that although attached to the military operations, the nurses were not *of* the military in any way. In 1885, those civilian nurses came from Winnipeg and Toronto, and some from a religious order. Subsequently, they were all decorated with the campaign medal. In addition, in the Yukon expedition, some nurses came from the Victorian Order of Nurses (VON). The idea for the VON came from the Vancouver Local Council of Women, who drew the attention of the National Council of Women to the needs of rural and remote areas for nursing services. Established in 1897 from discussions at the National Council of Women, the VON was conceived of as a civilian organization providing nursing services outside hospitals of Canada.[4]

---

4. See, for example, Barbara Dundas, *A History of Women in the Canadian Military* (Ottawa: Art Global and Department of National Defense, 2000); Strong-Boag, *Parliament of Women*; and Griffiths, *The Splendid Vision*.

In the South African War of 1899–1902, Canadian women participated as nurses under contract to the Canadian government but under the control of the British. From January 1900, each Canadian nurse was appointed to the rank of lieutenant. This rank set the remuneration levels.[5] Along with this officer rank, they were known as "nursing sisters." Why Canadian nurses were appointed as officers and British nurses were not may be explained by the very different recruitment strategies of the two countries. The first very few Canadian military nurses were recruited largely through their high political connections, although each was a trained and qualified nurse. The British did not always require the same standards.

Mann's biography of the exceptional Canadian nurse Margaret Macdonald describes in detail the long-term significance of this first war engagement for Canadian nurses.[6] Macdonald was sent in the second group of nurses in 1900, returned in 1901 to Canada, and then later, with seven others, was returned to South Africa for a few months in 1901. Only a handful of nurses were sent to that war; they were provided as a result of the participation of Canadian soldiers in the South African War.[7] While treatment of the very sick soldiers was the nurses' purpose, military action was not. Mann records one instance of Margaret Macdonald coming under fire: working in a field hospital, housed in a tent, Macdonald was hit by a piece of shrapnel. Although she was not seriously wounded, Macdonald, like the other non-combatants accompanying the armed forces, risked her safety in the course of her work.

---

5. See Dundas, *History of Women*, 22.
6. Mann, *Margaret Macdonald*.
7. One of those soldiers was the poet John McCrae, with whom Macdonald was friendly. McCrae is author of the World War I poem "In Flander's Fields," which is read on 11 November memorial services each year in Canada.

In 1904, the Canadian military established both the reserve Army Nursing Service, to which civilian nurses belonged, and the Permanent Army Nursing Services. The
eight women who had served in South Africa were founding
members of the permanent service. During these wars, and
long afterwards, the wounded and disabled required care at
home. When Canada brought nurses into the military hospitals in Canada, they drew on those in the reserves as well
as the permanent members. Professional nursing was an expanding occupation for Canadian women.

World War I (1914–1918)

Because of Canada's colonial status, when the British declared war on Germany in 1914, Canada was automatically at
war. Canadian troops were again extensively involved under
the control of the British. The government of Canada, however, had to organize who would go to the war in Europe as
well as how they would get there. This work included not only
the regular army and those enlisting for the war, but also the
non-combatant personnel, of which there were many.

Canadian nurses were chosen from the Permanent Army
Medical Corps as well as the reserve Army Nursing Service,
along with other trained Canadian nurses, for the Canadian
Army Medical Corps (CAMC). In this war, the nurses
formed their own unit with their own commanders and with
unique Canadian standards. While thousands of volunteers
who came forward served with the CAMC, all those selected were professionally trained (unlike the British who took
in untrained volunteer women to nurse), and all Canadian
nurses continued to be appointed at the rank of lieutenant.
While they were established in European war zones, nurses
worked in Canadian hospitals under a complex command.
Margaret Macdonald was promoted to rank of major and ran

the Canadian nurses under a complicated line of authority shared with the head of the British nurses and the Canadian military commanders. Among a wide variety of complex duties, Macdonald managed the language issues for Quebec nurses, finding assignments for them in the two Canadian hospitals staffed by Quebec doctors in France. Like all Canadian hospitals in France, these were under British authority. Complications like the command structure, arising from unique Canadian values, highlighted the importance of managing our own affairs. Macdonald was no doubt the "imperial daughter" Mann describes, but it is clear she and many others saw that practical matters needed to be carried out by Canadians dealing with Canadians.

World War I nurses were not combatants, but some were killed in the line of duty when their hospitals and other workplaces were hit. An enormous loss occurred when the *Llandovery Castle*, a Canadian hospital ship, was torpedoed in 1918. Among the 234 who died were all 14 of the nurses on board.[8] The postwar influenza epidemic also killed some nurses. Despite these shared tragic circumstances, the gender-differentiated roles between women and the men in the army and other forces were not only clear in recruitment, training, and deployment, but also insisted upon in daily life overseas and in Canada. Killed and wounded women might be, but men were still the focus of concern and took precedence in the military world.

On the home front, women were drawn into paid employment to replace men not only in munitions factories and elsewhere, but also in expanding economic sectors. In 1917, J.O. Miller, then principal of Ridley College, edited a book of essays titled *The New Era in Canada: Essays Dealing with the Upbuilding of the Canadian Commonwealth*. Among

---

8. See Debbie Marshall, *Give Your Other Vote to the Sister: A Woman's Journey into the Great War* (Calgary: University of Calgary Press, 2007), 218.

the essays was one titled "Women and the Nation" by Marjory MacMurchy, described as a member of the Ontario Unemployment Commission. In this essay, MacMurchy makes a vigorous case for the fundamental importance of the work—both paid and unpaid—of Canadian women in the service of the nation. She not only advocates the recognition of women's work in paid employment and in the household during the war, but also argues that Canadian women will not go back to the pre-war conditions when the war ends. She points to the fact that the vast majority of women in Canada are either in training or education or already in the labour force. Following a review of the census numbers on women in various categories, MacMurchy insists, "It must be recognized that the leisured class of women in Canada is very small." Women are skilled and "have a genius for organization." While bowing to the primary importance of child care and home life, she maintains that education and training for this skilled work is required, as it is for all other occupations. Furthermore, in light of the rise of skilled work in the Canadian economy, and for women in particular, every young woman should prepare herself for skilled employment. "Canadian women themselves, by their efforts and good judgment, their willingness and fitness, should see that their opportunities for paid employment are maintained and extended. This is one of the economic contributions which they can make both during the war and afterwards."[9]

All of the work women carried out professionally and as volunteers during the war had a major impact on the consciousness of Canadians, Canadian parliamentarians, and sectoral leaders. The men running the factories, the farmers, the senior civil servants, and the businessmen were

9. Marjory MacMurchy, "Women and the Nation." in *The New Era in Canada: Essays Dealing with the Upbuilding of the Canadian Commonwealth*, ed. J.O. Miller (London: J.M. Dent, 1917), 213–16.

impressed with the accomplishments and contributions of women in Canada. What these men—as a group—could not overcome was their deeply held view of "women's place" and "women's sphere" in society as supporters, helpmates, housewives, mothers, and wives of men.[10] This was not true of all men, of course, but even those men and women supporting women's rights were not all heralds of equality. The ideas of maternal feminism in that period reveal that Canadian women were for the most part moderately progressive rather than radical or revolutionary in their approaches to the changes in gender roles in the economy and in war.[11] Most people saw it as a case of women "pitching in" and "all pulling together" during the crisis, rather than a permanent change in the status and roles of women.

The more militant views came from those concerned about the economic conditions of women. By World War I, a fairly large proportion of women were in the paid, wage-earning economy. An even larger group of women—usually married or older single women—earned money for the household through the home-based labour of keeping chickens, taking in laundry, or offering room and board, sewing, or paid child care. In the factories and offices, there was a great deal of anger about the inequality of both wages and opportunities, which manifested in strikes and work stoppages both before and during the war. The concern of the labour movement for these unfair conditions was considerable and expressed in

10. See Alison Prentice, Paula Bourne, Gail Cuthbert Brandt, Beth Light, Wendy Mitchinson, and Naomi Black, *Canadian Women: A History* (Toronto: Harcourt Brace Jovanovich, 1988), 144.

11. There were women with politically and socially radical views such as Flora Denison in Toronto. See Deborah Gorham, "Flora MacDonald Denison: Canadian Feminist," in *A Not Unreasonable Claim: Women and Reform in Canada, 1880s–1920s*, ed. Linda Kealey (Toronto: Women's Press, 1979). By 1913, the members of the National Council of Women were debating women's rights not on the basis of maternal feminism but as equals. These debates are found in Griffiths, *The Splendid Vision*, 107ff. The revolution in Russia in 1917 was of great interest to many Canadians, including feminists.

one of the many suffrage bills introduced into the Ontario legislature in 1912 and 1913. The Member sponsoring the bill argued that without the vote and labour law protection, women had to sell their labour more cheaply than men and this would significantly undercut the labour markets.[12]

Suffrage as a Consequence of War

In some places women had municipal votes as property owners, and there were long-standing calls for women's suffrage, which had both preceded and followed Confederation. Those advocating suffrage—having been beaten back many times—were now very closely aligned, and sometimes even merged, with the temperance movement, and sometimes with the workers' movements.[13] In any case, through their organizations, women expressed their views publicly and forcefully in a range of settings.

After years of rejecting suffrage proposals, several provinces had granted women suffrage during World War I,[14] and it was a matter of debate in Parliament whether provincial suffrage automatically granted women the right to the federal vote. The Conservative government of Sir Robert Borden equivocated in the face of calls for female suffrage, and the history of the period from 1916 to 1920 is both complex and nuanced. Prior to these years, many bills advocating suffrage had been introduced into legislatures across the country and vigorously debated on both sides; all had been defeated. Even those arguing in favour of the vote for women—who pointed

---

12. See Catherine Cleverdon, *The Woman Suffrage Movement in Canada*, 2nd ed. (Toronto: University of Toronto Press, 1974), Chapter 2 on Ontario.

13. For a detailed account of women's suffrage at the federal level, see Cleverdon, *The Woman Suffrage Movement*, Chapter 5. See also Carol Lee Bacchi, *Liberation Deferred? The Ideas of the English-Canadian Suffragists, 1877–1918* (Toronto: University of Toronto Press, 1983).

14. See the detailed discussion on gaining suffrage in Chapter 5.

to women's intelligence and increasing education, their role in and their increasingly important contribution to the formal economy, and their significant stake in the future of their country—seldom made arguments about the intrinsic equality of men and women. The "separate spheres" beliefs were widespread. Women's work was segregated in both the paid labour force, in volunteer work, and in the household, and it was the exceptional legislator who based his arguments on concepts of equality. Arguments that women would improve the standards and morality of legislatures, improve society, and represent the interests of women were far more common. Even more common were arguments against suffrage on the grounds that women did not want the vote, that their views were reflected in their father's or husband's vote, or that they did not understand public affairs. There was extraordinary hostility to feminists, especially those considered radical, and accounts show that even the moderate women whose husbands were respected public figures were treated with disdain or plain rudeness.[15]

The government of Canada faced a serious challenge during World War I to recruit sufficient men for military needs. In 1916, as savage fighting in Europe led to a climbing death toll, politicians realized conscription was required. This was highly controversial. Most in Quebec and many in the West opposed conscription, but conscription was not the only problem and pressure facing the government of the day. It was pressured for more railways, for a coalition "union" government, and for women's suffrage.[16] The leaders of the

---

15. For more detailed information, see, for example, Prentice et al., *Canadian Women*, Chapter 6 on the "women's sphere."
16. One of the Members calling on Borden to give women full suffrage was William Pugsley, MP Liberal (1907–17), from New Brunswick, whose many speeches are referred to in Cleverdon, *The Woman Suffrage Movement*. Sadly, this aspect of his work is not mentioned in his official biography. Cf. Robert Craig Brown, *Dictionary of Canadian Biography Online*: Pugsley, William, 2000, http://www.biographi.ca/009004-119.01-e.php?&id_nbr=8335 (accessed December 15, 2011).

two main parties saw the divisions that the necessity for conscription was creating as both serious and filled with potential political dangers. In the end, Prime Minister Borden and Wilfrid Laurier (the leader of the opposition) each solved his political problems in the course of the controversy surrounding the creation of a union government, proposed by Borden and opposed by Laurier.

During this controversy, the Wartime Elections Act was passed on 20 September 1917; it was condemned by the Opposition and the press for its discriminatory features. Under this Act, women who were 21 years of age and British subjects or naturalized since 1902 (not conscientious objectors or those born in enemy countries), and who had a close relative serving in the armed forces of Canada or Great Britain, could vote in the wartime election. The Opposition believed the Act was designed to return the union government under Borden to power in the imminent "conscription election" of 1917, and so it did in December of that year. The conscription crisis was most pronounced in Quebec, and in opposing conscription Wilfrid Laurier both lost and won supporters. He won over those opposing conscription and lost those Liberals for whom winning the war took precedence over party loyalty.[17] But it was not only political parties that were divided.

In Montreal an umbrella organization of 44 women's organizations, the Montreal Council of Women, was badly divided on the issue of conscription, as were women's organizations across the country. The president of the Council put full suffrage for women ahead of Borden's Military Service and Wartime Election's Act. There was a concerted effort

---

17. For an analysis of these complications, see John English, "Conscription," in *Readings in Canadian History Post-Confederation*, 2nd ed., eds. R. Douglas Francis and Donald D. Smith (Orlando, FL: Holt, Rinehart and Winston, 1986), 337–47.

to impeach the president for her convictions. This is only one example of how difficult these issues were for men and women, and for suffragists of all political parties and of both maternal feminist and the equalitarian feminist viewpoints.[18] Not all women agreed, nor did all feminists and suffragists agree. The pressure of war and each woman's personal circumstances strained the loyalties and values of all.

By the following year, 24 May 1918, under continued pressure and perhaps with a change of heart, Borden had introduced and passed a new bill which gave every woman who was a British subject and age 21 or older the right to vote in federal elections *provided she met the same qualifications that a man would require to vote in her province.* This law came into effect on 1 January 1919 and was in many ways a step forward except for two issues: first, the provincial–federal differences, so troublesome throughout Canadian history, again prevented many from voting; and, second, the law did not allow women themselves to stand for election. The first issue caused tremendous complications in establishing the qualifications for voting and counting the votes. All this created inequalities across the country. The second issue was modified in the By-Elections Act of 1919, by which women eligible to vote were also eligible to stand for election. Then, finally in 1920, the Dominion Elections Act made both women and men eligible to vote provided they were 21 years of age, British Citizens, and resident in Canada for a year and in the electoral district for two months. This 1920 bill, introduced by the Borden union government, had some limitations, but it removed the requirement of meeting provincial conditions and so extended both the franchise and the right to stand for office.

---

18. Tarah Brookfield, "Divided by the Ballot Box: The Montreal Council of Women and the 1917 Election," *Canadian Historical Review* 89, no.4 (2008): 473–501.

This bill did not begin to move Canada to universal female suffrage, however. Not all provinces had legislated
the right of women to vote in provincial elections, although
by 1916 Manitoba and Alberta had done so and British
Columbia followed in 1917. Not all provinces had given
women the right to stand for office. While Ontario gave
women the right to vote, the right to hold office did not
come for another two years. Women were enfranchised
in New Brunswick in 1919, but the right to hold public office was granted only in 1934. Quebec gave neither right to
women until 1940.

On the basis of race, entire categories of people were not
enfranchised in 1920, such as Asian, Indo-Canadian, and
Aboriginal peoples registered as Status Indians. Only in
1947 did Chinese and Indo-Canadians get the vote. With
the franchise for Status Indians (including women) in 1960
and the rights of prisoners to vote in 1993, virtually all
women older than 18 years of age gained access to the ballot box.

But in 1917 provincial differences prevailed. In Alberta
one of Canada's overseas military dietitian-nurses, Roberta
MacAdams, was elected from a special constituency formed
from the soldiers and nurses from Alberta serving overseas
in the war. This made her one of the first two women elected
in Canada and the British Empire (Louise McKinney was
the other Canadian). MacAdams was a remarkable woman
whose life story is recounted in *Give Your Other Vote to the
Sister: A Woman's Journey into the Great War.*[19] Given the
ideological barriers she successfully challenged, she is an
important figure in Canadian history. Her election is also
significant given the overwhelming support to win the election she received from men in the military. Clearly, the war

---

19. Marshall, *Give Your Other Vote.*

was changing the perceptions of women in a most fundamental way. But it is worth noting that before this vote,
MacAdams had never been in favour of suffrage—her ad-
vocacy of issues facing women had been built around her
"separate sphere" beliefs. Her ideas about equality emerged
from her work in the legislature after her election. The
MacAdams story supports the argument that the war experience had more impact on the advance of equality views
than might have occurred without it.

Would the federal women's suffrage bills have passed
without the pressures on the government of Robert Borden
to achieve conscription? Probably, but it would undoubt-
edly have taken longer. With the opposition Liberals in
support of women's suffrage, no doubt it would have happened; although, as Cleverdon's account of suffrage debates
in Canada makes clear, equality rights for women were not
central in the suffrage debates. The work and commitment
of women during World War I was the basis of arguments in
favour of suffrage from many members of Parliament both
in Canada and in Britain. Many were of the view that women
had "earned" this right, rather than noting that women had
paid taxes and voted in municipal and other elections (and
in many places) for generations. Nor did many profess the
intrinsic equality of women, as had John Stuart Mill in 1867
in Britain or John A. Macdonald in 1885, among others who
argued for women's equality.

At the war's end, men and women returned from Europe
to face the devastating effects of the influenza epidemic at
home. Recognizing the sacrifices of servicemen, government worked to find employment for them. Government domestic policies were adjusted accordingly. Many women left
their employment voluntarily or were forced to leave their
paid employment to create opportunities for returned combatants. In the 1920s, even with sex-segregated workplaces,

women's labour force participation increased, especially among single women for whom employment between school and marriage became the norm. But within a few years, the onset of the Great Depression and the belief among many Canadians that men should have precedence in employment led to what historian Veronica Strong-Boag has described as "ruthlessness" in hounding women from jobs.[20]

World War I, known as the Great War for its unprecedented scale, had changed the lives of Canadians in many ways. Among those changes was an expansion in the role and status of women. Some changes were permanent and some fleeting. Having worked in some traditional "men's" jobs during the war and having run organizations of significance, most women were pushed back into their secondary status once more, but they did not forget their experiences.

The significant permanent changes for women were in political rights and military roles. Suffrage for the majority of women was secure at the federal level and in most provinces. Women could stand for the federal Parliament and hold public office. Women were now clearly established as nurses and officers in the military. Despite the disbanding of the women's military service units in the postwar period, their status during the conflict was well acknowledged. Because of the work women had undertaken in wartime, attitudes had broadened toward women's citizenship. Unfortunately, that did not include any significant break in the patriarchy in relation to governments, heads of institutions, or the household. Women in the labour force were still highly segregated from men in the civil service as well as in the private sector. "Separate and slightly less unequal" was the postwar reality for women in employment.

---

20. Veronica Strong-Boag, "Janey Canuck": Women in Canada, 1919–1939, Booklet No. 53 (Ottawa: Canadian Historical Association, 1994), 9.

World War II (1939–1945)

This time Canada made its own declaration of war, decided by its own Parliament six days after the United Kingdom declared war on Hitler's Germany. This was possible as a result of changes between Britain and its old imperial colonies leading to the creation of the Commonwealth in the 1931 Statute of Westminster. This Act described the ties between Britain and the dominions, but essentially granted them independence in many ways. Legislators in the provinces of Canada could and did modify their laws, but the path to amending our own constitution still lay in the Parliament of Britain.

In the case of Canada and Australia, however, the division of powers between the federal and provincial governments was unresolved by the Statute of Westminster. Could Britain continue to have legislative power or relations with the provinces? Could the provinces go directly to Britain to amend their own legislation? In practice, without resolving the question constitutionally, Britain refused attempts by the Australian states or Canadian provinces to bypass their federal governments. However, it was only through further constitutional change in Canada in 1982, and Australia in 1986, that this question was settled in favour of the national governments of those countries. By that time, women were playing a much more influential role in parliaments and governance at all levels.

In this unresolved aspect of the 1931 Statute of Westminster lies the roots of the constitutional changes in Canada in the 1980s, through the patriation of the Constitution of Canada. There was considerable resistance in the provinces to the proposed patriation and the amending formula brought in by Prime Minister Trudeau. He was forced to accommodate the provinces and they, in turn, took a case to Westminster. It was the same concern about provincial and local historical rights that was prominent in the

Charlottetown Conference of 1864, undiminished by more than one hundred years of confederation.[21]

Canadian women intervened vigorously and successfully in the wording of the Charter of Human Rights and Freedoms that was part of the Constitution of 1982. However, in the 1920s, during debates about the Statute of Westminster, women constitutionalists were not involved in discussions or in the debates between the provinces and the federal government, or part of the delegations that appeared before the British Parliament. This is all the more surprising given that in 1928 and 1929, when these discussions were underway, the Persons Case, led by the Famous Five women and resulting in further rights for women, was a key public and constitutional issue. The decision on whether women were "persons" in Canada was fought before the British Judicial Committee of the Privy Council in London. It is clear that many women recognized the constitutional problems they faced.

Between 1931 and 1982, three amendments to the Canadian Constitution were all related to universal economic measures, providing the federal government with powers over unemployment insurance, old-age pensions, and supplementary pension benefits. Further action—for example, on family allowances and health insurance—did not take the form of a constitutional amendment but rather was carried out through the spending powers of the Government of Canada.

By the time of World War II and the end of the long and brutal Great Depression, women occupied non-combatant positions in the armed forces. In addition to nurses, these positions included ciphers, intelligence officers, map-makers, and map-readers. Some war artists were women

---

21. See the powerful defense of provincial rights in many post-Confederation speeches in Virginia E. Robeson, ed., *Debates about Canada's Future, 1868–1896* (Toronto: Ontario Institute for Studies in Education, 1977). Of particular force is the speech by Honoré Mercier, 1884, 10.

(e.g., Molly Bobak), as well as filmmakers, photographers, journalists, and war correspondents.

Women's work in the economy in Canada was equally crucial in the production of food, war weapons, and other supplies.[22] In 1939, while only two women were in Parliament, women were nonetheless active in the main political parties and in electoral debates and politics. Having survived the privations of the Depression, most women welcomed the opportunities to earn their livelihood in the jobs now opening up in war production and in replacing enlisted men in the civilian labour force at home.

In 1939, Canadian Parliament declared war on Germany and threw the resources of the nation into the effort. While contributing to the war effort on the side of the Allies, Canada was not prepared for the variety of the demands of war, such as decisions about the internment of Japanese from the West Coast and of Italians and Germans in Central Canada. Internment policies and refusal to accept Jewish refugees in 1938 (and throughout the period) divided the population at home and abroad, incurring long-term consequences for the nation.[23]

Recruiting for the military was a sensitive issue in light of the conscription of World War I, and at first only volunteers went overseas. Again, the pressures of war aided the

---

22. It should be noted that prisoners of war (POWs) were also used in agricultural work toward the end of World War II: "During 1945 about 2,200 POWs were employed in sugar beet work and the hoeing of crops" in Alberta and Ontario. See John Joseph Kelly, "Der Deutsche Kriegsgefangener auf Alberta: Alberta and the Keeping of German Prisoners of War, 1939–1947," in *For King and Country: Alberta in the Second World War*, ed. K.W. Tingley (Edmonton: Reidmore Books, 1995), 285–302.

23. On the long-term consequences for the interned Japanese, see Pamela Sugiman, "Passing Time, Moving Memories: Interpreting Wartime Narratives of Japanese Canadian Women," *Social History* 37, no. 73 (2004): 51–79. The consequences of denying Jewish refugees in Canada in 1938 has been extensively documented but see Irving Abella and Harold Troper, eds., *None Is Too Many: Canada and the Jews of Europe, 1933–1948* (Toronto: L&O Denny, 1983).

movement of women into the armed services and this time in a range of occupations in addition to nursing. Once more, military nurses were much more likely to serve overseas, and less than 10 percent of the other women in the armed services did so. Many women were decorated for their services, and 71 women were killed during their service.

Unlike the circumstances in 1914, many women were well informed about international affairs and were ready to serve. In 1938, Canadian women were voluntarily forming paramilitary groups that were training in a variety of military and other war-related skills. When war was declared in 1939, this training intensified, and Canadian women, observing the involvement of British women, asked the government if they could join the British services or be auxiliary to the Canadian armed services. The Canadian government did not want these paramilitary groups associated with the military, but there were nearly 7,000 of them and they were in contact across all the provinces in both languages. Some response had to be made.

The result is that by 1941 the Canadian government was recruiting women for the armed forces; in the end, nearly 50,000 women were in uniform. The view of the government was that the women would replace male clerks, administrators, cooks, telephone operators, drivers, and similar non-combat duties in Canada rather than overseas. But their views changed.

The Royal Canadian Air Force (RCAF) created a "women's division," although married women with children and permanent civil servants were ineligible. With the exception of medical officers, women were paid less than men, despite the appeal of an air vice-marshal.[24] By 1942, some of the RCAF (Women's Division) was going overseas.

---

24. See Dundas, *History of Women*, 52.

The army created the Canadian Women's Army Corps (CWAC). With the exception of ranks, the conditions were similar to those in the RCAF. The pay gap between men and women, with some exceptions, was significant. By 1942, some CWAC were going overseas, and eventually they served—21,000 strong—in virtually all the theatres of war, as well as in Canada.

The Women's Royal Canadian Naval Service (WRCNS), also created in 1942, eventually grew to about 6,000 volunteers and, as were members of the other armed services, many were posted to Britain, Newfoundland, Washington, and New York.

Canadian women in the services undertook tremendous amounts of vital work. So did the civilian women who worked in the factories, farms, and offices of Canada to replace men in the services. But the attitudes toward these women reflected both the sexual division of labour that pre-existed the war and the pay differentials similar to civilian practices. Also similar—and perhaps even more strident— were the requirements that women's personal and social behaviour uphold a model of female virtue.

Just as the nurses had kept a reserve after the South Africa War in 1902, which was called into action in 1914, so it was that the nurses maintained a reserve presence in 1918, when all other women's military groups had been disbanded. In 1939, this reserve list consisted of more than three hundred nursing sisters, while the Royal Canadian Amy Medical Corps had only one matron and 10 nursing sisters.[25] Women medical doctors and other medical therapists were also recruited for World War II, serving the armed forces as well as civilians.

Canadian nurses were exceptional in their service for a variety of reasons. First, their enlistment pattern was well

---

25. Dundas, *History of Women*, 38.

in excess of that of men. As Cynthia Toman in her study of nurses in World War II points out,

> Trained Canadian civilian nurses volunteered again during the Second World War in numbers so large that the military placed a moratorium on their enlistment only ten days after the call to mobilize medical units, contradicting military historian C.P. Stacey's pronouncement of Canada as a very "unmilitary community."[26]

She notes that this enthusiasm for enlistment among Canadian nurses was in contrast to the experience of Canadian men or the enlistment—and finally conscription—of American nurses in the late years of World War II when the United States entered the war.

Why this difference between the men and women of Canada and between Canada and the United States in these enlistment practices? The values of the two North American countries had diverged widely for many years with respect to foreign policy. This difference was reflected in the attitudes and values of many Canadian women toward war in Europe. Canadians did not want war, but they were not isolationists.

As the war ended and troops returned, government made special efforts to create positions for the men, such as in university programs where veterans had opportunities that would not have been open to them before the war and in the civil service. Women veterans were also eligible for these opportunities. The inclusion of women after this war honoured those who had been killed and created opportunities for the many other women who had gone overseas, some of them decorated for their service.

While the women armed services units were disbanded again shortly after World War II (temporarily, as it turned out, since the Korean War and a series of wars followed), the

---

26. Cynthia Toman, *An Officer and a Lady: Canadian Military Nursing and the Second World War* (Vancouver: UBC Press, 2007), 4.

benefits created for those serving in the armed forces were available for women. As Pierson points out, there were several

> sex-typed inequalities. As pensions were based on service pay and as servicewomen's pay was only four-fifths that of servicemen's, the pension rates payable to former members of the CWAC, RCAF-ED, or the WRCNS, were four-fifths of the standard men's pensions. Furthermore, the preference that ex-service personnel were to be given in the civil service applied only to those who had seen active service overseas or on the high seas.[27]

Of the nearly 50,000 women in uniform during World War II, only 7,000 women had been overseas in active service and none had been on seaborne vessels. However, Pierson notes that a higher proportion of women in armed services took advantage of the educational opportunities than did men.

In the familiar postwar reaction, many woman left the labour force after 1945, but they did not leave in numbers similar to women in the United States. The proportion of women plunged to a quarter of the workforce in 1946, only to return to war levels in 1966.[28] Nor did married women leave the paid labour force as they had done before the war. The numbers of working married women declined, of course, but by 1951 a third of working women were married. It was also the period of the "baby boom," although this was the result of marriage at young ages, and of the economic opportunity and prosperity that enabled men to earn a "family wage" again (in which the husband/father earned enough to keep his family). This had often been an impossible feat during the Depression. Women's double day is ascribed by some to the immediate postwar period when many women were committed to their careers and determined to retain their own economic independence.

---

27. Pierson, *Canadian Women and the Second World War*, 23.
28. Ibid., 25.

The lives of women in prison camps, refugees, and internees in Canada and abroad, were permanently changed by the wartime experiences. For civilians in Europe, North Africa, and the Pacific, the years during and after the war were terrible, filled with suffering from which many never recovered. Refugees, displaced persons, and war brides came to Canada in relatively large numbers in the postwar period, changing the composition of cities, the requirements of settlement, and the diversity of the country. They brought, along with their sorrows and broken lives, new ideas, skills, and energies, and so added to the postwar recovery. While they may not have brought new ideas about women's equality, their experiences of immigration created many activists for fairness and social change in later years.

Taking stock at the end of World War II, women would have noted that suffrage was now held in all provinces, including Quebec,[29] although not for all women. As noted earlier, Canadians of Asian origin and Indo-Canadians won the right to vote in 1947, but Status Indians had to wait until 1960. Women were now recognized in all branches of the armed forces. They were not combatants but occupied a wide range of roles vital to the military. Therefore, women took note of their entitlement to further education in vocational, secondary, and post-secondary education programs, as we noted above, opportunities taken up by women at a

---

29. Women gained suffrage in Quebec in 1940—the last province to legislate it. Women owning property in Quebec had the municipal franchise in 1840 (on the principle of "no taxation without representation") but lost it in 1849. When, during the World War I period, all other provinces granted women suffrage, Quebec did not under the heavy influence of the Roman Catholic Church, but by 1940, Liberal Premier Godbout was able to get passage of a suffrage bill for women against Church opposition. This was partly due to the fact that virtually all other jurisdictions had already done so and that Quebec women were already participating in many walks of civilian life and, of course, had had the federal vote since 1918. A detailed account of the long struggle for the vote in Quebec is to be found in Cleverdon, *The Woman Suffrage Movement*, Chapter 7, and some description and analysis found in the chapter on social change.

higher rate than men. While many women veterans went to university or other forms of further education through this bill, the majority prepared for occupations traditionally viewed as suitable for women. Some would also have had the experience of wartime government-funded child care, although this disappeared at the end of the war. Women's range of experiences in the paid labour force had radically increased through wartime work.

But by war's end other changes had occurred in Canada. The introduction of the family allowance put some cash into the hands of mothers, a small comfort to those used to earning a proper income, but a comfort to stay-at-home mothers who had previously had access only to what their husbands chose to give them.

This measure of social reform was only one of the recommendations of the Marsh Report on Social Security for Canada.[30] This study was created by the federal government during the war as a result of the concern by many Canadians that the country might return to the inequalities and deprivations of the Depression years. They feared the potential for more widespread social unrest that had preceded the war arising from the dire poverty and injustice of the period. While the unions and many social reformers across the country were most concerned with wage rates and the ability of workers to earn a family wage to support their children, the federal government seized on the family allowance as a way of putting cash into the hands of families with children. It realized that the cash would be spent unquestionably on the types of goods that, produced during the war for the armed forces, could now be produced in the form of children's shoes, clothes, and goods. In a special victory for Quebec mothers, widespread outcry by women's

---

30. Leonard Marsh, *Report on Social Security of Canada* (1943; repr., Toronto: University of Toronto Press, 1975).

groups, social reformers, and others overturned a federal–provincial arrangement that would have had the allowance delivered to mothers everywhere except Quebec.[31] Wages remained a serious concern, and a wage freeze at the end of the war meant that the family allowance became even more vital to the household economy.

The social reforms advocated during and between the wars in Canada had maintained the paramount importance of the family. Nonetheless, the importance of women in the economy, as well as the rights of women, was a strong current in the debates on social and political reform in the period. The Marsh Commission was concerned with wage rates for family support, unemployment, and the reintegration of women after the war. Despite many strong arguments by community and national organizations—as well as in the academy, social agencies, and the civil service—sex segregation in the workforce and the primacy of the male breadwinner continued unabated at the end of the World War II.[32] This sex segregation came in the face of the much higher proportion of girls graduating from secondary education and of women graduating from post-secondary education.

What was evident to women who had worked during the war is that the participation of married women with children in the labour force, while a reality, was not widely accepted except under conditions of economic necessity or in occupations such as nursing. It was also clear that government funding for universal daycare for children was ephemeral—not institutionalized either as an idea or a policy. This was the case, as Pierson tells us, in spite of the fact that

---

31. For a comprehensive look at the welfare state in Quebec throughout and after World War II, see Dominique Marshall, *The Social Origins of the Welfare State: Quebec Families, Compulsory Education, and Family Allowances, 1940–1955* (Waterloo: Wilfrid Laurier University Press, 2006).
32. See, for example, Nancy Christie, *Engendering the State, Family, Work and Welfare in Canada* (Toronto: University of Toronto Press, 2000).

"A 1944 Labour Department survey showed that 28 per cent of the women, as compared with 2 per cent of the men, intended to quit work after the war, but that meant that 72 per cent of the women wanted to stay in the work force."[33] For single women, working for pay between schooling and marriage was an expected part of their lives, but this had been the case well before World War II. For married women without children, a career or full-time work was acceptable. For women, once their children were in school, the labour force was a possibility but not yet institutionalized. The institutionalization of mothers in the paid labour force came only later in the years when family size dropped and the rights of women, married or not, became once more a matter of public debate and action. Two generations later universal child care is still not institutionalized as a public service—with the exception of Quebec—despite the dramatic increase of mothers in paid employment throughout the country and the dire needs of working parents.

In the years after the war, women married at younger ages, and many had several children closely spaced, making work outside the home very difficult. A drop in the labour force participation rates for women with young children followed. At the same time, there was a rise in the expectations of higher education for women, in terms of not only school completion, but also post-secondary education. This came, first, through specialized secretarial, teaching, and nursing schools and then, later, in more specialized programs at universities. The world was changing for women but not as a direct result of the war. It was the more indirect, secondary effects of postwar prosperity, large family size, and population growth through immigration that led to vast changes in the lives of women in Canada that were manifest in "the Second

---

33. Pierson, *Canadian Women and the Second World War*, 24.

Wave." All those baby boomers going to school in the 1950s and 1960s created the enormous demand for school teachers and related occupations, but in the years immediately after World War II, there were other preoccupations.

After the colonial wars and the two European wars, Canada's war efforts changed. Subsequent to World War II, Canada's participation in wars has been with United Nations or other international forces in Korea, the Middle East, Bosnia-Serbia-Croatia, Chile, El Salvador, Guatemala, Lebanon, Israel, Syria, Cyprus, the Falklands, Rwanda, Haiti, the Gulf War, and Afghanistan—the latter being the first occasion during which our combat forces overseas have included several hundred women, and the first time women combatants have been killed. But in all these wars, during the Cold War period, and subsequently, Canadian women have served in the armed forces and very often overseas. Dundas's detailed description of women in these missions shows that while women were recruited, trained, and involved, there was nonetheless a sexual division of labour that confined women to separate roles in most instances.

In previous wars, women nurses and others came under enemy fire and were killed and wounded, although they were not in combat positions. In the post–World War II era, and especially after the Royal Commission on the Status of Women (1970) examined the roles and status of women in the armed forces, the momentum for equality, the strongest value of the Second Wave of the women's movement, led to the demand to open the armed forces to women in a much wider range of occupations. Consistent with the views held during both world wars, the military authorities began a first stage by replacing men with women in a wider range of occupations than previously. They created a separate personnel division for women and permitted few overseas or mission-based postings.

In a second stage, as women in many occupations were posted overseas and, especially, in peacekeeping operations, the armed forces began to face up to the realities of a gender-integrated force. Persuading both senior commanders and all other ranks and services that women were capable not only of the physical and technical demands but also of serving as colleagues on an equal footing was a long struggle. Persuading the international forces with which Canada was serving that women should not be "special" but should be "equal" is an even more difficult task.[34]

Eventually, after long study and debate, trials were established to determine whether the integration of women into combat could be successfully achieved.[35] After the 1987 results of these studies, women won positions in combat roles, including air, sea, and land roles.

Consistent with the need to create organizations to institutionalize change, the Canadian Human Rights Commission was a powerful force not only in interpreting the rights of women and men, but also in reviewing the implementation of change. In the case of the armed forces, a landmark tribunal ruling of the Commission landed in 1989. This came four years after the implementation of the Charter of Human Rights and Freedoms into the revised Constitution of Canada. It was a dramatic case. Five complainants argued that there was gender discrimination in the armed forces—four women reported that they had been denied access to some areas of employment based on gender, and a man argued that he was required to serve in combat while

---

34. See Donna Winslow and Jason Dunn, "Women in the Canadian Forces: Between Legal and Social Integration," *Current Sociology* 50, no. 5 (2002): 641–67.
35. The "Swinter" trials were a careful and thorough testing of the question. See, for example, Rosemary Park, "Overview of the Social/Behavioural Science Evaluation of the 1979–1985 Canadian Forces Trial Employment of Servicewomen in Non-traditional Environments and Roles," Research Report 86–2 (Willowdale, ON: Canadian Forces Personnel Applied Research Unit, 1986).

women were not. This was a powerful challenge for the tribunal. It ruled that only submarine service and Roman Catholic chaplaincy service could be closed to women on the grounds that there were bone fide occupational requirements for male service in those occupations. Since 2001, women have been permitted to serve in the submarine service as well.

There have been many women in combat roles in our forces in Afghanistan (230 in 2008), and 2006 marked the death of Nicola Goddard, the first Canadian woman killed while serving in a combat role. Sadly, other women also number among the serious loss of Canadian lives in that war. But has this change been institutionalized and accepted? One might say the military has accepted women in combat positions, but it is still unclear if the broader society has accepted this as "normal." It remains to be seen if this change will be reversed under some set of circumstances. The value of Canadian women serving in combat roles and leadership roles in our armed forces has been accepted very widely and provides a model to some other cultures. It is institutionalized in law and practice through the actions taken by the armed forces and the Canadian Human Rights Commission. Increasingly, it is becoming embedded in our culture, as can be seen in the CBC radio drama series *Afghanada*, which dramatizes the work of the armed forces in Afghanistan and features women in both leadership and regular roles.

The changes in the role of women in the armed services since Confederation have been extraordinary—from nursing to virtual integration in just over a century. Despite traditional views of the role of women that prevailed long after the views had changed in civilian workplaces, the new concepts of gender equality have arrived in the Canadian armed forces in a clearly defined and embedded fashion. These changes stemmed from many different sources: the demands made on Canadians by war; the far-sighted actions of people such as military nurse Margaret Macdonald and many women who served in and with the forces; complaints to the Canadian Human Rights Commission, and also by the pressure applied on governments and the attitudes of all Canadians by organizations in the women's rights movements.

Another path to change in the Canadian armed forces and a special part of the women's movement was the spouses of members of the military.[36] The sacrifices in pay, standard of living, and social services made by the spouses of members of the armed forces had been a serious matter for a long time. Throughout our history, military families have faced higher rates of marriage breakdown and divorce than civilians, as well as family violence and alcoholism. Snell, in his study of divorce in Canada, points out that New Brunswick and Nova Scotia had divorce courts before Confederation and that New Brunswick had "been active in this field as early as 1786."[37] Early regiments had been stationed in those Maritime provinces and the high rate of divorce in these nineteenth-century provinces no doubt stemmed from the need to deal with the failure of military marriages in those areas.

In 1914, members of the armed forces were assured by the Government of Canada that they would be cared for upon their return to civilian life. Veterans' pensions and allowances were instituted, but widows and wives and families of the disabled always struggled to achieve access to those pensions and allowances. The armed services may have provided housing, schools for children, and health services

---

36. See Deborah Harrison and Lucie Laliberté, "Gender, the Military, and Military Family Support," in *Wives and Warriors*, eds. Laurie Weinstein and Christie White (Westport, CT: Bergin and Garvey, 1997).
37. Snell, *In the Shadow*, 49.

on the bases, but enlisted men's incomes were low, wives were prevented by location and frequent moves from building careers or even working for pay at all, and the complex problems now called post-traumatic stress disorders were not recognized or properly treated.

The pressures on the family led to much misery for everyone. Many attempts at care for family of members of the military were made for veterans of the two world wars and the Korean War, and for those in NATO and NORAD engagements as well as in peacekeeping missions. However, the assertion of the rights of spouses (mainly wives) of members of the military emerged in the post-Charter era when the Organizational Society of Spouses of Military Members (OSSOMM) was established. That organization took its case for the rights of women to organize and lobby for change to the Parliamentary Committee on Equality Rights in 1985. When no response was forthcoming from that body, OSSOMM went to the Special Senate Committee on National Defense in June 1986, where LEAF—the Women's Legal Education Action Fund—intervened on its behalf. A flurry of activities followed on the civil rights of the spouses and families of the military. Despite some progress, there continues to be a number of unresolved problems. Stacey Douglas has traced the continuity of issues for Canadian military spouses or "camp followers" throughout history, commenting in detail on the current issues of spouses' rights.[38]

Through OSSOMM, women have profiled yet another aspect of women's lives in the military and reflected the changes in the status of women within the highly structured confines of military life. While their work and the work of numerous committees and policy changes that followed

---

38. Stacey Douglas, "Readiness and Rights: Developments in Canadian Military Family Politics and Policy," Proceedings of the Fifth Annual Society of Military and Strategic Studies Student Conference, Calgary, February 2003: 28–41.

have not solved all the problems, the civil rights of military families have been institutionalized in Canada, at least for spouses living on armed forces' bases.

Is it war or is it any crisis that changes opportunities for women in Canada? Other crises, such as economic depression and recession, the collapse of the East Coast fishery, and the dramatic social changes in Quebec in the Quiet Revolution, have certainly changed women's lives in regions of the country or for some groups. War is a period of national mobilizations and, as tragic and as undesirable as it is, it has given women new chances.

>–♦⟩O⟨♦◃

Women and War

A Chronology

1884	Canadians at the Siege of Khartoum, the country's first overseas conflict and the first time women at the home front are affected by war.
1885	Northwest Rebellion at which Victorian Order of Nurses present.
1899–1902	South African War: Canadian nurses present from 1901.
1904	The Permanent Army Nursing Service and the Reserve Army Nursing Service are established.
1914–18	First World War, the "Great War": Canadian nurses serve and one is elected to the Alberta legislature by Albertans serving overseas.
1939–45	Second World War: women serve overseas, and women's divisions gradually formed in all the armed forces, so by 1942 the air force, army, and finally the navy had such division.

IV

Demographics Change Women's Lives

Any individual life is different from another, but collectively, the patterns of life are of consequence because we live in groups and every day observe the lives of others. We model our behaviour on those who we know and respect or admire. Girls observe the life patterns of their mothers and their sisters, as well as other women in their spheres. They react by judging their own social position relative to others.

Three major changes since Confederation have altered the demographic patterns. They have also led to greater scope for women in some important aspects of their lives. First, the prevention of deadly diseases and improvement in health conditions has increased life expectancy. Second, effective and now legal forms of birth control have resulted in predictable family planning, along with improvements in the treatment of infertility or low fertility. Third, these first two changes have meant that women have more years available for the paid labour force, and the economy has changed at the same time so that women's labour is valued. Together these events have led to a transformed structure in the lives of women in Canada, with important implications for their social and economic roles in public life and in the family. All this has happened gradually and within a complex set of social changes since 1867.

For most of our history, women have had only limited control of child-bearing and almost no preventive medicine, and were guided—sometimes forcefully steered—in their choice of marriage partners. The demographic patterns they observed were very powerful. The census data show that until 1951 about 90 percent of women married in Canada. Even in the 1941 census, 83 percent of women who had ever married had given birth and, of those, 20 percent had given birth to six or more babies. These data were gathered before the years of official recognition of cohabiting relationships or births to single women.[1] There were probably far more babies born than are shown in those data.

The Vulnerabilities of Our Women Ancestors in Canada

A young woman looking at her future in Canada toward the last quarter of the nineteenth century would be conscious of her life prospects. Those prospects would include creating her living through marriage and family responsibilities or, for a few, through religious orders. The prospects for the majority would include child-bearing and family management, which were seen in those times as the main purpose of any woman's life. Her education, her family's material circumstances, and her own ambitions might vary the outcome of her life but only within the confines of the available and suitable marriage partners.

Death was an ever-present possibility for babies and the elderly, but also for young adults. Death in childbirth or

---

1. See Thomas, "The Census and the Evolution," 40–46. Common-law relationships were first included in the 1981–86 census questionnaires.

shortly thereafter was not unusual. Communicable diseases swept through communities, carrying off young and old, men and women. Typhoid, typhus, measles, tetanus, whooping cough, and even smallpox were added to the usual influenza, tuberculosis, and other dangers. Young men, then and now, could be exposed to fatal accidents and to war service, leaving widows and families to fend for themselves. How long could a woman expect to live?

Calculations made from 1831 show a steady increase in the proportion of women surviving to age 65. This ranges from 302 per thousand women in the population in 1831 to 861 per thousand in 1980 to 1982. If we look at women surviving just past the years of fertility, the story is different. In 1871, only 543 Canadian women of every thousand were alive at age 45, whereas 965 were still alive in 1982. Ellen Gee, a Canadian demographer who compiled a history of women's life course, points out that not only were the numbers of survivors much better, but also life became far more predictable. "It is 'unexpected' life course events such as the loss of one's husband in one's 30s or death of a child that create severe psychological trauma and stress," and those unexpected events are far fewer in the population than they have ever been.[2] But our young woman in the late nineteenth century could not be overly optimistic of her life chances.

Women's vulnerability to diseases was increased by bearing children in quick succession, as well as by the conditions in which she worked and lived.[3] She would know that many women died before their husbands, and she would have observed from the community around her that she would be

---

2. Ellen M. Gee, "The Life Course of Canadian Women: An Historical and Demographic Analysis," *Social Indicators Research* 18 (1986): 265.

3. George Emery, "Age-Parity and Marital Status Compositional Influences on the Maternal Mortality Rate in Canada, 1930–1969: A Regional Comparison," *Social History* XXV, no. 50 (1992): 229–56.

doing well if she lived into her late sixties. Equally, if she were beyond her child-bearing years and foresaw living into very old age, she would want to have children who would look after her both financially and in day-to-day life. She would want to, or have to, live with them or other relatives in her old age.

Until into the 1920s, young women's life expectancy was only slightly higher than that of men in their age group. Only if women survived to their post-child-bearing years could they be expected to outlive their husbands. Women died in childbirth or of puerperal fever afterwards, or of tuberculosis or epidemics.[4] Because birth control was unreliable even when used, too many babies with too little spacing between them lowered women's resistance to infection. When sick, no antibiotics were known, and in poor or rural areas hospitals and good health care would be the exception.

Abortions were not legal, although they were probably frequent; and subsequent infections or bleeding proved fatal all too often. We know this because in 1892 a member of Parliament inveighed against birth control and abortion in the House of Commons: "Improper and obscene or semi-obscene literature is imported into this country and openly sold. Drugs and instruments for procuring abortion and for kindred purposes are advertised secretly and are sold by agents."[5] The 1892 Criminal Code made it an indictable offence to advertise, sell, or dispose of any means of birth control. Women and men were left on their own when it came to preventing births—either by highly unreliable "natural" methods or by illegal actions.

---

4. Emery points out that it was not until after World War II that maternal mortality dropped dramatically in Canada; pre-1940, five to seven women per thousand died because of pregnancy or childbirth and more if the indirect causes of death are included. See "Age-Parity and Marital Status," 229n.
5. Angus McLaren and Arlene Tigar McLaren, *The Bedroom and the State: The Changing Practices and Politics of Contraception and Abortion in Canada, 1880–1980* (Toronto: McClelland & Stewart, 1986), 9.

Women who had children outside of marriage would suffer more or less depending on their circumstances. Children might be given out for adoption, brought up by relatives, or in some cases killed at birth. In this Victorian era, it was not acceptable for the children to be formally acknowledged. Sex was a source of terrible anxiety for a large proportion of women, single or married. Much advice about chastity for the unmarried and submission to one's husband for the married was given. There was little advice circulated about the pleasures of sexual intercourse.

Furthermore, young women lived with the knowledge that husbands usually remarried upon the death of a wife. It was to be expected, as indeed a widow might well remarry. A second family from the second wife might well displace the first wife's children.[6] When John A. Macdonald (soon to be prime minister of Canada and eventually to be knighted) remarried in early 1867 to Agnes Bernard, it was a very public event and not at all unusual. His surviving child, Hugh John, from his first wife Isabella, was only a few years younger than Agnes. Her role as stepmother to Hugh John and then as mother of her own daughter was not uncomplicated. Despite the ongoing support of the extended family and the position of power and privilege the Macdonald family occupied in society, according to the accounts,[7] it was a difficult time for Agnes.

Taking on children from a previous marriage and then adding to the family with one's own children complicated the lives of many women. It is complicated today, although these days this situation is most probably caused by divorce rather than widowhood. Now we call this sort of unit a "combined" family, and if possible, support includes shared child custody, child-care services, and counselling. In the nineteenth

---

6. Emily M. Nett, "Canadian Families in Social Historical Perspective," *Canadian Journal of Sociology* 6, no. 3 (Summer, 1981): 239–360.

7. For an account of Agnes's life, see Louise Reynolds, *Agnes*.

century, however, the kinship network was stronger and badly needed in many circumstances for care of the children and the sick, or in times of crisis. In addition, as Anatole Romaniuc points out in a review of fertility in Canada, that kinship network ensured the passing of the values of the family from generation to generation, for good or for ill.[8]

Because most mothers were dependent on the income of their husbands and relied on the charity of their church or family in times of need, it must have been painful for a mother to consider the future of her children in the event of her death. Even if her husband was loyal and generous, it would be a stepmother or other female relatives who would have to take on the care of her infants and young children. For other women whose husbands were not sensitive to children, it must have been much more painful to contemplate, and yet husbands had absolute control over any decisions pertaining to the children.[9] Given the lack of legal rights and economic opportunities for women in the country in the period between Confederation and World War I, widowhood at a young age was not an enviable nor, for many, a sustainable situation for women. Remarriage was, if not attractive, at the very least necessary for survival.

The Vulnerabilities of Women Reduced

By 1960, young women would expect to outlive their husbands by a considerable number of years. This knowledge would have changed their outlook considerably. They still

---

8. Anatole Romaniuc, "Fertility in Canada: Retrospective and Prospective," *Canadian Studies in Population* 18, no. 2 (1991): 56–77.

9. See Katherine Arnup, *Close Personal Relationships Between Adults: 100 Years of Marriage in Canada.* paper for the Law Commission of Canada, March 2001, 13, http://epe.lac-bac.gc.ca/100/200/301/lcc-cdc/close_personal-relation-e/html. Arnup points out that one of the reasons for the rise of the doctrine of maternal feminism in the nineteenth century was to support the campaign of feminists to remove the absolute rights of fathers over the children.

did not have access to truly reliable birth control (the pill would not be legalized for birth control purposes until later in the decade); nevertheless, through barrier and chemical methods, they were better able to control their fertility and plan their family size. In the 1930s, the birth control movement in the country had greatly advanced the general knowledge of how to control fertility by providing widespread information. In the 1937 dismissal of a court case against Dorothea Palmer for disseminating birth control, two things became clear: first, that unless there were complaints, charges for teaching or using birth control would not be laid, and second, unless birth control became acceptable in Quebec, the law would not be changed. That did not happen until after Quebec's Quiet Revolution.

For wives in the 1960s, marriage breakdown and divorce were more likely to threaten the stability of their lives than the death of their husbands. Divorce usually meant economic hardship, and so young women had to consider the necessity of training for some sort of career. Even the daughters of well-off families could no longer rely on the economic support of their parents or significant divorce settlements. Especially following World War II, many parents urged their daughters to acquire skills with which they could re-enter the labour force if the marriage failed. Fortunately, the demand for workers in "women's" occupations such as teaching, nursing, office work, and factory work was high. Public sector jobs were favoured because they provided security and pensions. Women with no access to any advanced education or training kept their jobs in service and manufacturing or office jobs as long as possible. Wages were lower for women than men but would provide some income for them. By the late 1960s, their benefits would include membership in the Canadian Pension Plan (1966), but most benefits would depend on the social programs of the province in which they worked and the policies of their employers and union status.

Despite the incremental reforms that had occurred in various provinces since the nineteenth century, marital property laws were still egregiously unequal, child custody was still problematic, and child support and alimony were unreliable.[10] Many women in this period of history had borne the baby boom children and had several children to support. By this postwar period, a significant number of social relationships had changed: the sense of duty in the earlier strong kinship network had evolved; there were more nuclear families and working mothers; the number of extended households had declined; migration patterns had altered; and cultural and religious practices had declined. In the last half of the twentieth century, many women were left in highly tenuous situations.

When the birth rate fell, as it did during the Great Depression, it was in part because couples married later and used abstinence to avoid bearing children they could not afford to look after. Although many women of child-bearing age had participated in the war effort in both wars, times when sexual behaviour was less constrained and more women had children outside marriage, ignorance about sex and birth control was still widespread in Canada. Despite wider access to birth control since the 1930s and the legalization of the birth control pill (known as "the pill") in the late 1960s, many young women were not served because of the values of their doctors and pharmacists. These professionals controlled access to chemical contraception and would not prescribe birth control if they disapproved of birth control in marriage or if the patient was unmarried. Eventually, after the "sexual revolution" of the 1970s, sex and fertility became separated and birth control widespread. But the

10. See Arnup, *Close Personal Relationships*, and the discussion of the Murdoch case in Chapter 2.

change in attitudes and values is recent, and the refusal of doctors and hospitals to perform abortions in many parts of Canada shows us the limits of these changes.

It was not only birth control that was controversial but the acknowledgement of pregnancy. The memoirs of one of Canada's great public servants, the late Arthur Kroeger, give us an example. Kroeger was the son of a Mennonite family from Russia who arrived on the Prairies in 1926. His description of their settlement in the Palliser Triangle in those dustbowl years before and during the Great Depression is particularly poignant. He describes the work of his mother, Helena, and his sisters. In Russia, his mother had given birth to six children, two of whom had died (one of measles) before they emigrated. In Canada, two more sons were born. Kroeger's mother not only did all the housework to look after a large family in terrible conditions in the abandoned farmhouses they were forced to occupy for many years, but also cleaned the schoolhouse and other people's homes when she could get the work. Kroeger himself was born in their small farmhouse in 1932. His mother, who was 46, was attended by two neighbours serving as midwives. Arthur was the youngest.

> When my mother's labour pains began, most of the children were at school, and Peter, age four, was taken to a neighbour's. He recalls that when he was brought back hours later, he saw me lying on a little table, covered with a flour sack, being spoon-fed sugar and water by Mrs. Holmen. My father was pleased and excited. That afternoon, when Helen, Anne and George came home from school, they were surprised to find a new baby in the house. *They had not known that their mother was pregnant.*[11]

---

11. Arthur Kroeger, *Hard Passage: A Mennonite Family's Long Journey from Russia to Canada* (Edmonton: University of Alberta Press, 2007), 135; emphasis added. These memoirs were based on family documents, the recollections of Kroeger's older siblings, and other studies of this migration.

Even those who were knowledgeable did not discuss these matters in a public setting. Sex was not a topic of teaching or "polite" conversation. While mothers might prepare their daughters more or less well for marriage and child-bearing, if they did not, doctors would not necessarily take up that task.

Schools stuck to the biological "facts," even during the 1950s, and embarrassed teachers often showed films to avoid having to talk about human reproduction. The Victorian values were not abandoned quickly. Children born out of marriage were still called "illegitimate" and were often placed for adoption, brought up by other family members, or ostracized. They had no legal rights in the family unless subsequently adopted by a marriage partner of the mother.

>—۱—◆>—0—<◆—۱—<

Only a generation later, by the 1990s, women were in quite different circumstances. They expected to live longer than ever before, have communicable diseases cured, and be immunized for diseases their mothers could never control, such as measles, hepatitis, and tuberculosis. They also knew that they would be likely to die, when they did, in a hospital or institution of some kind rather than in the home of their children. The life expectancy of men rose, and so the long widowhood of wives during the twentieth century was slightly reduced. The speed of travel connected parents and children more easily than ever before. Many old parents could have some care by their children. End-of-life palliative care was a major concern for the public purse and the private individual. Recognition by employers of family care issues was being formalized so that some time or benefits were provided by some employers.

Not only was a wide range of reliable birth control available, but also legal, safe abortions in hospitals were available in some parts of the country.[12] As services became available among the majority of communities, attitudes changed remarkably. Some religious groups maintained their traditional requirements for abstinence. Others updated their constraints on sex, birth control, marriage, divorce, and abortion. *Illegitimacy* was a concept and term no longer applied to children born out of wedlock in Ontario and Quebec, but four other provinces still do retain the distinction. In many communities, young women who had babies were supported through their high school years. Sex was widely discussed in the media and taught in schools, and the focus was on "safe sex," sexually transmitted diseases, and health, rather than only moral and biological issues.

Public campaigns to find the cure for cancers of all kinds, for HIV/AIDS, and for other diseases or conditions feature high-profile individuals talking openly and explicitly about their diseases on television. Graphic explanations of the workings of the body's systems, body parts, and the link between mind and body are addressed regularly in the public media. Attitudes toward women's bodies have been revolutionized, although sexism can still be found in abundance.

Sex has become separated from marriage for all but some segments of the population. Interestingly, the rates of teenage pregnancies and motherhood were much lower in Canada than the United States even among similar types of populations, and overall fertility was lower in Canada.

---

12. Some of the activists and public debates on abortion are described Chapter 5, but this service was not gained without great pressure on unwilling legislators and judges. Abortion is not a positive right for women in Canada to this day, but the absence of an explicit law makes it a health service. However, some provinces still do not make abortion available, forcing women to travel for the procedure.

As Belanger and Ouellet[13] have pointed out, although Canadians and Americans say they want a family size that is similar, Americans have a larger average family size than Canadians. Or, put another way, Canadians are far less likely to achieve their desired family size. The lives of Canadian women are different from those of women elsewhere.

Now women are truly their own decision-makers. To form a "traditional" family of a married mother and father with children is a conscious choice rather than assumed to be a future for everyone. Many make that choice, but if they do not, few eyebrows are raised. Many couples choose to be childless,[14] and those unable to have children have medical remedies to explore. In the last few years, same-sex marriages have become legal, although in some jurisdictions marriage laws and customs make that difficult. Adoption by single people and by same-sex couples has become possible. Child care and child rearing are public issues, as most mothers are in the paid labour force, but publicly provided child care remains scarce in most jurisdictions. But each individual parent in any kind of family has to prepare to be on her or his own again with all the social and financial implications of that condition.

All this change could occur despite fairly constant backlash against these reforms, because the value changes of the post–World War II era have become embedded in our institutions of marriage, family, health care, and community. After significant periods of deliberation, many laws have changed with respect to marriage; custody and care

---

13. Alain Belanger and Genevieve Ouellet, "A Comparative Study of Recent Trends in Canadian and American Fertility, 1980–1999," *Report on the Demographic Situation in Canada 2001* (Ottawa: Statistics Canada, 2002). As this study shows, the fertility of US teenagers (aged 15 to 19) is extraordinarily high, at least in this time period, and Spanish-speaking US women have a higher than average number of live births.

14. Susan Stobert and Anna Kemeny, "Childfree by Choice," *Canadian Social Trends* 69, Summer (2003): 7–10.

of children; health care; and access to procedures heretofore forbidden, such as chemical birth control, abortion, and in vitro fertilization. Divorce laws and procedures changed along with the attached issues of property rights and child custody. Equally important, dominant attitudes in most communities changed greatly. The ideas about equity and equality for women (and other marginalized groups) have become widely accepted, if not always practised. They have become the ideal just as "separate spheres" between women and men had been the ideal for much of Canada's history.

>–⊷–○–⊶–<

The changes came about for a complex set of reasons but not without pressure from women and their organizations, as well as health providers and legal institutions. But some issues remain privatized in the family or household for women to resolve.

In all these changing times and values, women have struggled with the competing demands of children and their other obligations of earning a living, contributing to the household, or caring for the extended family. Whether contemplating or forming personal partnerships such as marriage, adjusting to the immigrant experience, or preparing for their old age, women were responding to the demographic facts of their times. No one woman knows exactly how long she will live; how many pregnancies she will have; what diseases she will contend with; or how many moves, across which boundaries, she will take. She does know what most women experience, however, and that common knowledge affects her planning, her decisions, and her participation in the community. For example, knowing that life expectancy is the highest in history and that a third of marriages in Canada end in divorce, she may stay in school to gain a qualification because she expects to support herself at some point. She may change her diet and lifestyle to avoid an associated disease or simply to fit into Canadian life. She thinks of her own interests in current-day society and may hold different views from her partner or husband. She may support a group or a politician promising her child care, tax benefits, or more rights, even if the men in her life disagree.

Official Data Sources

Beyond observing their circle of family and neighbours, how do women know the situation of other women or communities?

In the years since Confederation, Canada has developed a large and sophisticated statistical office rich with data both contemporary and historical. Although censuses had been taken in the pre-Confederation years, vital statistics for birth, death, marriage, and divorce were not collected by the government until 1921, limiting our ability to look at the nineteenth-century world as clearly as we would like. The survey of the labour force that greatly helps planning for government, employers, and individuals became available only in 1946. Nonetheless, other statistical records and historical accounts provide a great deal of useful information. Using census data records, demographers have been able to reconstruct many of the vital data from the nineteenth century.

For example, empiricism on the situation of women in Canada has been greatly assisted by the early and systematic use of the census. Presenting numbers to governments and employers on women's status with respect to education, to health care, and to jobs is highly effective in a liberal democracy. As services in health and education, for example, became publicly funded, programs and services were based on those official data. Countless briefs have been written by members of groups such as the National Council of Women, the National Action Committee on the Status of Women, and other national and local groups. Using the data to make their case, the groups present their briefs to government officials and legislators, school boards, and employer and union groups. This approach has been a keystone to social movements, including the women's movement throughout our history. McDonald's study of empiricism in the thinking of early women social scientists shows how women learned to use these data sources to make their case heard.[15] Since the French have a very long tradition of accurate record-keeping and demography, and since censuses were taken from the earliest times in New France, we began with astonishingly good records well before Confederation. This tradition continued after Confederation, so the evidence of gender equalities and inequalities can be accurately traced in some spheres of Canadian life, and has been. In a rational democracy, accurate data carry weight in decision-making.

Basic data on the lives of women and families were taken in the censuses every 10 years from 1871 forward. A five-year or quinquennial census began in 1956. The collection of vital statistics through registration was first begun in 1921. Time series data are very important, and so the limitations of census data and the many changes in the questions concerning the lives of women present a serious challenge in documenting social changes.[16] Without longitudinal data, it is difficult to make the case concerning equality or in-

---

15. MacDonald, *Women Founders*. Lynn MacDonald herself has used such data for many years as a feminist activist and as a member of Parliament, and has helped others to do so.

16. For a short synopsis of census data, see Statistics Canada, *History of the Census of Canada*, http://www.12.statscan.ca/census1/info/history.cfm. For a discussion of the problems of using census data, see Roderick Beaujot and Don Kerr, *Population Changes in Canada*, 2nd ed. (Toronto: Oxford University Press, 2004), Appendix A.

equality. Women, therefore, have a vested interest in the continuity of these data.

Marriage and the Sex Ratio

One simple fact of life is that for a marriage between a man and a woman to take place, there must be people of each sex present and they have to meet each other. In short, the sex ratio and the age distribution in the community are key factors. The ratio becomes obvious in school or in community groups. If, as a teenager, a girl saw there were more girls than boys in her high school, community group, or community, she would realize she might have to look further afield for a marriage partner.

Even in the 1860s a young women of marriageable age would be conscious that the sex ratio in the country favoured her chances of marriage: there were somewhat more men than women in the colonies that became Canada. Given that her living depended on men's livelihood, she would take this knowledge into account in her planning. Even if the men would not be considered "marriageable" in her community of origin, circumstances were different in the new world. Women might be willing to marry "below" their expectations, as marriage and family were their source of livelihood. No doubt this was common in second marriages by widows.

The sex ratio changed back and forth in the 1870s and first half of the twentieth century, but by the 1960s, there were more young women than men in Canada, and that ratio has continued to prevail. This was all the more reason for young women to prepare to be self-supporting. Not all women who wanted it would find a mate and marry.

Since immigrants were a much larger proportion of a small Canadian population, and since most people show a preference for marrying someone of the same general cultural and

immigrants in total population (%)

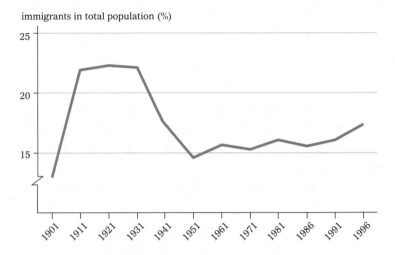

Figure 4.1   In the Early Decades of the Twentieth Century, One in Five People in Canada Were Immigrants
Source: Boyd and Vickers, "100 Years of Immigration in Canada," 80.

ethnic background, it is useful to note that until the 1970s there were more men among immigrants than women. The numbers imply that marrying a partner from a different culture or ethnicity was very likely to occur in Canada.

It is equally important to note that interracial marriage was strongly discouraged by some authorities in early periods, and this opposition even included the use of deportation of one or both of the intended spouses. For Aboriginal women, once the Indian Act was passed in 1876,[17] marriage of a Status Indian woman to a white man resulted in her loss of Indian status with all the property, family, and other rights that entailed. This requirement was not reversed until 1985.[18]

---

17. The Indian Act of 1876 was based on earlier federal legislation of 1868 and previous colonial laws. See Historica-Dominion Institute, *Canadian Encyclopedia*: Indian Act, n.d., http://www.thecanadianencyclopedia.com/index.cfm?PgNm=T CE&Params=A1ARTA0003975 (accessed December 6, 2011).
18. See Arnup, *Close Personal Relationships*.

number of men per 100 women

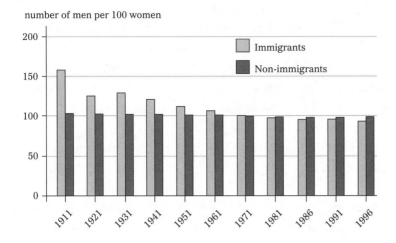

Figure 4.2   The Ratio of Men to Women Immigrants Stabilized with Family Reunification Programs and Changed Modes of Immigration
Source: Boyd and Vickers, "100 Years of Immigration in Canada," 80.

In female-dominated workplaces, the arrival of a male worker was a matter of great interest in certain communities where the sex ratio was unbalanced in favour of women. For example, in the textile industry of Paris, Ontario, women employees dominated: "As it was more girls than men, if a man got a job in Penman's they thought it was something smart, the girls did—'oh,' they would say, 'we've got another man in town.'"[19]

By the twenty-first century, the significance of a balance of women and men in the community was less important. Not only was the marriage market widened by freedom to migrate to other workplaces, but also marriage was far less tied to livelihood. A woman might have several partners in a lifetime as she became more self-supporting.

---

19. Joy Parr, *The Gender of Breadwinners: Women, Men and Change in Two Industrial Towns, 1880–1950.* (Toronto: University of Toronto Press, 1990), 84. This study is described more fully later in this chapter.

Given the cultural practice of men to marry younger women, the sex ratio was salient only for newly single middle-aged women. At older ages, the death rates for men begin to be higher and finding male partners becomes more difficult. Only in old age was a majority of women a significant topic in social and public debate, as in the sex ratio in retirement and nursing homes.

In Britain after World War I, middle-class women who had lost their marriage prospects in the devastating number of deaths of the men in their age and social class faced a daunting future.[20] But in Canada, while the losses were great, the dominance of men in the population still promised marriage prospects. A considerable number of single British women immigrated to Canada because of this opportunity.

Population Growth: What Women Did

In the 1861 census—just before Confederation, when our own story of Canadian women begins—the population of the provinces that became Canada was just over three million, excluding the Aboriginal population (which was in any event quite small in that territory).[21] Ontario and Quebec had a population of 2.5 million, the balance being primarily in the Maritimes, with fewer than 20,000 in the "West."

By the turn of the century, in the 1901 census, population in the country had grown to more than 5.25 million, with population growth in all regions and most dramatically in the West. Ontario and Quebec continued to dominate in population numbers, as they do today.

---

20. Virginia Nicholson, *Singled Out: How Two Million Women Survived without Men after the First World War* (London: Viking, 2007).
21. Numbers vary depending on the source. The numbers here come from McInnis, "The Population of Canada," 373 and 376. When the western territories came into Canada, the numbers and proportion of the Aboriginal population grew; however, the numbers are still estimates.

population (millions)

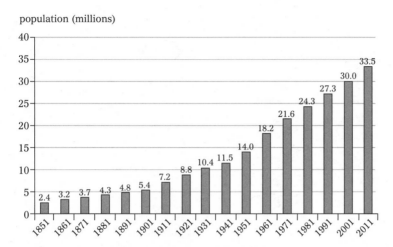

Figure 4.3   Population of Canada, 1851–2011

Source: Adapted from Statistics Canada, Census of Population, 1851–2011

growth rate (%)

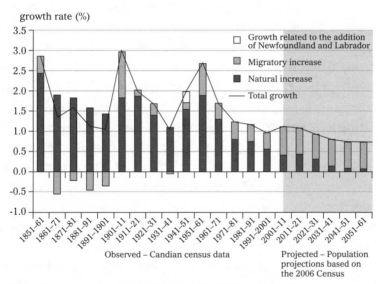

Figure 4.4   Population Growth in Canada, 1851–2061

Statistics Canada, *Population growth in Canada: From 1851 to 2061*.

This growth is remarkable because it was, in contrast to the pre-Confederation years, a period of massive emigration, largely to the United States. Canada received very large

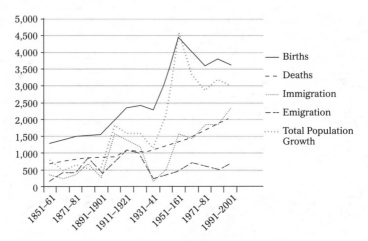

Figure 4.5   Population and Growth Components (1851–2001 Censuses)
Source: Adapted from Statistics Canada, *The Canadian Population in 2011.*

numbers of immigrants, mostly from Britain, but thousands left the country. Contrary to later periods and the present time when immigration accounts for much of the population growth, in the first years of Confederation, it was exceptionally high fertility that drove population growth. Thus, it was down to the women to "grow" Canada for the first years of Confederation and that is what happened.

While the demographic facts of an individual life are of great interest, the population data also paint a picture of what constrained the lives of women in Canada. They reveal how long they were likely to live (life expectancy), what might cause their deaths (age-specific mortality rates), and the family size they might have (total fertility rates).

It is true that the key demographic facts of the lives of Canadian women follow those of the developed world.[22] Like women everywhere, women in Canada marry or form "close personal relationships,"[23] and they have children. Like other parts of the developed world, the life expectancy of women is

22. McInnis, "The Population of Canada."
23. Arnup, *Close Personal Relationships.*

greater than that of men, and the causes of death in women show patterns similar to those in most developed countries.

In the classic demographic transition, from the end of the nineteenth century to the 1940s, mortality declined—particularly infant mortality—but so did fertility. This slowed the growth of the population by natural causes, and immigration eventually replaced the excess of births over deaths as the chief element in our population growth.

At present, like other developed countries, the population is aging. The pattern in Canada is similar to that in England, Europe, the United States, and Japan, albeit with different rates of aging. So men and women in developed economies have shared the major population shifts at roughly the same time in roughly the same way. However, it is important to note the actual population numbers are different. For example, McInnis points out that in 1901 Canada was one of the smallest nations in the world by population; its population was just 7 percent of the population of the United States, which was, and still is, our nearest comparator because of the intertwining of our land and economies.[24] Now Canada has roughly a tenth of the US population. However, there are some important differences in the way our populations have grown.

Canada's Unique Child-Bearing History

It is in fertility that women in Canada have shown some historically famous behaviour, the explanations for which are intriguing. In the nineteenth and early twentieth century, history shows us an overall picture of women living lives more healthy than the women of Europe: Canadian women were marrying young, having many births, and remarrying

---

24. McInnis, "The Population of Canada." This and his article on the nineteenth century in the same volume are essential reading for those interested in the population history of Canada pre- and post-Confederation. As with other areas of intense study, some of his data are disputed by other specialists.

quickly if widowed. Around the time of Confederation, the crude birth rate (the number of babies born per thousand population), was about 41. In 2009, the crude birth rate was 10.28. The birth rate at Confederation was a vigorous number indeed and is the explanation for much of the growth in population at the time. Of course, despite the decline in the birth *rate* to the present time, the *number* of births is higher because of the growth in overall population size.

A woman's life experience is radically altered by either having a large number of children or by immigration to a new land. In the period since Confederation, Canadian women's lives have been affected greatly by one or the other experience, and quite often both. Child-bearing was almost unavoidable for married adult women until the development and distribution of reliable methods of contraception in the last half of the twentieth century.[25] Both historically high fertility among married women and historically high rates of immigration are observed at some points in the history of women in Canada. As the graph on page 107 shows, a very large proportion of the women in Canada were immigrants, many of whom had arrived much later than their husbands. Immigration patterns shifted with both policy changes (e.g., the introduction of family reunification or requirements for certain skill levels) and with easier transportation.

It is true that both high fertility and high rates of immigration are found in other countries. However, many interesting aspects of the lives of women in Canada are different from elsewhere. These variations are of real importance because, to some extent, this history shapes the lives of women

---

25. The Palmer case concerning the distribution of information about birth control in 1937 indicates that the courts by that date were not willing to prosecute advice on birth control, but it was not until the Trudeau-sponsored Omnibus Bill of 1968 that access to chemical contraceptives became legal in Canada and came into effect the following year. (See Prentice et al., *Canadian Women: A History*, 2nd ed. [Toronto: Nelson, 2004], 295.)

in Canada today. These are expressions of our values and our culture, if not in general then certainly in the particular segment of the society in which it is found.

The very high proportion of women who married stands out, for example, as a feature of nineteenth and early twentieth century life in Canada.[26] McInnis points to the high rates of nuptiality in Canada in the 1860s and concludes that the Canadian birth rate was very high not because each woman was having such a large number of children but because such a large proportion of women in the child-bearing years were married.[27] In Europe in the same period, by contrast, child-bearing was reduced by delayed marriage and the much larger proportion of never-married women. In this regard, the life experience of women in the period before and just after Confederation was structured differently in the population than that of the countries of origin of the women or their parents and ancestors.

The exception is Quebec where marital fertility was high but nuptiality lower than in the rest of the colonies. Even that is a simple account since there were both cultural (francophone and anglophone; Catholic and Protestant) and rural–urban differences. Where there were lower rates of marriage in some rural areas, the birth rates were lower, with the few exceptions discussed below. The three urban centres in Quebec had higher rates of fertility. In some Ontario counties, the rates were as high as Quebec's, but not in the urban areas. It was a complex pattern tied closely to marriage patterns.

---

26. In 1899, the newly formed National Council of Women had a Committee for the Better Protection of Women and Children. That committee convenor wrote to the Minister of Justice asking that the legal age of marriage be raised to 16 and that the age be raised to 18 for marriage with the consent of a parent. See Griffiths, *The Splendid Vision*, 59.
27. His calculations can found in McInnis, "The Population of Canada," 389–402, and repay reading for those interested in this distinction.

Immigration usually has the effect of reducing family size, always depending on the time and circumstances of immigration. In the early part of our history, it was not unusual for families to arrive at several different times. Often the breadwinner would establish a base before the rest of the family came. Since the breadwinner was most often the man, the separation of the parents would reduce the number of births, and there was quite often a gap between the children born in the land of origin and those born in Canada.[28] For refugees and immigrants fleeing persecution, the number of children is likely to be even lower as they are leaving dire circumstances that are not conducive to building a family. Many immigrants to Canada came under these circumstances.

There have been periods when single women immigrated usually for work opportunities. This type of immigration has been well documented in Joy Parr's study of Paris, Ontario, 1880–1950.[29] The owners of the textile mills there recruited women from the textile mills of England to work in their factories between 1906 and 1928. Women from England and other parts of Canada came in sufficient numbers to dominate the town. While many married, they had fewer children than the Canadian average. While mothers usually kept on working, many had delayed their marriage to look after aged parents; and after their mid-thirties, many remained single. The average of one child per family was very low by Canadian standards of the day, although the range was wider. But four children were considered a large family for a long time in Paris, Ontario.

Immigration depressed family size both because of the separation of the partners and by the necessity of earning

---

28. The award-winning novel of Nino Ricci, *Lives of the Saints*, beautifully illustrates this theme in our history. See also Kroeger, *Hard Passage*.
29. Parr, *The Gender of Breadwinners*.

wages to support the family. Immigrants have lower wages, on average, than the native-born Canadians in most periods of our history and certainly in the early twenty-first century.[30] All this made it difficult for couples to support large families, at least in the first generation.

By the time of Confederation, Canada was beginning the familiar demographic transition but with some differences. Nuptiality was high then, leading to higher birth rates, a situation that was repeated in the postwar baby boom. The important social fact is that, throughout our history, in general, women in Canada could and did expect to marry.

These expectations would be increased by observing that a much larger proportion of women would marry in Canada than in the United Kingdom or Europe, for example, where detailed studies of fertility show higher rates of never-married women.[31] Rates of marriage were also high in comparison to the United States. Getting married, then, was part of the culture of the colonies and then the country. It was part of the official expectation of life, similar to how Canadians now expect to own a house. It was institutionalized in laws and behaviour. Marriage was simply expected, and non-marriage was the surprising alternative.

By the last decade of the nineteenth century, cities were offering opportunities for jobs to unmarried women in factories and offices. Many young women moved off the farm to these jobs. As a consequence, rates of marriage declined and with that urban fertility rates. Toronto made this demographic transition early on, Quebec cities much later. But some Ontario counties, such as Prince Edward *County*, had very low rates of marital fertility. Prince Edward *Island*, by contrast, in the same period, had low rates of nuptiality

---

30. See Beaujot and Kerr, *Population Change in Canada*, 118–23.
31. Ansley Coale and Susan Cotts Watkins, *The Decline of Fertility in Europe* (Princeton, NJ: Princeton University Press, 1986).

but high rates of marital fertility. Where they settled in Glengarry County in Ontario and Antigonish in Nova Scotia, Scottish Catholics had, in the words of McInnis, "maximally high marital fertility with outstandingly low nuptiality."[32] In other words, a smaller proportion of that population married, but those who married had very large families.

Of course, the opportunity for marriage and bearing children was affected for any individual woman by her religion, culture, age at marriage, geographic location, and health. For example, opportunities were quite different for French Canadians in comparison to Anglo-Canadians, quite different in Quebec from Ontario and the rest of the country. Much of this difference is accounted for by religion. To illustrate, Henripin shows the number of Catholic births in Quebec in 1867 to be 43,757 and the number of non-Catholic births to be 5,516, reflecting the ratio of Catholics to non-Catholics in that province. The birth rate in Quebec in the decade 1861 to 1870 is 45 per thousand, down markedly from the rate of 65.2 per thousand population a century earlier but still higher than in the rest of the country. Rural and urban differences were significant in some parts of demographic life, such as infant mortality.[33] In short, economic opportunity, religion, sex ratios, and age distributions all count in explaining demographic differences and the wide variations in women's lives.

Fewer Infant Deaths

An additional profoundly touching factor in the lives of women in the first half-century after Confederation was infant deaths. While many infants died in their first year of life, the cause of death in Canada was less likely than in

---

32. McInnis, "The Population of Canada," 402, n. 36.
33. Jacques Henripin, *Trends and Factors of Fertility in Canada* (Ottawa: Statistics Canada, 1972), 354.

Europe to be the external factors of disease such as communicable diseases or infected water, although those were still causes of death in some cases. In Canada, causes were more likely to be complications of birth or some infrequent genetic condition. As a consequence, Canadian women would have many children over their child-bearing years and a high proportion of the babies lived, contributing greatly to population growth. The average completed family size is calculated to be about seven per married woman, but with very wide variation. This has to be contrasted with the current total fertility, or completed family size, of under two children on average.

The mortality rates in the last half of the nineteenth century varied widely. In their study and building of new birth cohort life tables from 1801 to 1991, comparing Canada and Quebec, authors Bourbeau, Légaré, and Emond show that after 1881 infant mortality fell and continued to fall.[34] These life tables are a way of calculating probabilities of deaths in a cohort and in this case retrospectively, so they cannot be read as actual historical data. But they do illuminate the past where vital data were not recorded. For example, the graphs on page 118 from their study show the probability of dying by birth cohort with the U-shape illustrating the life course of all cohorts. That is, we are much more likely to die in our earliest and our last years of life than at any other time of life.

Of course, at all ages females have a better survival rate than men, and so one can see that a higher number of boys die at birth (age 0) and in the first few years of life although

---

34. Robert Bourbeau, Jacques Légaré, and Valerie Emond, *New Birth Cohort Life Tables for Canada and Quebec, 1801–1991*, Statistics Canada, Demography Division, 91F0015MPE no. 3, 1997. These are calculated life tables, not actual data, since such data were not collected in those years; however, they are nonetheless instructive. For methods and a fuller explanation, this article can be found online through the Statistics Canada Library, BiblioCat.

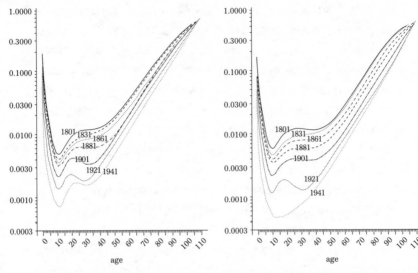

Figure 4.6   Probabilities of
Dying for Selected Birth Cohorts,
Canada, Males, 1801–1941
Source: Bourbeau, Légaré, and Émond,
*New Birth Cohort Life Tables for
Canada and Quebec, 1801–1991*, fig. 4.5

Figure 4.7   Probabilities of Dying
for Selected Birth Cohorts, Canada,
Females, 1801–1941
Source: Bourbeau, Légaré, and Émond,
*New Birth Cohort Life Tables for Canada
and Quebec, 1801–1991*, fig. 4.6

these remain dangerous years for both sexes. Look carefully at the differences between young men and young women.
Starting in about 1901, there is a "bump up" in male deaths
in young adulthood. These deaths are mostly violent, rather
than disease, driven.

In 1891, the calculations show that infant mortality was
much higher in the Quebec cities than in the rural areas or
the anglophone areas. These Quebec rates of infant mortality are reported in McInnis to be higher than those of
black Americans in the same period.[35] The rates were also
high in Ontario cities in this period. For example, McInnis
shows the infant mortality rate in Montreal to be 285 per

---

35. McInnis, "The Population of Canada," 405.

thousand, in Quebec City to be 275, and in Toronto 199. Vancouver's infant mortality rate was lower at 122, and outside the cities it varied from 173 in Quebec to 105 in Ontario. But in 1919, it was Alberta that had the highest infant mortality rates in Canada. There was nothing intrinsic to the cities except the conditions of life experienced by mother and child at any point in our history that led to these sad mortality facts. In the years since, we began to keep careful records of vital data. We see in the graph on page 120 the very rapid decline in infant mortality. Now, we expect that virtually all children will live through those early vulnerable years.

While all these factors continue to be important in women's lives and choices, the results in the late twentieth century were dramatically different. Quebec in the 1970s and thereafter has the lowest rates of marriage and fertility in the country.

Women themselves played a major role in changing the patterns and institutionalizing those changed patterns of marriage and child-bearing. They did so by their use of birth control, by their economic activity, and through a profound change in their culture and values.

The Demographic Importance of World War I

World War I changed so much in our country. The war killed many young adults—about 60,000—and most of these were men; this affected the lives of many families and many young women. It was followed by a devastating influenza epidemic that killed about 50,000 people in Canada. It spread across the country with the return of troops and other war workers in 1918. Unlike other influenzas, this one killed young adults, rather than the frail and elderly (although the sickness itself was widespread). Particularly vulnerable were

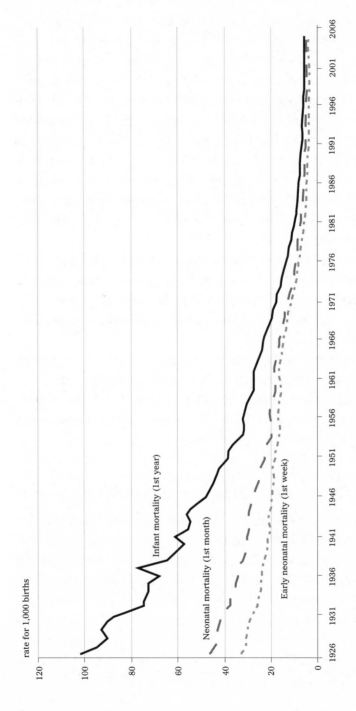

Figure 4.8   Infant, Neonatal, and Early Neonatal Mortality Rates in Canada, 1926–2006

Source: Statistics Canada, *Report on the Demographic Situation in Canada 2003 and 2004*, fig. 3.4

First Nations people, whose death rate from this virus was much higher than other parts of the population.[36]

The war brought women into war work in substantial numbers; it delayed births in some marriages; it changed the relationship of Canada to Great Britain;[37] it led to the vote for women; and it led to great social reforms, a ramp-up of social and economic change in Canada not completed until well into the 1960s.

Women did not initially see their lives changed by delaying child-bearing but rather by the changed opportunity structures. Part of the change was the greater acceptance of women—at least single women—into the paid labour force and part was the arrival of new barrier contraceptive methods. Both these occurrences had the effect of delaying marriage and child-bearing.

In her biography of two Canadian women who nursed in World War I, Susan Mann notes that it was only in this period that fully trained women nurses replaced male orderlies serving during wars.[38] It was a breakthrough for the profession in Canada. There were several elements to this breakthrough that distinguished Canadians. As noted in Chapter 3, thanks to the determination of Margaret Macdonald, the nurses were made officers, unlike nurses from Britain for example, and they were properly uniformed in a distinctive way. They set a high standard. Canadian nurses were all single, older than 21 years and their behaviour was monitored by Macdonald, who served as matron-in-chief with the rank of major throughout World War I. Of the almost 3,000 nurses who went off to the war, 39 died. This work and sacrifice was noted by everyone, but particularly by

36. J.M. Bumsted, *A History of the Canadian Peoples*, 3rd ed. (Toronto: Oxford University Press, 2007), 328.
37. Bumsted, *A History of the Canadian Peoples*, Chapter 8.
38. Mann, *Margaret Macdonald*.

Canadians, including Canadian politicians. The work and sacrifice of Canadian women was one of the more convincing reasons given for extending the franchise to women in Canada in 1917. It is important to remember that when the vote was held in the 1917 conscription election in Alberta, one of Macdonald's nurses won a seat in Alberta.[39] The attitude toward women had changed. Women themselves recognized a change toward more independence that was not previously widespread. Life took on other dimensions as important as marriage and child-bearing.

Interwar Changes in the Family

Why is the marriage and fertility behaviour of Canadian women so particularly interesting in the interwar period? This was an era in which women's activism in labour union organizing, in politics and in social welfare, was especially high. The twenties did not "roar" for most women. Incomes were distributed very unevenly, and even in the manufacturing regions of the country, prosperity was confined to a few. As is typical of a postwar period, the demand for resources was diminished and therefore Canada's economy suffered. Inflation soared.[40]

Women in all parts of the economy suffered—from those in the domestic, household economy where shortages and low incomes were widespread, to women in all occupations forced out of their positions by a government campaign to ensure that men had jobs with a family wage. The assumption that women's place was in the household still held sway with a large proportion of Canadians and, despite bitter disappointment, even single women, such as Margaret

---

39. See the story in, for example, Marshall, *Give Your Other Vote.*
40. It was to avoid a similar economic downtown that planning for postwar Canada was so vigorous during World War II. As a consequence, after 1945 Canada's economy was strong, resulting in other further changes in the lives of women, such as a lowered age of marriage and therefore the baby boom fertility.

Macdonald (the Canadian military nurse) were quietly "let go." Fortunately, Macdonald could cope financially and even had a pension.[41] Many others did not. Middle-class educated single women (or widows) were encouraged to take "women's jobs" in social welfare and white-collar occupations and, of course, to marry and have children. Different wages based on sex were the norm. Racial prejudice was open and active against black women and Asian women.[42] And there were the thousands of postwar immigrant families who left a devastated Western Europe, a revolutionary Russia, or a depressed Britain for the opportunities of Canada. There are many memoirs and histories of those immigrant families and the terrible struggles they went through to survive in those years.[43]

In that period, fertility control became essential for economic survival. The methods women used and the new forms of contraception are vividly described by McLaren and McLaren. Women went to great lengths to control their fertility "but they were plagued by the fear that methods might fail,"[44] as they often did. The emotional, moral, and physical burdens on women were still extraordinary. It was the twentieth-century changes in the lives of women that increased the pressures to control their fertility, for now almost all women were expected to be in the paid labour force, to have careers of some sort, and to contribute to the household income to a greater extent than before.

In the 1930s, when the birth control movement began to make serious inroads across Canada, many of the arguments were eugenic—for example, birth control could

---

41. Mann, *Margaret Macdonald*, 169–70.
42. See Prentice et al., *Canadian Women*, 2nd ed., 256.
43. See Kroeger, *Hard Passage*. See other biographies of British, American, Ukranian, and other European and Asian immigrants in the literature of the Depression period.
44. McLaren and McLaren, *The Bedroom and the State*, 30.

"assist" the poor in having fewer children, prevent the birth of children with "mental deficiencies," and stop the spread of venereal diseases. Sterilization of the mentally ill and those with Down's syndrome was carried out without the consent of the patients in a startlingly large number of cases.[45] Mr. A.R. Kaufman from Kitchener, Ontario, was strongly committed to the cause of practical birth control that could be and would be used by the poor. As a eugenicist, he wanted to ensure that the middle classes continued to have children. But this period in the history of birth control was also a showdown between the Protestant and Catholic communities and leaders.

It was the Protestant clergy and supporters, along with doctors and scientific experts testifying at the trial of Palmer, a birth control advocate, in 1936, who brought birth control into wide public acceptance, although the law remained unchanged for many years. That is, while women had been using all available means of contraception for generations, and while birth rates and family size had been declining for a long time, including in Roman Catholic families, what changed in the 1930s and afterwards was the institutions— the churches, the professions, the scientists in universities— incorporating the ideas of birth control into their thinking.

But in Canada the law was not changed to make chemical or mechanical contraceptives legal until the late 1960s. Already other countries had legalized the use of birth control, including education and prescription by health practitioners. In Canada, women and couples were using all means of mechanical and chemical contraception they could get—and using them illegally. This legal lag was attributed to the very large proportions of Canadians identified as Roman Catholic, but the gap between individual behaviour and the institution

---

45. McLaren and McLaren, *The Bedroom and the State*, 148–49.

prevailed far longer in Canada than in Britain or the United States—until the revisions to the Criminal Code in 1969. While many doctors did prescribe the pill or the diaphragm and condoms, at the same time many feared that they might be charged under the Criminal Code; women were left to cope with a most complicated situation, except for those who had access to a progressive family planning clinic.

In fact, the birth rate and family size among Catholic women in Quebec was cut dramatically from the late 1950s, well before the law was changed. This, as analysts point out, was the result of economic changes to industrial society, including mandatory education for children, as much as it was to the availability of contraception, which was already in widespread use by those who wanted to use it. People made decisions about their own family size and how many children they could raise under modern requirements. It was the law and the institutions that had to catch up to the desires of the people.

The desires of the people were expressed again on the matter of abortion. After long years of protest over its illegality, the criminal law was changed in 1969 to make abortion legal when performed in a hospital under certain conditions. The issue was almost as difficult after the changes to the law as before. The conditions required a panel of doctors to decide, case by case, whether a therapeutic abortion was allowable. Many hospitals failed to establish a committee, which meant that women, especially in small provinces and rural areas, had to go to the large cities to even get their case before a committee. This was a situation of demonstrable inequality.

While several pro-choice organizations existed whose members fought the requirements, it was the trials of Dr. Henry Morgentaler and his team in the 1970s that finally caused abortion rights to be addressed in the courts. Morgentaler publicly declared that he performed abortions to test the legal system. He was charged and acquitted more than once before an appeals court overturned a jury-based acquittal. He served some months in prison. He was charged again in the 1980s, again acquitted by a jury and again an appeals court overturned that judgment. He then appealed to the Supreme Court in 1984. In 1988, the Court ruled that, under the Charter, the 1969 law on abortion was unconstitutional. They did not rule that abortions were legal, but this decision left Canada without a law on abortion. Some attempts were made to introduce a law to restrict access to abortion, and one such bill passed the House of Commons but was defeated on a tie vote in the Senate. While access to abortion is subject to provincial regulations and hospital practices, there is no criminal law restricting the practice. The Supreme Court decision of 1988 coincided to a large extent with public opinion. Both these instances of reproductive rights—on birth control and on abortion—followed by many years the demands of a majority of Canadians for legal change.

The Baby Boom

Much is made of the rise in births from the end of World War II to the mid-1960s. The popular view of the baby boom of the postwar years is that this large cohort drove many changes and events in Canada, from an increase in schools to accommodate baby boomers as youngsters to pension crises as baby boomers began to retire.[46] It was war, once again, that resulted in this phenomenon. The Great Depression of the 1930s suppressed births as couples struggled to feed their families, but the birth rate was rising as the economy recovered in the late 1930s in areas where economy prosperity was returning. When the war broke out in 1939, many

---

46. This was a large cohort, especially compared to the small cohorts of the previous decades of the Depression and wartime struggles.

couples had what is referred to as the "now or never" babies, as women faced the end of their fertile years and men joined the forces. During the war, separation of couples, postponed marriages, and the widespread use of condoms (intended to prevent venereal diseases) decreased births. Once the war was over, couples "made up for lost time." They did so by marrying at younger ages and having children earlier and more closely spaced. In general, they did not have larger families than before but a larger proportion of women of the age group married and had babies in a few short years.

This birth cohort was highly visible all across Canada, although in Quebec this transition was particularly interesting. Historically in that province a larger proportion of women were celibate than in the rest of Canada, but in the war and postwar years, as fewer young women went into convents, the proportion of women who married increased. While the number of Quebec families having very large families was always a minority, and they were usually in farm families in which many hands were required, in the postwar period the farm family size dropped by half, while the proportion of Quebec women having children rose. The effect looked dramatic, but the causes are not remarkable. Farming gave way to industrial jobs in many rural areas, and schooling became compulsory in 1943. It was not economically feasible to sustain very large families and the ideology of maintaining the Quebecois population—an ideology that continues to the present in many communities—was no longer as attractive. Quebec families came to resemble families across the country. By the 1970s, the number of children born per thousand women was dropping as the demands of post-secondary education and the labour force escalated.

In the immediate postwar prosperity of the 1950s and early 1960s, across the country it was possible for families to live on one income while the children were young—and have a house, a car, and a "modern" life. The images of family life in that period were captured by the media in advertisements and television shows. The long-standing dream of the family wage earned by a husband to support the family, which had reoccurred ever since industrialization, was reinforced in this short period of Canadian (and indeed North American) history. But it was still a dream for most.

By the mid-1960s, this was becoming less possible and family incomes were stretched. The demands for service-sector workers, especially in the public sectors of health, education, and administration, were rising. Women were pushed and pulled into the labour force. The baby boom became an economic matter more than a fertility matter—it meant there were schools to be built, then universities, and then jobs to be found. By the beginning of the twenty-first century, there were escalating fears of both a health funding and pensions crisis because of the baby boom cohort that governments were forced to address. It was not that the postwar years produced such extraordinarily large families, but that so many produced families at all, and as the pent-up demand for marriage and family formation slowed, the subsequent family size became even smaller. By the late 1970s, women were spending more years both in post-secondary education and in the paid labour force creating lives of their own.[47]

From Religion to Science

As the control of fertility became medicalized and child-birth even more so, and as treatment for infertility and then genetic research became available and widely used, the

---

47. For an analysis of this change, see Jones et al., *Lives of Their Own*.

institutions controlling women's reproductive health were no longer those of churches so much as the professions. The answer to many of the health issues facing women was to attract more women into medicine as well as nursing and other health professions. It was also to focus more research on the issues of women's health, and not only reproductive health. The health charities—heart, lung, cancers, and a range of other female or female-dominant diseases and conditions—ramped up their focus on women, thereby benefiting research institutions at universities and hospitals. Once again in our history, just as in the birth control movement, the battles for women to control their own bodies were the subject of social organizations and protest movements.

The rise in women's labour-force participation after the 1970s has become, like the baby boom studies, a subject for economists, policy-makers, and public debate. The charts show the rise in women's levels of education and consequent rise in the labour force. At the same time, family size and spacing has become the focus of attention by families as well as employers and the state. There is no longer a public view that a family wage can be earned by a husband while a wife rears children and manages a household. That possibility is lost to all but a very few couples. There is now social pressure on all women to participate in paid work and the pressure on men has eased only slightly. Parenting leave for both parents, even where it is provided, is not widely used.

One of the significant changes that occurred was evident in the small and then very large recessions of the period from the 1980s to the first decade of the twenty-first century. Whereas in the earlier recession—including the Great Depression and many recessions thereafter—public policy concern was with the men who had lost their jobs and whose work was crucial to the family well-being, in the recent recession of 2008–2011, it became very clear that women were the income earners for many families and it was their income that sustained the family through periods of high unemployment of men. Especially interesting was the rise in employment among Aboriginal peoples. Although unemployment is still very much higher in the Aboriginal than in non-Aboriginal populations, women's employment increased to over 50 percent and the percent of women unemployed in the population was lower than for Aboriginal men.[48]

Thus, in the period from Confederation to the present day, we have seen the transformation of women's lives in their health, life expectancy, total fertility, and means of controlling their fertility (spacing of births); the expansion of their paid labour-force activity; and the increase in the similarity of the life experiences of women across the country. Even in vulnerable populations—such as many Aboriginal peoples who have lower life expectancy and higher fertility rates, or new immigrant groups who struggle with jobs, language, and poverty—the patterns of women's lives in education, work, family life, and retirement are more similar across the country today than they were a generation ago. Thirty years ago, the more usual pattern was school, followed by labour market work, then marriage and child-rearing years outside the labour market, a return to paid work, and then retirement.[49] Now the entire life-cycle pattern is more similar for men and women than it has ever been, certainly since Confederation. That is, schooling and higher education are followed by work in the paid labour market until retirement. But throughout these decades, the demographic patterns have shaped the public perception of the issues before them and therefore the individual's expectations within his or her

---

48. Jacqueline Luffman and Deborah Sussman, "The Aboriginal Labour Force in Western Canada," *Perspectives*, Statistics Canada Catalogue no. 75-001–XIE, January (2007): 14–15.

49. Jones, Marsden, and Tepperman, *Lives of Their Own*.

social group and social class. Although these expectations have changed dramatically, women are still the primary caregivers for children and their double burden of labour-market and domestic work has only intensified.

>–†–‹›–○–‹›–†–‹

Demography

A Chronology

1871   Census is taken in 1851, but first census after Confederation is 1871.

1892   The Criminal Code makes it an offence to advertise, sell, or dispose of any means of birth control and abortion is illegal.

1921   Vital registration data are required: registration of births, deaths, marriages, divorces.

1937   Decision in the Palmer case makes the use of birth control easier. The court decision made it clear that prosecutions would not be used unless there was flagrant use of birth control.

1969   Justice reform makes the pill legal, and abortion is permitted under very restrictive conditions.

1978   Concept of illegitimacy is abolished in Ontario and now in most but not all common-law provinces.

1982   Under the Civil Code in Quebec, the concept of illegitimacy is abolished.

1988   Supreme Court decision in Morgenthaler case means the abortion law is struck down and further attempts to legislate abortion fail in the senate on a tie vote in 1990.

2005   Civil Marriage Act of Parliament makes same-sex marriage legal in Canada.

V

How Women Changed Canada

In the late 1800s the majority of women in Canada would not think of themselves as equal in any profound way to their fathers, brothers, husbands, or even their adult sons. Only a few would think of women's equality as we now conceive of it. But most, like women today, would think about a better world for their families and themselves, whether because of a better income, or better schools, or a better place to live. Many would think of improving social conditions for the poor, or badly educated, or helping with immigrant settlement or assisting the sick. Hundreds joined temperance associations as a widespread reaction to the devastating influence of uncontrolled alcohol manufacture and consumption on families and on towns and villages. Where it was permitted, women became school trustees and volunteered in hospitals. So we know that many women thought of improving civil society as well as their own lives. Men and women were concerned with aspects of the emerging democracy, such as responsible government, freedom of religion, and language rights.

Whatever women thought about social change, a remarkable number of them were involved in bringing about changes that directly or indirectly made a difference to their lives and the lives of their children. In doing this, they also changed the nation. The relationships between men and women were modified; laws were changed; the culture of male domination was greatly reduced; women joined the legislatures and senate; health improved in both sexes; family structures changed; military life improved; and Canada emerged as a different country. In this chapter, therefore, we look at some illustrative examples, such as the entry of women into universities and gaining the right to hold public office, thus breaching two preserves of men. We look at the changes in health services that women provided in civil and military situations. Women used the courts and a willing male doctor to deal with the problems of illegal abortion. From demanding equal wages and gaining access to more education, women changed the workplace and diversity in occupations. We also see how women's understanding of the weaknesses of the Constitution led them to insist on improvements in the Charter of Human Rights and Freedoms in the 1980s. These are only some examples of the work that changed our country.

Women persuaded or joined with the men in their lives to be allies in the search for a better life for women. They joined organizations of activists. They appealed to authorities in person or through their family connections. They marched in protests. They went out on strike. They contributed money, time, and talent. They sat in legislative galleries and town halls to bear witness to the debates. They challenged institutions such as churches and universities to listen to women and admit them to their ranks. And they drew on their expert knowledge to insist on change. All this occurred within the dynamics of population and economic changes and of established laws and international connections. We see the struggle for equality rights as a long process that fuelled ideas that changed the status of women.

In this chapter, illustrations of how it all brought us to where we are today are found in terms of women's rights, equality, and life experiences. These examples highlight the key methods by which social change in this arena has occurred and will continue to occur. The stories we recount have to do with women organizing nationally to communicate their key message to the country, mobilizing provincially to get the vote, and working locally to address immediate needs. The way girls became formally educated was a fortunate combination of economic and geographic circumstances. The education of girls was important in all the subsequent struggles for equality. We learn that the effective use of social networks linked elite women to powerful advocates resulting in major changes, and that attention to the details of legislation won equality by small steps at strategic moments. Finally, the chapter considers the playing out of these factors in the Second Wave of feminism with examples from that period and, in particular, the impact of a large group of women experts who focused on gains in equality.

Early Knowledge of Equality Rights

The idea of equality for women was not born easily. It was born very early on, however, as studies of the early woman philosophers and social scientists tell us. It was used and debated by a number of intellectual women and men in the seventeenth and eighteenth centuries.[1] Mary Astell in the seventeenth century, Mary Wollstonecraft in the eighteenth, and Virginia Woolf in the twentieth stand out among others. Included in those early debates were the problems of women's education, violence against women, property issues, and general human rights.

---

1.   For a clear discussion, see McDonald, *Women Founders*.

In France, Olympe de Gouges's "Declaration des droits de la femme and de la citoyenne" of 1791 exposed the profound hypocrisy of the French Revolution in the phrase *the rights of man*. And what of the rights of women? Her bold public stance influenced some, but it appears neither to have come over to the colonies in North America nor to have had a sustained effect on the public discussion of women for long.

For Canadians, the very early debates are more clearly addressed to the issues of equality and the roles of education, property, and culture. Ruth Roach Pierson, in "Two Marys and a Virginia: Historical Moments in the Development of a Feminist Perspective on Education," however, focuses on the reactionary thinking of the Victorian period that had such a key influence on Confederation and on what was considered appropriate in women's behaviour.[2] All these influential early writers dealing with equality for women assumed, and in some cases reaffirmed, social class differences or destinies. For example, many asserted that the vote should go to those who were "educated."

The elements of their agendas for equality gradually came to be part of discussions in the Western world. These powerful ideas of sexual equality, of "separate spheres," or of the mental superiority of the educated, which had been advanced and debated over the centuries, were part of the Canadian culture. Elements of them were most certainly entrenched in the thinking of our lawmakers and intellectual leaders throughout most of our history.

These very early thinkers in Europe—principally in Britain and France—influenced the development of what might be called a feminist agenda. The broad headings

---

2. Ruth Roach Pierson, "Two Marys and a Virginia: Historical Moments in the Development of a Feminist Perspective on Education," in *Women and Education: A Canadian Perspective*, 2nd ed., eds. Jane Gaskell and Arlene McLaren (Calgary: Detselig Enterprises, 1987), 203–22.

included access to education, economic opportunities ranging from marital property rights to work in the paid labour force, compensation and equal treatment in law, and representation in governing and decision-making bodies—in short, full citizenship on the same basis as men. The specific ideas developed under those headings ranged widely and changed over time. They took a particular expression in Canada as women participated in building the nation.

Confederation was born during a period of movement toward improvement in the rights of women in North America and Europe, although *equality* for women was not a principle of those movements. In the 1880s, women's organizations in Canada invited speakers from the United States and England to address those rights; suffrage bills were introduced into the legislatures in Canada; and supporters came from a broad range of individuals and groups. The rationale for suffrage turned not on the equality of men and women but on the moral superiority of women, the rights of property owners, the need for legislation concerning temperance or prohibition, and the relationships between women and children.

The concept of equality has a precarious life even in contemporary Canada. Its development should be seen as a very long-term series of pressures mostly by women to gain ground in the minds of the people (often thought of as "consciousness raising") and then to get the gains institutionalized in law and custom. Sometimes the minds of the elites such as legislators and religious, union, or corporate leaders were the focus, as unremitting pressure for suffrage on some provincial legislatures discussed later in the chapter illustrates. Sometimes the focus was to capture the minds of women in general, women who had to be persuaded out of many generations of conceiving of themselves as subordinate, incapable, or outrageous should they want the vote, equal pay, or representation in civil society. In the debates of the National Council of Women from 1893 forward, one can see differences in views about what constituted equality. Should domestic science courses in schools be taught only to girls or should boys also receive this training?[3] In Quebec in the 1930s, women's organizations ran a campaign to persuade women in the rural areas that suffrage was important. Women already had the federal vote, but the organizations pressing for provincial suffrage were let down by the lack of support outside Montreal. The "general education" of women was and remains important to equality gains.

Post-Confederation Rights

Social change derives from a complex intersection of ideas, action, and organization. As we have seen in earlier chapters, in some instances externally imposed events such as war or economic collapse have opened up opportunities for women to change their circumstances both individually and collectively. One example of this was winning the vote for women during World War I (see Chapter 3). Wars opened up occupational opportunities that have only expanded since. With these changes in women's behaviour, thinking about the status of women changed. The thinking of decision-makers and activists is essential to expanding the rights of women.

At the end of the twentieth century, one of the most sweeping changes occurred with the patriation of the Canadian Constitution from Great Britain to Canada (the Constitution Act of 1982). Within that Constitution is embedded a written Charter of Human Rights and Freedoms. Women activists

---

3. See Griffiths, *The Splendid Vision*, 66.

and their supporters fought hard to get a precise wording in that Charter, including in particular two sections, sections 15 and 28. Section 15 deals with equality of the sexes "before and under" the law, and section 28 says that all Charter rights are guaranteed equally to men and women. Why did they fight so hard over particular wording? Why were they so determined to get women's rights into that Charter? It was because women had learned so much from history since Confederation about the importance of the way ideas become written laws and about the interpretation of the wording in those laws. What are some examples of why they were so concerned?

The idea that males were dominant over females in all statuses except motherhood represents an ideology about social structure that is the opposite of equality. The "separate spheres" and the "separate but equal" ideas underpinned the view of the sexes during much of Canadian history. These ideas were entrenched in laws that in some instances prevailed until the debates and changes of the late twentieth century. For example, being able to pay women less than men for the same or very similar work was a long-standing employment law. The idea that women, and other minorities, should occupy quite different statuses has not altogether disappeared.[4] The groups excluded from the exercise of rights were whole segments of the population, including at various points those without property, ethnic minorities such as the Chinese and religious or visible minorities, women, people with disabilities, and Aboriginal peoples.

Changing those ideas has been a gradual process. However, from well before Confederation, women formed organizations for the purposes of social service. Those

---

4. It is interesting to note, however, that in the economic crisis of 2008–11, when so many lost their jobs in the manufacturing sector, it was women who were more likely to be the breadwinners for the families.

organizations, through women's leadership, reached into virtually all the elites in the country. In a small town, the woman heading up a shelter for women escaping domestic violence may not seem very powerful, but through regional or national associations of transition houses, she can reach governments, news makers, businesses, and religious organizations. An individual woman's problem with property rights may not seem important, but when an association of lawyers takes up the case, it may be the impetus for major reforms.[5] A reporter for a local newspaper may cover a story that becomes the reason why girls are admitted into a male-only sport, or a television report on a woman saying "Goodbye Charlie Brown" may trigger or crystallize the consciousness of a nation.[6] In most cases, however, many individuals worked many years to raise ideas and find a way to put them into action.

Post-Confederation Action

Turning points toward greater equality for women in Canada have come when pressure is exerted on policy-makers and legislatures to change law, regulation, or practice in the lives of women. How that desire for improvements is expressed by women has not changed very much since Confederation. Women still present briefs to governments; agitate through large organizations; support politicians who share their goals; write letters; make visits; form

---

5. The Murdoch case was taken up by women's groups and women lawyers. It was unsuccessful in court but hugely successful in triggering concern and agitation for legislative changes.

6. In 1985, an organized protest of seniors against the de-indexing of the Canada Pension Plan took place on Parliament Hill. Cameras caught Solange Denis telling Prime Minister Brian Mulroney that if his government carried through on de-indexing pensions, seniors would not vote for his party, that it would be "Goodbye Charlie Brown." The moment and phrase have gone into Canadian history, symbolizing the political effects of single-issue voters.

single-purpose organizations to show concern; and, if necessary, create drama on the streets or legislative grounds. Pressure sometimes comes from international events, such as economic recessions, or social movements, such as suffrage movements. Occasionally, pressure comes from the clash of political ideologies in the Canadian legislatures. Often, the change in women's lives is a by-product of such other changes. Mostly, however, women were themselves pressing for change through one means or another.

This chapter stresses how women approached problems very differently from men in the nineteenth and early twentieth centuries, and although the expressions of it are modern, there remain significant gender differences to this day. This is largely because women as a group not only had, and have, a different status from men in Canadian society, but also because social class operates differently between the sexes. Stratification theorists have examined this subject. For many years, gender inequality in various institutions dominated the discussion.[7] Researchers looked at differences in education, the labour markets, and health, but within socio-economic classes, gender differences continue. So a middle-class woman might have more wealth and social power than a working-class woman, but relative to the men in her social class she was and is much less wealthy and powerful.

In Canada, John Porter's major study of social class and social structure, *The Vertical Mosaic*, was published in 1965. It was, to a very large extent, a study of elites—the powerful members of the corporate, political, and social elite who shaped Canadian institutions and society. By elites, scholars mean those creating ideas and holding decision-making positions in everything from religious organizations, to sports federations, to social organizations, to business. They are

---

7.   See, for example, Alfred A. Hunter, *Class Tells: On Social Inequality in Canada* (Toronto: Butterworths, 1981).

the gatekeepers, the influentials, the representatives at the top of all the pyramids that make up the complex society in which we live. Porter contended that Canadians elites were a notably homogenous group who formed an integrated social unit.

Women did not form any significant part of this analysis. It is the very rare woman who stood out as an elite member of Canadian society in the nineteenth century, or even in the twentieth century, although a few have done so.[8]

In social class ranking, whether defined in relation to the means of production or in socio-economic terms, men were seen to hold the social class position for the family. This is one of the reasons that marriage used to be such a crucial matter for daughters and their parents. Social actors are "unitized" as it were—husband and wife, parents and children, members of clubs, religious groups—all were treated similarly and held to be motivated and to act in generally similar ways. Even now, when women retain their birth family names upon marriage and lead quite independent lives in the public sphere, in the private sphere, their families of origin and of marriage continue to be important in their social placement. It is still popularly thought that the daughters of the rich and powerful and the wives of powerful men have career assistance by virtue of their fathers and husbands and seldom the other way around.[9] It is still the case that a woman who "marries down" finds life more difficult than a man who does the same. The independence and power of women is greatly increased in the economic life of

---

8. Lady Aberdeen, wife of the Governor General (1893–98) is one such woman. She founded the National Council of Women in Canada as well as other organizations assisting girls and women. Once women were able to become judges, parliamentarians, medical doctors, lawyers, and professors, many more participated in elite positions and, in postwar Canada, women increasingly occupy elite social, economic, and political positions.
9. See Hunter, *Class Tells*, 146.

Canada and this has improved the status of all women, especially unmarried career women. Nonetheless, family attachments remain important in the economic and corporate, social, and political elite structures.

If changes are often the result of negotiation between those with the power to make change and those who want it, how did women in the post-Confederation years who were forced to work through men with status operate? Taking a broader and more gender-neutral view of elites to include those individuals who lead organized groups in institutions such as religion, education, economic life, or the community leads us to visualize many more people in the pool of elites. For a social movement such as the women's movement, this is important because it was the people who headed the suffrage, worker, social welfare, or school organizations who wielded considerable power and swayed opinion in communities in the nineteenth and most of the twentieth century. This becomes even more important to understanding Canada when we consider the hundreds of communities that are distant from other communities, the number of time zones, and the federated state. In a country such as Britain or most European countries with one time zone, one language, and shared newspapers, as well as the ability to gather together quickly from around the country, local or segmental elites may be less significant than they are in Canada. Furthermore, in such countries, elites tend to know one another. In Canada, for much of our history, even national leaders of important institutions might never meet one another. In the period before widespread air travel, electronic communication, and shared media, leaders below the level of premiers or heads of national organizations would probably not meet or not meet often. This meant that whoever was the leader in the local community was the party to negotiations, and quite often that was a woman. She would be the school teacher, the wife of the minister, or the woman who ran the farm when her husband was away or had died. Many women led organizations, wrote for the local newspaper, and organized charity drives. In some senses, it was the sparse population in an enormous country that created opportunities and made demands on women for leadership. In their communities, women did influence ideas and values, make representation to governments and corporations, raise funds, and were sectoral elites.

While men predominated in the notable institutions and organizations, for most of our history women gained access to discussions with decision-makers through their fathers or husbands and some still do so. Before women could hold public office, they were forced to work through male representatives. Even after women could hold public office, they were still forced to work through male representatives in many cases because in Canada women have never numerically dominated government at any level, nor corporations, nor unions, nor religious organizations.[10] But organizations were crucial to giving women a voice and a means of changing their society. This chapter looks at two ways in which organizations of women changed Canada.

Organizations: A Key to Change

A woman in Canada almost certainly has some type of civic engagement. Her membership in occupational, religious, or service organizations has been motivated rather differently at different times in our collective history, but her involvement is almost certain. In certain periods of our history, from the

---

10. This does not imply that men were not sympathetic, helpful, and instrumental in many issues concerning women's equality. Indeed, one of the fascinating outcomes of writing this book is to find what a diverse group of men introduced suffrage and related bills to legislatures. We know little about these men and their motivations.

post-Confederation years until after the Great Depression, the community was a woman's major source of assistance and social welfare (in addition to her opportunity to see people outside her family and household). Since the French regime of the eighteenth century, women had been creating and maintaining organizations to support the sick, the poor, new immigrants, and young women on their own. There was no social safety net so they carried out this crucial work through their dozens of religious and community groups. From the nineteenth through to the late twentieth centuries, girls and women would probably belong to a religious organization— a church, chapel, temple, or synagogue—and be a member of the associated organizations for girls and women. In the twenty-first century, many girls and women are still involved in religious organizations, although not nearly as many as would have been at the time of Confederation. Increasingly, the work extended to national, or Canadian, branch organizations such as the Young Women's Christian Association (YWCA), created in 1870 in Saint John, New Brunswick, by Agnes Blizzard. The YWCA spread quickly to major Canadian cities where young women needed the support of such organizations. The Women's Christian Temperance Union, created in 1874 by Letitia Youmans, was established nationally in 1885, primarily for the abolition of alcohol. There were other groups formed of this nature.

As women began to work in industry, they might join their union, as women entering the professions would join their professional association.[11] A woman might be a member of a

---

11. As we see later in Chapter 7, journalism was one profession that played a key role. Until the Canadian Women's Press Club was formed in 1904, there was no professional association, and there was no training program in a university until much later. See Kay Rex, *No Daughter of Mine: The Women and History of the Canadian Women's Press Club, 1904–1971* (Toronto: Cedar Cave Books, 1995), and Marjory Lang, *Women Who Made the News: Female Journalists in Canada, 1880–1945* (Montreal and Kingston: McGill-Queen's University Press, 1999).

literary or arts society. Political parties, children's organizations such as Scouts and Brownies, charitable organizations
of all kinds count on the voluntary work of women. It has
been, and remains, a major part of our civic culture.

By Confederation, the demands for social changes to address increasing industrialization were intensifying. Housing
conditions were disastrous for the urban poor and hard for
the rural poor. Schools had to be expanded and the local
people were the builders. Protecting the old, women, and
children was a family and community responsibility. If there
was the need for more workers for farms, households, or factories, the employees would have to be recruited, often from
abroad, and then provided for. In many communities, individuals or groups gathered to right an injustice. As the population grew and became more concentrated in towns and cities,
the organizations became larger, and with a provincial and
a federal government in place, the desires of people could be
expressed directly to their local legislators and civic leaders.

Despite uprisings, strikes, and the occasional rebellion, social changes in Canada have been achieved largely
through peaceful means. There is no crisis of revolution in
post-Confederation Canadian history. Rather, it is a story of
negotiation, elite accommodation, incrementalism, political
necessity, or cultural change.

The question that many women in organizations must
have faced was how to connect their group or community to
the regional or national leadership. National organizations
such as the temperance union, the service groups, or the
church groups played this role. However, toward the end of
the nineteenth century, a new form of organization arrived
in Canada that created a powerful new institution: the non-
aligned umbrella organization to which other organizations
could belong for the purposes of exchanging ideas and communicating. This led to a common understanding of issues,

the formation of powerful alliances, and a powerful voice for women who could not yet vote, hold public office, or occupy the public sphere. This new form of organization was introduced through the International Council of Women (ICW), which established a branch in Canada in 1893 under the guidance of Lady Aberdeen, wife of the Governor-General of Canada.

Lady Aberdeen arrived in Canada as wife of the Governor General in 1893 and was a committed and experienced social reformer. In the year the Aberdeens arrived, Lady Aberdeen, age 29, was elected president of the ICW at its Chicago convention, a position she held for more than 40 years. Canada had been well represented at the founding meeting of the ICW in Washington, D.C., in 1888. Six Canadian women were delegates from their organizations.[12] The idea of the Councils was a relatively new one in that it was to serve no *particular* interests but to provide a means of communication among existing women's organizations and to provide the means of exchanging views on the welfare of families and people throughout the world. So the Councils were not tied to any religious, political, or other views, and the national and international council was a talking shop among women's organizations.

When the next ICW met in Chicago in May 1893, in addition to those who had attended the 1888 meeting, there were many other Canadian delegates—22 in all, including Adelaide Hunter Hoodless (leader of the YWCA).[13] Of

---

12. They were Dr. Emily Howard Stowe (the Dominion Women's Enfranchisement Association), Betsy Starr Keefer (from the WCTU), Mrs. Willoughly Cummings (journalist), Mrs. Foster, Mrs. Hardy, and Mrs. Mary McDonnell.
13. Hoodless was another fearless organizer. Later that year, she become first vice-president of the YWCA, and still later founded the Women's Institutes to support and educate farm and rural women. Sadly, she died suddenly on the stage of Toronto's Massey Hall in 1910 while speaking to the Federation of Women Councils. This is one of several famous feminist events that took place in Massey Hall.

course, all those women in Chicago met and talked with the newly elected president of the Council, Lady Aberdeen. Canada already had a base of support for new ideas, and now it had a connection with the ICW president.

These 22 Canadian women in Chicago set about organizing the National Council of Women of Canada (NCWC), with Mrs. Mary McDonnell as interim president. They spent the summer of 1893 contacting women's groups for a formal founding meeting that fall.

The arrival of the new president of the ICW as the vice-regal spouse must have been very welcome to these organizers and all who were in support of the NCWC. There was a well-established and widespread concern in Canada for the conditions of working people in health, the workplace, and the community. There had been two Royal Commissions on these issues: the Royal Commission on Mills and Factories in 1882 and the Royal Commission on the Relations of Capital and Labour in 1889. The women of Canada had been instrumental in making representations to governments at all levels about the conditions of life for everyone, but particularly for women and children. Women's organizations, and many men, recognized the importance of women's views in the building of the country. Women were very effective but spoke in several different, often competing, voices, depending on the particular goal of their organization. So the non-partisan, inclusive structure of a national council was an obvious advantage.

When the NCWC was established in October 1893—and later incorporated through an Act of Parliament in 1914— its particularly Canadian characteristics showed very clearly. The NCWC is still a key organization that women use to advance their issues in Canada. It has continued over a century as Canadians have been torn by religious, political, and ethnic identities, provincial struggles, wars, strikes, and ideological divisions. How has a voluntary organization survived all this? It appears that the organization's constitution was built to accommodate all of Canada's strengths from the beginning.

Lady Aberdeen, in addition to her other qualities, was what we would now call a "political junkie." Doris French's biography *Ishbel and the Empire* details Aberdeen's meetings with all the major politicians of Canada and her interventions in Canadian politics.[14] She was a strategist and a tactician with considerable political experience. Because women could not hold public office, she used the instruments available to her—that is, the power she derived from her husband's position.

One of her friends was the famous clerk of the House of Commons John Bourinot (later Sir John Bourinot), whose rules and procedures are still used and adapted in the Canadian Parliament. In these early days of Confederation, Bourinot understood the particular challenges facing the national government of a group of former colonies with not a lot holding them together. He wrote extensively about the early days of Confederation and, from his positions as clerk of the Senate and then of the House of Commons, developed the procedure of the Canadian Parliament. He delved deeply into comparative politics. He gave advice on municipal, provincial, and federal procedures. Indeed, his entry in the *Dictionary of Canadian Biography* says, "During Lord Aberdeen's term as governor-general, Bourinot frequently gave advice both to him and to Lady Aberdeen on constitutional matters as well as on procedure at the meetings of organizations with which Lady Aberdeen was associated,

---

14. For example, Aberdeen's husband never went to Parliament except on official occasions, but she liked to go and hear the debates. When she went, she sat in a chair beside the Speaker at the front of the Chambers, a place reserved for the Queen's representative.

such as the NCWC and the Victorian Order of Nurses. His friendship with the Aberdeens continued until his death."[15]

Certainly someone with such a depth of understanding of Canada's constitutional arrangements could help create a national organization that suited the basic elements of the country: local concerns, language and ethnic diversity, regional interests, and a barely tolerated powerful national government. But, much more important, the NCWC and its constitution reflected the type of vagueness and flexibility that not only typify many of Canada's constitutional arrangements, but also that some see as essential to peace, order, and good government.[16] This "vagueness" took the form of not really defining words so precisely that they could be interpreted in only one way. For example, the NCWC constitution stated that meetings should be opened with prayer. Lady Aberdeen decided to interpret this requirement as silent prayer so as to be able to include Jewish women who she saw in attendance at an early meeting of the Council. She did not consult her colleagues about this decision, and the wording was sufficiently vague that she could defend her decision.

The NCWC was "flexible" enough to accommodate powerful local concerns, struggles with provincial interests—as well as religious issues—that sometimes threatened the existence of the organization. Local and even provincial councils of women joined and then withdrew from the NCWC at times. The flexibility was such that the local councils carried on with their work and, in time, they were welcomed back to the national meetings.

15. Margaret A. Banks, *Dictionary of Canadian Biography Online*: Bourinot, Sir John George, 2000, http://www.biographi.ca/009004-119.01-e.php?&id_nbr=6573 (accessed December 12, 2011).
16. This argument is put forward by John Ralston Saul in his book on Louis-Hippolyte LaFontaine and Robert Baldwin.

In this way, the NCWC has had a powerful influence on the history of women in Canada and continues to do so. Historian Veronica Strong-Boag called it a parliament of women. The "umbrella organization" concept was taken from the ICW in the nineteenth century, but the way in which the NCWC was designed created in this country a new sort of institution. This volunteer, civic, big-tent organization was created to bring people together for the purposes of the exchange of ideas; it was tolerant of differences and even of different purposes; it was non-exclusive and, indeed, widely inclusive; and it encouraged its members to be active in a wide range of other organizations and to take ideas back and forth from one to another. Another national or local organization could affiliate with the NCWC and still not lose its members to NCWC work. Lady Aberdeen and her colleagues could create the Victorian Order of Nurses and other organizations and yet not dilute their work in the NCWC. In more recent years, having been crucial to the creation of the Royal Commission on the Status of Women (RCSW) in 1967, the NCWC welcomed the creation of another umbrella organization, the National Action Committee on the Status of Women. Led by Laura Sabia and her colleagues, who had urged Prime Minister Lester B. Pearson to establish the RCSW, this new umbrella organization was formed to press for the implementation of the recommendations of the Commission when it reported in 1970. Instead of seeing the new National Action Committee as a rival, the NCWC supported this new organization in a generous way.

The structure of the NCWC is an extraordinary solution to the problems of diverse interests, language, and religions in a small, geographically disperse population. It was adapted from an international form to create an enduring, responsive, and Canadian solution. Indeed, it was a new form of institution for Canada, which has been emulated in subsequent organizations, such as the Canadian Federation of University Women.

Suffrage Came through Persistence

The struggle for suffrage took different forms in different provinces, but it always involved the efforts of some women.

The concept of the right to vote had evolved a great deal in the years leading up to Confederation. There were a variety of views in the nineteenth century in Upper Canada and elsewhere. Should all property owners—whether male or female, Aboriginal, or not British subjects—be entitled to vote? If so, could the same property be the basis for voting by more than one person in the household, by both a husband and a wife, for example? How old did people have to be to exercise the vote? Was suffrage a privilege bestowed by the State or an inherent right of citizens? All these ideas and the expansion of suffrage in Great Britain were debated in the colonies of British North America. Women property owners did vote in some of the colonies in some periods. But which women? Only widows or spinsters, or could married women vote? Could they vote in all elections or only municipal elections?[17]

Here we look at the achievement of suffrage as an example of Canadian women's social movements and organization styles. Achieving the right to vote depended on many issues: ownership of property (often real property), which was an important municipal—and sometimes provincial—requirement for voting in many cases; whether single women with property or married women or both should have the vote; the wording of legislation and especially the interpretation of

---

17. For a thorough discussion, see Garner, *Franchise and Politics*.

the word *person*; the enthusiasm with which the Opposition in a legislation wanted to immiserate the Government or vice versa, which often did not reflect a special commitment to suffrage but the use of suffrage as a convenient stick with which to beat the other side; church and newspaper support or opposition as voices of authority in the debate; the expressed desire of the women of the municipality or province to have the vote; the right of women if enfranchised to hold public office, which was separated by some years from the right to vote, for example, in Prince Edward Island; and the social or political connections of the women's leaders within the province. All these variables, and many others, influenced the progress of suffrage in each province. Each province has a different and interesting story.

To look at the simple dates at which women achieved the vote and the right to hold elected office in Canada is to obscure the organization and constant effort that went into that achievement. Catherine Cleverdon's painstaking description of the process explores the situation in each province as well as federally.[18] But several exceptional cases are important to note.

---

18. Cleverdon's *The Woman Suffrage Movement in Canada* was her doctoral thesis for Columbia University, submitted in 1949 and published first in 1950. It is an extraordinarily well-researched and documented thesis on Canadian suffrage struggles, but it is important to note that consistent with the times in which it was written those excluded from the vote—Canadian Asians, Indians, and those who were not British subjects—were not on Cleverdon's radar anymore than they appear to have been on the minds of those working toward or those finally passing legislation for the vote for women. It was not until the 1960s that all free citizens had the vote, and it was even later than that for prisoners. Garner (*Franchise and Politics*) points out that only in British Columbia and Nova Scotia were Indians specifically disenfranchised, but a lack of individual property holding by Indian people had the same effect elsewhere. A different view of the same events concerning women, and including an excellent review of the literature, is found in Bacchi, *Liberation Deferred?* Bacchi points out that the situation was considerably more complex among women with diverse views than Cleverdon's description suggests.

Quebec: The Longest Struggle

In the case of Quebec (or Lower Canada, as it was called for part of this time), women had the right to vote, which many exercised, from the time of the 1791 Constitution Act until 1834 when an act was passed excluding women. The reason women could vote in Quebec, New Brunswick (until 1848), Nova Scotia (until 1851), and Prince Edward Island (until 1836) hung on the interpretation of the word *person*. Since women were not presumed to be excluded from the category of "persons," some women exercised their voting rights until women were excluded by amendments to the law.[19]

In Quebec, women were excluded at the municipal level in 1834 and more definitively in 1849.[20] It appears clear that women had voted in Quebec (and Nova Scotia, although scholars find no evidence that women did so in the other two provinces).[21] The vote of Quebec's women at the provincial level was not restored until 1940, coming into effect in 1941.

That does not begin to describe the story that Cleverdon tells so well of the 14 bills for suffrage introduced into the Quebec legislature from 1915 until the fifteenth bill was finally successful in 1940. Since only men held elected office, these bills and the petitions, resolutions, and amendments were put forward by the male members of the political parties from time to time. It is important to note that in Quebec, as in all the other provinces, men in all the political parties sponsored the suffrage activities at one point or another. The leading voices for

---

19. Federally, this interpretation became famous as the Persons Case in the late 1920s when the Supreme Court of Canada found that women were not included in the definition of *persons*. This case is discussed later.
20. John Ralston Saul attempts to explain why women lost the vote in the Province of Canada in 1849 as a matter of voting reform. Saul, *Louis-Hippolyte*, 207ff. This is also explained in Garner, *Franchise and Politics*.
21. See also Bradbury, "Women at the Hustings,"73–94. See also Saul's assertion that women in Upper Canada who owned property voted in provincial elections until the late 1840s. The most thorough review of the entire system is found in Garner, *Franchise and Politics*.

suffrage behind the elected men sponsoring bills in Quebec in the 1880s were the Women's Christian Temperance Union (WCTU) and the Montreal Council of Women.[22] In 1892, widows and spinsters with property were given the right to vote for schools and those municipalities that allowed it in their charter. The legislature then went quiet on the subject until 1915 when a franchise bill was introduced. But the Montreal Council of Women was not quiet in those intervening years; it sponsored suffragist speakers from outside the country and raised petitions. The Montreal Suffrage Association was formed in 1913 and had on its executive women and men, one of the latter being the Anglican dean. Since this association was largely from the English-speaking population, it disbanded in 1919 to be replaced in 1922 by the Provincial Franchise Committee, led and composed of women in both language groups. The newspapers were solicited for support and women took up—unsuccessfully—the fight of the admission of women lawyers to the bar.

In 1927, the Provincial Franchise Committee divided. Professor Idola Saint-Jean led an organization with roots in the working class and feminist circles called L'Alliance canadienne pour le vote des femmes du Québec (the Alliance); and, in 1929, the Provincial Franchise Committee was renamed the League for Women's Rights (the League). With the Local Council of Women, various versions of the suffrage associations and the WCTU in Quebec worked unrelentingly for the cause. When required, they got publicity, such as in a petition to the King of England, and they used the radio as a way of informing the rural women about their interests and activities. Both the leading groups were highly imaginative in the methods—all peaceful—used to achieve their goals. Although the majority

---

22. The National Council of Women, founded in 1893, did not support votes for women until 1910, although local councils in some areas did so earlier. See Griffiths, *The Splendid Vision*, 106.

of Quebec activists were found in the cities, countless women were involved over the 91 years between the time women were excluded and the achievement of the franchise again.

It cannot be said that gaining the vote in Quebec was a populist movement. Cleverdon points out that when the franchise was finally achieved in the spring of 1940, the League had only 47 members. The leaders of both the Alliance (Idola Saint-Jean) and the League (Thérèse Casgrain and others) were well-connected women with different viewpoints and focus but a common goal in suffrage. In Quebec, as in other provinces, the interaction of the leadership with the political parties at the top level was a major contributing factor to their success.

Prince Edward Island

The other extreme case is that of Prince Edward Island, which never had a suffrage association but where women gained, without asking for them, the municipal franchise in the two cities by 1892; a married women's property act in 1895 (described by Cleverdon as "very liberal"); and the right to sit as school trustees in 1899. In 1922, as a result of a "quiet" campaign, women gained suffrage. The style of pressure in politics in Prince Edward Island differs most significantly from the Western provinces. The male legislators introduced these rights without any obvious populist or public pressure. Indeed, it seems that women could have had the vote in 1918 had they shown any enthusiasm for it.[23]

Ontario

Ontario had women campaigning for suffrage at Confederation, greatly enhanced by the return of Dr. Emily Howard Stowe with her medical degree from the United States in 1868. In Cleverdon's account, one finds descriptions of 28 bills

---

23. Cleverdon, *The Woman Suffrage Movement*, 202.

calling for one type of suffrage or another (married or single, property or not, municipal or provincial), which were presented until the successful bills for the vote in 1917 and then for holding elected office in 1918. This was in addition to hundreds of other actions, such as forming societies for suffrage, winning the support of other like-minded organizations, mounting an extensive campaign for the support of women in the rural areas and small municipalities, petitioning the legislature, meeting with elected members of Parliament, sponsoring suffrage speakers from the United States and Great Britain, getting women admitted to the bar, and staging a famous mock Parliament in 1896 and the inaugural performance of the play *How the Vote Was Won* in 1911.

New Brunswick and Nova Scotia

New Brunswick, having denied women the vote in 1848, found itself with a Saint John Women's Enfranchisement Association in 1894. The pressure on the legislators continued with bill after bill (all defeated), petitions, resolutions, and delegations in all the cities until women were enfranchised in 1919. At this time, women got the vote but not the right to hold public office, which occurred in 1934. Next door in Nova Scotia, women were excluded from the vote in 1851 until the franchise was won in 1918. A separate bill allowing women to hold office was passed in the same year. The women and their male supporters, again including the Protestant churches, petitioned, campaigned, organized, and appeared in committees of the legislature. They suffered the same setbacks, indignities, and abuse as the suffrage workers in most of the other provinces where activism was outspoken and strong.

Newfoundland

Newfoundland, at the time of the struggles for suffrage in Canada, had not yet joined Confederation. It was an

independent dominion within the British Empire. It joined
Canada in 1949. However, in remarkably similar efforts to
those in the Canadian provinces, women formed a WCTU
in the 1890s and this organization and others petitioned and
argued for suffrage for many years. Their tactics, at first lively,
were toned down when the press came out against them. Their
efforts in World War I were widely lauded, but even though
their contributions were recognized, it was not enough to get
them the vote. In 1921, women property owners in St. John's
were given the right to vote, although there were precious few
of them. In 1925, the vote was given to women 25 years of age
or older. Men could vote at 21 years of age. Finally, in 1946,
just three years before Newfoundland joined Confederation,
suffrage was given to men and women aged 21 or more.

British Columbia

In British Columbia, the first suffrage petition appeared
in the legislature in 1885, and 11 bills for suffrage of one
kind or another were introduced and failed before 1899.
Even before then, several pieces of legislation permitted
the municipal franchise to single and then married women
with property qualifications, followed by the vote for school
trustees and then by the right to be elected as trustees. After
much hard work and continued activism of a muscular variety among women in Victoria and Vancouver with support
from women throughout the rest of the province, the vote
and the right to hold public office was won in 1917. This led
to a very long list of legislative reforms for women for which
women had petitioned over the years.

Yukon, the Northwest Territories, and Nunavut

The Yukon had become separated from the rest of the
Northwest Territories in 1898 and the history of women
in the Yukon tells us about a determined group. Their

territorial government gave women the vote in 1919, and in 1935, Martha Black became the second woman elected to the House of Commons in Canada.

In the Northwest Territories, it was not until 1951 that women were given suffrage. And when Nunavut was created in 1999, a gender-based representative and voting plan was proposed by the Commission setting up the new territory. At the end of the day, however, the people voted down those proposals, so the Nunavut electoral system is similar to that of the rest of the country. It is important to note that in their very first election men and women had the vote and stood for public office. One woman served in the first cabinet, and women continue to be active in politics and the legislature.

>-+-+>-+-O-+-<+-+-<

All these roads to suffrage were travelled by men as well as women, and it is interesting to know why. It seems that some of the men supporters came from the temperance cause; some church leaders held the desire to see more social reforms, and others, no doubt, had been influenced by their family members who were active in the cause. Some made it clear they believed in the principle of gender equality. Others believed in women's suffrage but not gender equality in all spheres.

The accounts of the struggle for suffrage also show that the chief opposition in some times and places came from women who were indifferent, hostile, or afraid to speak out. The lesson in all cases, however, is that women activists had to find and use male allies to achieve their goals. Those allies sometimes came from personal relationships but sometimes from institutional bases. For example, the support of the established Protestant churches was important, while the opposition of the Catholic leadership in Quebec and Manitoba was important in its own way. Of course, individuals associated with these major institutions might exercise different views, but their religious organizations had a position on the matter. In some provinces, university leaders were supportive, and in others, it was the professions—medicine, law, journalism—that brought their institutional positions in support of suffrage. Cleverdon makes the case that on the Prairies it was the practice of men and women working together on their farms and in their businesses that led to the close working relationship on suffrage. She also believes that the stronger influence of the United States on those provinces was a factor. However, Cleverdon demonstrates that it was the big producer associations of farmers that carried great weight with the politicians.

Manitoba: First for Suffrage

In Manitoba the story is familiar to many since it was the first province to enfranchise women under Confederation. The ethnic Icelandic women in that province had been petitioning for the vote for a long time, and in 1893, they were joined by the WCTU. Throughout the 1890s, the activity continued, including motions in the legislature, a bill that died at second reading, and a bill the following year that was defeated. Women—both married and single—had won the municipal vote in 1887 and the school vote in 1890. After a hiatus, the suffrage cause emerged in 1910, again from the Icelandic women associations, the WTCU, and the Grain Growers Association. The Grain Growers endorsement in 1911 resulted in the formation of the Winnipeg Political Equality League, distinguished by the number of men and women journalists who were members. Mary Crawford, yet another medical doctor, led the Winnipeg Political Equality League. When the League was formed activism was the result. An unpleasant meeting with Premier Sir Rodmond Roblin in January 1914 was followed by vigorous high-profile action, including Nellie McClung playing the role of premier in an enactment of a women's parliament. Her wit resulted in good humour toward, and respectability for, the cause, and the League raised significant funds. Nonetheless, an opposition suffrage bill was voted down. But, as the suffrage proposal was endorsed at the Liberal Convention, followed in 1915 by the Grain Growers Association offering membership to women, organizing of petitions across the province increased. Again an opposition bill was defeated, but an election later in the year led to the defeat of Roblin's government and the election of the Liberals. In December, in an exciting denouement, the draft bill was seen by one woman activist who realized that it contained the vote but not the right to hold elected office. Her sister, the well-known journalist Frances Beynon, then attending the Brandon Grain Growers convention, was informed, and she threatened to reveal this inequity unless the bill was changed. Under this pressure, the bill was changed and passed its third reading—unanimously—on 27 January 1916. This province was the first to give women the right to vote and hold elected office in Canada.

Alberta and Saskatchewan Are Next!

Alberta and Saskatchewan soon followed. Their associations—the United Farmers of Saskatchewan and the Saskatchewan Grain Growers Association—played key roles organizing the rural support. By February 1916, the women of Alberta had the provincial, municipal, and school franchise, and the same passed in the following month in Saskatchewan. In Alberta, the women later known as the "Famous Five" were leaders in the suffrage cause and many other improvements for women. In Saskatchewan, it is notable that the University of Saskatchewan, by organizing Homemakers' Clubs in its extension division and by bringing the women together for an annual meeting, greatly enhanced the effectiveness of the suffrage movement at the same time.

The pattern in the Prairie provinces, then, was quite different from the rest of the country. They worked extremely hard to gain the support throughout all the farms, villages, and towns with the support of the major producer associations. They had the support of the press and a few key women leaders such as Nellie McClung, Francis Beynon, and Emily Murphy, who were known across the region. While they faced legislative opposition, they were not ridiculed and tormented as women in the Eastern provinces were on many occasions, and their provinces had already made progressive moves toward women's citizenship and rights in the earlier years.

All the struggles for suffrage required women leaders to gain the support not only of male allies but of a significant proportion of other women. Petitions signed not only by large numbers of citizens but from across many regions of the provinces were the favoured instrument to demonstrate support. The famous Francis Beynon commenting on the success in Manitoba said:

> If there is any lesson in the success of the women of Manitoba for the less fortunate provinces of Canada, it is the necessity of getting a great body of people working for this reform. Every such movement will have its outstanding women, who by their force of character and platform ability will make a magnificent contribution to the cause, but back of this there must be a great body of quiet workers who act like a leaven upon the solid mass of public opinion . . . Their work is complementary and both are essential to the success of any great movement.[24]

It was not always the case that the "solid mass of public opinion" was required to express itself for change to occur. Prince Edward Island's path to suffrage is an example of

---

24. Cleverdon, *The Woman Suffrage Movement*, 65.

this. While the Western provinces had more populist support, the involvement of women who had education, political connections, and other social capital remained important.

To a great extent, the success of the NCWC and the suffrage organizations in the provinces, like the success of worker's associations and unions, depended on the literacy and education of women and girls. Support for this had come much earlier, well before Confederation, but the development and growth of education made many other gains for women possible.

Education for Canadian Women and Girls

The case of education is in many ways the best illustration of how change occurs in the lives of Canadian women, painful though it has been for many.[25] Without a high rate of literacy and competitive skills training, women are at a great disadvantage to men in any developed society. But unlike some other changes on the feminist agenda, schooling had widespread support in this country from before Confederation. By 1867, education was already an important and, in many areas, publicly supported institution for children of both sexes.

Education for girls and women began very early in the British and French North American colonies. Schooling, at least at the elementary level, was long established in Europe, and convent schools for girls began in New France very early on. The Ursuline nuns had created a boarding school for girls by 1642, and by 1789, "according to the Bishop of Quebec at that time, the number of literate women exceeded the number of literate men."[26] Just as the Roman Catholic

---

25. Being either forced into schooling—such as residential schools for First Nations children—or being excluded from schooling on economic, religious, or other grounds have caused pain for thousands of Canadians over decades.
26. Report of the Royal Commission on the Status of Women (Ottawa: Government of Canada, 1970), 162.

schools for girls existed in New France and then in Lower Canada, church-based schooling for children existed in the British colonies. Education was established in the BNA Act as a jurisdiction of the provinces, with the exception of the education of Canadian Aboriginal people, who fell under federal jurisdiction. By the time the colonies joined Confederation, some sort of schooling—or various sorts of schooling—had been developed in every province. Some children were excluded from the schools on the basis of poverty, or geographical isolation, religion, or ethnicity, but within the constraints of geography, family income, and the availability of teachers and classrooms, girls did go to school along with boys. Literacy, arithmetic, and a variety of other subjects were found in the early curricula. Furthermore, schools were governed and in many cases funded by the government. Prince Edward Island, for example, had established a public school system by 1852.

In the field of education, the most contentious factor was religion. Some schools were clearly established on a denominational basis, but even state-funded schools argued over bible reading or religious domination of one sort or another. By the 1860s, employers in all sectors demanded basic schooling, and girls had access for the most part (even if some parents did not take advantage of the opportunity). By the time the Western provinces joined Confederation, there were secular schools in many places along with denominational schools. School attendance was not compulsory, however, until the federal Family Allowance Act of 1944 tied access to the benefit to school attendance to age 16.

But the protection of minority rights, including language rights, was a hotly contested issue in the Confederation debates and in the years that followed. The "schools" question was highly contentious in all the provinces. Particularly in Manitoba, which on joining Confederation, had established a school system based on French-speaking Catholics and English-speaking Protestants. As the population shifted toward English-speaking Protestants, the controversy became the basis of the federal election in 1896 and was and remained a crisis for many years. If the gender of the students was not of concern, religion and language most certainly were.

School was only sometimes free. School fees were required in many schools and during periods when governments could not supply free education. So the movements for change in elementary education were less about rights or equality for girls than they were about religious beliefs and practices and funding. The latter no doubt had an effect on the education of girls but did not deny their admission to schooling. Local tax-based funding of the "common schools" was the usual pattern and, since most boys' grammar schools outside the major cities were the only source of secondary education, co-education was necessitated and government funding was underway.[27] Schooling was institutionalized through the church or religious group and local and then provincial governments.

For a long time in most provinces, secondary schooling was a matter of some form of classical education. This prepared a narrow band of the population, which did not extend much beyond the elites, for the church, the law, or teaching. After early schooling in home, private, or community schools, continuing on to some secondary education was not only a matter of money, but also of social class values and commitments. Gidney and Millar report that even in the 1850s many girls were going to the grammar schools at which boys were prepared in Upper Canada. In the cities, girls would go to ladies academies or private

---

27. Susan E. Houston and Alison Prentice, *Schooling and Scholars in Nineteenth-Century Ontario* (Toronto: University of Toronto Press, 1988), 329.

school, but outside the cities co-education was inevitable, and those schools accepted both sexes. While the grammar schools were publicly funded, the girls' schools were not. Educating a daughter at the secondary level was an economic disadvantage.[28] The "separate spheres" culture was also very strong, and in Upper Canada it was accepted that girls would earn their living as wives and mothers and therefore the knowledge required to achieve those goals was paramount.

The struggle for the education of girls whose families did not send them to private schools in the aftermath of Confederation was, as Houston and Prentice point out, the basis on which the rules for secondary education were created. They describe this as "both a victory and a defeat." Young women in co-educational schools had access to largely the same education as young men and could "aspire to quite different futures from those their mothers had known." The demand by some parents for a separate but different and equal education for girls was defeated. "For better or for worse, whether they attended public schools or private schools, girls increasingly would play the same game as the boys— but with boys' rules."[29] This important observation and its subsequent manifestation in the education hierarchy—male principals and inspectors, female teachers at the elementary level and in girls' schools, male teachers at the higher levels of education, segregation in vocational education and in careers and therefore career preparation at all levels—set the stage for the twentieth-century struggles by women and their allies for equality in the society. Girls were required to adjust to the boys' domination of education.

---

28. R.D. Gidney and W.P.J. Millar, *Inventing Secondary Education: The Rise of the High School in Nineteenth-Century Ontario* (Montreal and Kingston: McGill-Queen's University Press, 1990), 105–9.
29. Houston and Prentice, *Schooling and Scholars*, 329.

Vocational education in one form or another was available to learn the applied skills required in the labour markets of the period. Domestic skills and social behaviours were a large part of the teaching. This does not mean that the education desired for daughters was trivial or not rigorous. It was simply suited to "career" preparation as seen by the values of the times.[30] Preparation beyond the elementary school meant sex segregation for those with access to such schooling. Most often, it meant religious separation as well, because various Protestant denominations and Roman Catholics provided grammar or convent schools for young ladies. Apprenticeships remained dominant for many young people, and girls were far less likely to stay in school beyond elementary school, with one exception, until the demand for their labour by employers made "commercial" education widespread. As the Report of the RCSW points out, "However, the need for trained teachers was so great that by 1860 women were found in the normal schools of all provinces."[31]

Thus, we take elementary and then secondary schooling as an example of support of women's rights, brought about not through any broad conviction of women's equality, but because schooling was widely accepted as a necessity in Canada and geographic dispersion meant that in many communities school was co-educational. Even though some groups of families or communities had to struggle to get schools to serve their children, the idea of schooling was widely accepted by the time of Confederation as a desirable feature of the society. Schooling was institutionalized through the Church and local and then provincial governments.

---

30. See the interesting discussions in Gidney and Millar, *Inventing Secondary Education*, Chapter 2. See Houston and Prentice, *Schooling and Scholars*.
31. *Report of the RCSW*, 154.

For the pursuit of ideas of equality, however, it is important to note, as historians of the mid-nineteenth century
point out, that "Few any longer questioned (publicly at least)
whether women had the brains to undertake serious study,
although the wisdom of doing so would be debated for another two generations at least."[32] Scholars, looking back on
this period from the benefit of late twentieth-century equality concerns, can agree with Marjorie Cohen's description of
this period in Ontario as the "modernization of inequality."[33]
Others contemplating inequalities would call it "assimila-
tionist," suggesting that all minorities and women had to
adjust to a standard defined by white, male, heterosexual,
European, middle-class performance.[34]

Since education fell into the provincial jurisdiction, the
struggle for access to elementary and secondary education
for girls took different forms in each province. But the issue
was more religious than gender-based. That is, by the time
of Confederation, it was accepted that girls and boys should
go to school; the question was what sort of religious or
secular influence should the schools be under? Where girls
did not attend school because religious teaching was not
present—and this issue arose in puberty especially—they
were greatly disadvantaged in their adult lives. Not com-
pleting secondary education barred them from both higher
education and the social class position that arose from educational status.

Both the former Upper and Lower Canada had constitutional protection for "Protestant" and Catholic school systems. In the Atlantic provinces, Catholic and Protestant
schools were present in different forms at different times,

---

32. See Houston and Prentice, *Schooling and Scholars*, 326.
33. See Gidney and Millar, *Inventing Secondary Education*, 294.
34. Cf. Diana Majury, "The Charter, Equality Rights, and Women: Equivocation and
    Celebration," *Osgoode Hall Law Journal* 40, nos. 3 and 4 (2002): 298–334.

but this denominational division reflected the broader divisions in almost all the institutions of the region. Both the provinces of Quebec and Ontario formed in 1867 protected and funded their majorities, but their minorities fared quite differently. In the history of schooling in Ontario, for example, it was only when Catholic schools received government funding that most Catholic girls went to school, and then they went in large numbers. It was not until very late in the twentieth century that Ontario Catholic schools were funded up to the end of high school.

British Columbia joined Confederation in 1871, and by the following year, elementary schools had been legislated as public schools. In the two Prairie provinces, public schools were established by the time the Yukon and the Northwest Territories became part of Canada in 1905.

In all the struggles for education reform at the elementary and secondary levels, such a large proportion of the population was interested because of the social and economic benefits of education: better jobs, better incomes, and better security. In addition, the social benefits of upward social mobility into the middle class or even the upper class or the prevention of downward mobility into the working class or lower class were on the minds of parents.[35] Families may have been conscious of the social class implications for their daughters even more than their sons because until after World War II, most college women still thought of marriage and family as their major career. The industrializing world of the nineteenth and twentieth centuries led to demands for increasing levels of education for men and women. This education in turn brought about

---

35. Paul Axelrod, in *Making a Middle Class: Student Life in English Canada during the Thirties*, demonstrates the intersection of education, values, social norms, and class structure (Montreal and Kingston: McGill-Queen's University Press, 1990).

major social changes.[36] Parents and often grandparents, the major religious organizations, and the governments were all part of the debate about education and schools reform and change.

Even more recently women faced barriers to gain entry to the trades traditionally associated with men, such as plumbing and carpentry. Before these skills were taught in government-run colleges—that is, when apprenticeships were required under independent businesses—women had no chance to work in these fields at all. The exception came in wartime when women were recruited to do mechanical and technical jobs, replacing men. These jobs ended when the men returned. However, governments are more likely to be assessed in terms of their service to all taxpayers. Eventually, apprenticeships were replaced by technical colleges as the main means of training skilled workers. At this point, women had a better chance of entering these occupations.

Other skills and knowledge were divided along gender lines, such as occupations in the military services as was described earlier. Many occupations were closed to women because of a combination of social attitudes about the superior strength and "suitability" of men to those jobs and of protectionism from those already dominating the occupation who did not want additional competition. This is significant because when white-collar jobs opened for women,

---

36. For the English case, see Jane Robinson, *Bluestockings: The Remarkable Story of the First Women to Fight for an Education* (London, UK: Penguin Books, 2009). The "fights" that Robinson refers to were real no doubt but were by elite women into forms of post-secondary education, and then by bright and ambitious girls spurred on by their parents or teachers for entry into the Oxbridge circles, about which Robinson documents the inequality that carried on against the entry of women, then the granting of degrees, then the denial of entry to medicine (in the case of Cambridge until 1947). Because the class structure of Canada and the formation of universities was so different from that of Britain, the Canadian story is quite dissimilar, as we see later in this chapter.

it was because those jobs paid women less than men and the scope of the jobs had narrowed.

Acceptance into Universities

At the level of professional, occupational, and university education, women faced one of their major barriers and greatest struggles in Canada. Universities were created by and for a variety of elites, and to gain entry, women had to struggle within their own class position, as well as with competing social classes. Women wanting to further their education had to overcome the opposition of their fathers or other family members (within their social class) and those coming from working-class or minority families had to compete against the better placed students for resources and a place in the universities. Even more complex was the struggle for women to gain entry to male-dominated fields such as engineering, medicine, and law.[37]

The admission of women to classes and then to particular courses of study, and then, eventually, to degrees was decided by individual institutions. However, the main impetus came after Confederation when in the 1880s the majority of universities then existing in Canada admitted women to at least some classes. In the United States, by the mid-1850s, women's colleges (such as Vassar College, 1865), land-grant colleges, and theological colleges for women had been created that influenced many Canadians. In his detailed history of higher education in Canada, Harris shows that in 1881–82, 42 women were enrolled in 6 institutions, along with 2,555 men in 17 institutions. Harris reports that 10 years later there were 581 women in 11 institutions, compared with 4,168 men, and in the 1901–2 academic year, 798 women were in 14 universities, and 5,742 men were in 18

---

37. See, for example, Roger P. Magnuson, *The Two Worlds of Quebec Education during the Traditional Era, 1760–1940* (London, ON: Althouse Press, 2005), 217ff.

Canadian Universities that Accepted Women for Degrees Prior to 1900

Institution	Founded	Women Obtain Degrees
Mount Allison	1839	1875
Victoria*	1842	1883
Acadia	1838	1884
Queen's	1841	1884
Dalhousie	1818	1885
Toronto	1850	1885
Trinity*	1827	1886
McGill	1821	1888
Manitoba	1877	1889
New Brunswick (Fredericton)	1785	1889
McMaster	1887	1894
UWO	1895–96	1898

*Now part of the University of Toronto

institutions.[38] By the turn of the century, women were accepted in many but not all universities.

Harris also shows the expansion in programs for women, such as household science, nursing, social work, library science, and physical and occupational therapy, that sprang up after World War I.[39] In the academic year of 1920–21, he reports that 3,834 of the 23,418 university students were women, and by 1940–41, women were nearly 9,000 out of 37,000 students, nearly a quarter of all university enrolments.

The admission of women to degrees was a post-Confederation struggle but in an entirely different form from other struggles such as suffrage. The institution of higher education was located then, as now, in highly autonomous organizations: the universities. Up to a "tipping point," after which women were admitted as a matter of course, each university

38. Robin S. Harris, *A History of Higher Education in Canada, 1663–1960* (Toronto: University of Toronto Press, 1976), 624–29.
39. Harris, *History of Higher Education*, 398–99.

had to be won over to accept women as students, degree-takers, faculty, and administrators. As I shall show, this was a struggle of upper-middle-class women in the beginning rather than a popular movement for equality.

The struggle was also localized, not only because of the need to address each university separately, but because even within the provincial jurisdictions universities were autonomous from one another. Many universities were funded and run by religious organizations. There was no point in a national organization, such as the NCWC, pressing the federal government for university places for women in Canada since university education was outside that government's jurisdiction. In the early days, there was no point in assailing the provincial governments since so many institutions were run by autonomous religious organizations. Thus, one finds separate accounts of how this or that university came to the point of admitting women.[40]

In 1955, Canadian feminist leader Elsie Gregory MacGill wrote a biography of her mother, Helen, who was one of the women pioneers in university life in the late nineteenth century. In it, MacGill describes her mother's desire to become a concert pianist and how she was finally admitted to the new Bachelor of Music and then the Arts degree at Trinity College (now part of the University of Toronto).

> Barristers, priests and B.A.s were eligible to write the three examinations leading to the degree, while . . . musicians who lacked academic qualifications were accepted if they could show five years' musical study and practice. . . .
> In 1883, the Corporation [ruled] . . . that women might sit

---

40. There is a large literature on the admission of women to each of the universities, including a chapter in Martin Friedland's *University of Toronto: A History* (Toronto, University of Toronto Press, 2002, Chapter 9). For a detailed account of the struggle to create and then admit women to the University of British Columbia, see McClean, *A Woman of Influence*, 83–91, and many entries thereafter.

for the three Cambridge examinations but would be eligible only for certificates, not for degrees.

In September, 1884, Helen sat . . . for the First Examination. . . . Of the thirty Toronto aspirants only four passed. . . . Helen alone took First Class Honours.

. . . Helen now aspired beyond the certificate to the full satisfaction of the degree. . . . An argument in her favour was that the Corporation was now prepared to confer medical degrees on women. . . . There was no general breakdown of custom yet, however, and . . . each applicant for a "prohibited" degree had first to dig her way through the deposit of prejudice overlying the more conventional professorial minds.[41]

Helen had her distinguished lawyer grandfather on her side to prevail with the Corporation of Trinity. Women were permitted to seek the degree but with additional obstacles put in their way. In 1886, Helen passed the final music examination marked in Cambridge.[42] But now matriculation was required. Women were not permitted to attend lectures so preparation was complex. Furthermore Helen's application to take the degree was refused. Again, her grandfather was called in to help. Again, he won the case. In November 1886, Helen was the first woman in the British Empire to receive the music degree. She then enrolled, with another woman, in the Arts program, graduating in 1889. By that time, a number of women had enrolled at Trinity College in various courses. Helen went on to a career in journalism, social reform, and judging, while conveying her pioneering spirit to two splendid daughters. But the point here is that she "dug her way" into university degrees by brains, persistence, and influential family members. The change that occurred for her, as for other women pressing their cases

---

41. MacGill, *My Mother the Judge*, 42–43.
42. An E. Stanton Mellish had applied to Trinity College in 1883 and turned out to be *Emma* Stanton Mellish, a woman. In 1886, both she and Helen passed the final music examination.

at other universities, came by influence and courage rather than through a broad social movement. Quite probably others had tried and failed.

The admission of women to classes and degrees certainly had highly visible advocates. In Ontario, by the 1870s, the rights of women to university education, including co-education, were being advocated by Principal Grant and some distinguished male colleagues at Queen's University and John Clark Murray at McGill University. At the University of Toronto, co-education was opposed by the principal of University College, Daniel Wilson, but strongly advocated in the *Globe* by a graduate, William Houston. Women were already able to write the examinations but not take classes. As women began to petition to attend classes in the late 1800s, various other supporters of co-education emerged, including members of the legislature. Wilson favoured a separate college, such as McGill, but funding for such separate facilities never arrived.[43]

Sometimes the desire to keep the sexes separate prevailed, and this was clearly the case in Roman Catholic institutions. Sometimes it took the rather bizarre form of allowing women to listen to the lectures from a separate room. Dormitories and residences were almost always sex-specific until late in the twentieth century. This quest in universities to be open to women as equals in all available positions continues. The research data indicate that women are still considered marginal in some roles, such as top researchers. As recently as 2010, in the case of the federal Canada Research Chairs appointments, it was found that universities across the country were failing to recruit women to these prestigious chairs and pressure of various kinds is required to correct the situation.

---

43. See A.B. McKillop, *Matters of Mind: The University in Ontario, 1791–1951* (Toronto: University of Toronto Press, 1994), Chapter 6, "The Arrival of Women."

While co-education may have existed until puberty in secondary school and eventually in some university courses, throughout the Western world it was considered outrageous in such courses as medicine. In Toronto, the Women's Medical College ensured separation, although Augusta Stowe and other women graduated from the Victoria University medical school in 1883.[44] In short, the public attitudes toward sexual knowledge outweighed any interests in the equality of the minds of women and men.[45]

A later example demonstrates the persistence of these attitudes. In British Columbia, the university was established by an act of the legislature passed in 1908. It was followed by delays and complications so the eventual opening in 1915 of the University of British Columbia was an important event. There was a strong push by women in British Columbia for co-education in the liberal arts. In the postwar period, however, separate courses considered more suitable for women, especially nursing and home economics, were created first. Even in the twentieth century when women were accepted into universities, sex segregation in programs, especially professional programs, remained dominant.[46]

In Quebec, the situation was more complex because the sphere of education for the majority of Quebecers was controlled by the Roman Catholic Church in that province. While supportive of women and girls in many ways, the focus on the sanctity of motherhood made the Church in Quebec the foe of women's rights such as suffrage, any political roles, and any entry to professions that detracted from women's domestic priority. Whatever individual church

44. Victoria University was originally in Cobourg from 1836 but moved to Toronto and became one of the federated colleges of the University of Toronto in 1890.
45. See McKillop, "Professional Education and Maternal Feminism," in *Matters of Mind*, 132–36, for a description of the struggles of women to study medicine, and 136–37 for law.
46. See McClean, *A Woman of Influence*, 134–48.

leaders or members thought, the province's highest leaders waged campaigns that influenced thinking and actions in the province. This was true despite the views of Rome, which were supportive of women's rights. Education was considered preparation for girls' highest calling: motherhood.

For secondary school, Quebec boys had classical colleges, the necessary preparation for university. They also could attend the academies, both public and private. Among the 126 Quebec academies at the end of the nineteenth century, seven were co-educational, while most of the public academies were boys' schools and most of the private academies were for girls. At the time of Confederation, says Magnuson, the classical colleges

> whose origins reach back to pre-revolutionary France and the French regime in Canada shared a number of common characteristics: all were boys' schools which received boarding as well as day students; all were under the direction of the Catholic clergy; all were staffed by clerical teachers; and most offered an eight-year program of academic study anchored in classical languages and literature, which was capped by the baccalaureat, entitling its holder to enter university.[47]

While the academies held classes in the sciences, a "feature of the girls' academies, most of which were under the authority of religious orders, was their attention to sewing, embroidery, and other household arts."[48] Because elementary teaching was dominated by women, McGill University both admitted women to the Normal School from 1857—where they received a certificate to teach but no degree—and assisted in the creation of the High School for Girls in 1875, which prepared girls for university. They were admitted to McGill University in 1884 but, like the rest of Quebec education,

---

47. Roger P. Magnuson, *Two Worlds of Quebec Education*, 85–90.
48. Magnuson, *Two Worlds of Quebec Education*, 89.

on a sex-segregated basis. Women were "lectured, examined and housed separately from male students." The Royal Victoria College was opened in 1899 as a women's residence, and women were not permitted into any of the faculties except Arts. It took many years for women in either French or English, or Catholic or non-Catholic, communities to be fully accepted into Quebec universities. And yet, when the Quiet Revolution of the 1960s occurred, Quebec took the lead in graduating women in all the non-traditional fields for women except, of course, for the priesthood.

The story of women's struggle for higher education is one of courageous individuals and small groups of supporters taking on major established institutions that had powerful investments in men—men's education, careers, and dominance in public life. Traditionalists also had to cope with the discomfort of men who had to study with women, a cultural barrier that has not entirely disappeared. It is not dissimilar to today's struggles for the appointment of women to the boards of corporations and other organizations in which one sex wishes to remain apart. It is still an issue in many workplaces. Governments have limited instruments to enforce equality in these realms.

Equality Rights in Law

The search for rights is a long story. Certain rights and freedoms were first protected by employment and family law, but later by human rights legislation that came to exist in every province and territory. Provinces passed and amended their legislation from time to time—and still do so. Saskatchewan had a bill of rights by 1947 and Alberta in 1972. In 1975, Quebec passed a Charter of Human Rights and Freedoms. As people found, human rights and women's rights in provincial laws are uncertain because they can be repealed and changed. For example, rights in employment were to be found in all provinces at an early stage, although they would not promote the equality of men and women. Labour laws were enacted and then amended time and again as ideas about rights, freedoms, and equality changed and developed and citizens asked for changes. For women, the wage gaps between women and men in every occupational group and industry were historically frustrating from before Confederation, as the next chapter records. Women's groups and unions have exercised pressure to remedy the situation in provincial law time and again.

At the federal level, Prime Minister John Diefenbaker's government brought in the Canadian Bill of Rights in 1960, the first law to set out fundamental human rights in Canada at the federal level. As women discovered in the famous—or infamous—Lavell case in 1973, the Bill of Rights was inadequate to protect women's rights, or in sociological terms, the way in which "equality" was conceptualized did not allow for the recognition of the status of women. As recently as 1970 a wife was assumed to take on the status of her husband; the husband did not take on the status of his wife. Jeannette Corbiere Lavell lost her Indian status on marrying a white man in 1970, whereas when a Status Indian man married a white woman not only was his status protected, but also his non-Indian wife became a registered Indian. Lavell appealed but lost at the Supreme Court. The Bill of Rights was only a piece of legislation that did not trump other older legislation such as the Indian Act. This case and the not dissimilar case of Yvette Bedard[49] showed that

---

49. After the Charter became active in our Constitution in 1985—there was a three-year delay in bringing the equality provisions into effect to allow laws to be brought into conformity—the Indian Act was changed to allow women marrying to retain their Indian status, although complications remain. For a full description of the Lavelle and Bedard cases, see the *Canadian Encyclopedia* entries and Brandt et al., *Canadian Women*, 543–45.

whatever the intentions of the 1960 Bill of Rights it could not be used to change the provisions of the Indian Act.

Those court decisions about Status Indian women had a mobilizing effect on women as much as the later Murdoch case described in Chapter 2. Both those cases were seminal to the thinking of women in the development of constitutional rights. Attentive women learned the valuable lessons that well-intentioned legislation failed to either define equality rights for women or to protect them. They also learned that the precise wording of laws and regulations is material to their interpretation in the courts. This particular set of lessons was of crucial importance in the struggle over the wording of the 1982 Canadian Charter of Human Rights and Freedoms, when women realized that the proposed Charter, to be embedded in the Constitution, would not protect their equality. In the final 1982 constitutional transformation, the federal government set out to elevate the statement of the rights and freedoms of Canadians from legislation by embedding it in the Constitution. After much public outcry and determined lobbying, women were successful in changing the wording of the Charter to strengthen the protections for women.

None of the reformed legislation in the provinces or at the federal level was created without pressure from human rights and women's rights groups. None of the legislative changes escaped the attention of women's organizations. Women have learned to be very careful indeed and, with the Charter in the Constitution Act of 1982, they have had partial success. Even in the twenty-first century, not every equality issue can be brought before the Courts, and conformity with the Charter does not guarantee that equality rights are understood at the operational level.

While equality was not a new idea by the late twentieth century in Canada, its definition and use in laws, regulations, and workplaces remained ambiguous. It was in 1984 that an explicit operational definition of equality was accepted that merged into a variety of laws and labour market requirements.[50] It is important to remember that the idea of equality for women was available in the repertoire of ideas in the founding cultures of the European immigrants who populated Canada from the seventeenth century forward. It takes a long time to incorporate important ideas into social institutions.

Social Networks: The Persons Case and the Death Benefit

It was not only powerful women's organizations that changed Canada. It was also social networks built up among powerful individuals. The story of the Persons Case shows how women who were prominent through their work and leadership used their networks to change an important law. The story of the death benefit shows how those networks operate in changes in legislation on an everyday basis.

Although the vote had been won for many women by 1921, proposals to sit women in the Upper Chamber, Senate of Canada, were strongly opposed. This struggle, described in a variety of accounts,[51] shows the elements of principle and personal ambition, of networks of influence, of the determination of individuals—the Famous Five—and of the willingness of some men to take the case seriously and support it. The story of how that barrier was overcome illustrates the way in which social changes can be successful through the focused action of a relatively small group of determined individuals with access to a power elite, in this case Emily Murphy and her four persistent colleagues from Alberta.

Emily Murphy was appointed as a magistrate in Alberta in 1916. From there, with her work as a social reformer and a

---

50. See Abella, *Equality in Employment*, Chapter 1.
51. See Brandt et al., *Canadian Women*, 411–12, and Sharpe and McMahon, *The Persons Case*.

feminist on the suffrage, temperance, and law reform issues behind her, she pursued a seat in the Senate of Canada. When both the government of the day and the Supreme Court of Canada denied women's personhood and therefore the right to be called to sit in the Upper Chamber, Murphy organized an appeal to the Privy Council of Great Britain. This tells the tale of the powerful connections Judge Emily Murphy and her four well-known colleagues—Henrietta Muir Edwards, president of the National Council of Women for Alberta; Nellie McClung, a nationally known temperance and suf-frage advocate; Louise McKinney and Irene Parlby, both elected members of the Alberta legislature—rallied to their cause. All these women had important organizations behind them that gave them status, experience, and confidence. But this goal did not involve the active involvement of major groups in the way a broad social movement had done in the fight for the vote. The right to be called to the Senate began and ended with people at the top. The struggle involved letters to the prime minster, loyal friends and relatives, powerful judges, and well-connected and highly regarded lawyers. When the matter had been sent to Britain, where constitutional interpretations could be made in Canada's BNA Act, an independent Judge Sankey made the recom-mendations to the Judicial Committee of the Privy Council of Great Britain, to which the case was referred for decision. During these years, the action was directed by Murphy or-chestrating her friends and, when necessary, the pressure of petitions and letters from women's organizations. To carry out her goal, Murphy chose people of influence and high reputation at each step of the way and watched the case closely. Finally, with Canadian lawyer Newton Wesley Rowell putting the case in favour of women being included in the word *person*, Murphy won. The Sankey decision dif-fered from the decision of the Supreme Court of Canada in that he introduced the view that the Constitution should be interpreted consistent with contemporary times rather than with the times in which it had been written—it was a "living tree," as Sharpe and McMahon stress in their analysis of the case.[52] This decision resounded throughout Canadian law, not only for women. The Senate and a wide range of Canadians have Murphy to thank.

Nonetheless, this case is a clear example of high-profile pressure politics by an astute group of individuals whose actions finally changed the fundamental nature of the country.

Legislative Details and Rights

Another way to see how change occurs and is institutionalized is to examine the role of women in Parliament in bringing about social change. There are many examples. The effectiveness of women in legislative change benefiting women is strongly linked to their knowledge of key issues through their involvement with women's organizations. Reform to divorce laws in Parliament, including the Senate of Canada,[53] is one illustration, and another is the struggle for the death benefit in the mid-1950s.[54] In the latter case, a bill dealing with amendments to the Public Service Superannuation Act provided a death benefit for public servants. It consisted of a compulsory payment into a fund, with a limited government contribution, which provided universal coverage of workers at death dependent on age. The problem for women was twofold. First, married women were not permitted to work for the public service (unless widowed, divorced, or deserted), so the vast majority of

52. Sharpe and McMahon, *The Persons Case.*
53. See Lorna Marsden and Joan Busby, "Feminist Influence through the Senate: The Case of Divorce, 1967," *Atlantis* 14, no. 2 (1989): 71–81.
54. See Lorna Marsden, "The Senate and the Death Benefit" (paper, Canadian Sociology and Anthropology Association, Queen's University, Kingston, ON, June 1991).

women civil servants—making up about a quarter of the public service—were single. Second, the single women had to pay into the fund but would not benefit since they had no heirs as defined. A variety of women's organizations, but notably the Canadian Federation of University Women, that had been trying to remove the bar on married women in the public service, were upset about this provision. The president of the Civil Service Association raised the concerns of single women in committee by reading into the record a letter from a member. In response, some Members of the House made highly sexist comments against which there were protests in the public press. However, the bill passed the Commons unredeemed in this regard (there were five women in the House of Commons and there is no record of their objections) and moved to the Senate. There, the opposition was led by the new Senator Muriel Fergusson from New Brunswick. She was a lawyer, former public servant, and active member of several women's organizations. She had been well briefed on the issue. By second reading, objections to the bill came not only from women senators Fergusson and Carine Wilson but from male colleagues. In committee stage, the protests and representations continued to grow, despite threats by deputy ministers to fire any female employee who appeared or was present at the committee. In the end, an opting out amendment was made in the Senate. That, of course, required the return of the bill to the House, where the minister, in accepting the amendment, made derogatory comments about the "aggressive organization of maiden ladies here in Ottawa."[55] The case as a whole showed the tenor of the times in which Members of all three parties in the House supported this discrimination against women civil servants but a cross-party segment, supported

---

55. Marsden, "The Senate and the Death Benefit," 14.

by women's organizations and individual civil servants, won the day. It is, in the larger sense, a minor event in the movement of women's rights. Indeed, it was only to the benefit of single women public servants. But it does illustrate the effectiveness of a small group drawn from across the social spectrum and from organizations that focus their attention on a proposed legislative change.

It also shows the detailed and often difficult way in which changes are made (or fail to be made) in such a public institution as Parliament. Most people do not know about most changes to legislation or programs, despite the fact that those changes become embedded in law. Promulgation of those laws by the government of the day and their enactment in programs and regulation by the public service are equally important steps that can make change, or bury it, despite the will of legislators. But that is precisely how, then and now, most changes are made in our laws and regulations. It is why women's organizations who keep close watch on these matters are significant forces for greater equality.

The most familiar changes to the public are those brought about through widespread social movements that capture the public mind. These are important in our history but we need to remember that, at the end of the day, the fruits of social movements come down to ensuring that changes in law, regulation, and programs are made to carry out the popular will. We ignore parliamentary procedures and reports at our peril.

The Second Wave: New Talent and New Tactics

Much has been written about the revival of activism of women after World War II, but some examples illustrate the ways in which organizing changed the law and public attitudes to some key issues not previously addressed. Of course, domestic violence, rape, child care, workplace conditions and pay, and discrimination in a variety of spheres remained of concern in those years, as they have always been and are now.

The revival of activism that culminated in the last decade of the twentieth century, similar to that of women in the post-Confederation period that led to the vote for women, is usually referred to as the "Second Wave." This activism was widespread, especially in the United States, and in Canada it resulted in many changes but most particularly and by happy coincidence in important revisions to the Canadian Constitution.

It is significant that in Canada many women stayed in the paid labour force after World War II, that the State created benefits in the postwar period that recognized women explicitly (such as the family allowances), and that women had taken many leadership positions during the crisis of war and thereafter. More women had higher levels of education and were occupying positions of influence in politics, government, and the private sector than previously.[56]

Attention Establishment

In the revival of the widespread women's movement in the late 1960s and throughout the 1970s, many familiar issues emerged. It is important to point out, however, that many women's organizations had remained active throughout the entire period. In particular, national organizations were persistent in their efforts to improve the conditions of women and girls, including the National Council of Women, the Business and Professional Women's Associations, the University Women's Clubs, the religious and professional

---

56. Prentice et al., *Canadian Women*, 2nd ed., and more extensively in Brandt et al., *Canadian Women*.

associations, and other organizations not focused on issues for women, such as labour organizations, that nonetheless worked hard for gender equality. But, by the 1960s, interest surged beyond these groups in pushing forward reforms.

Once again women were pressing for equal pay, opportunity, benefits, and access in the labour markets. Once again inequality in the provincial domains of education, social services, health, and welfare were shown, province by province, to be inequitable. The well-established women's organizations were major drivers in this effort. But this time, there were two other forces for change. One was the new generation of women mostly not active in the established organizations seeking another "new day for women" and who saw the stark injustices in their workplaces, family lives, and communities. A second was wider access to education and the professions in a period of relative prosperity.

Women's organizations were strengthened by the new membership growth, and many had significant leaders. They were not happy with the status of women in Canada and saw other countries making gains they wanted. Their mobilization led in 1967 to the formation by Prime Minister Lester B. Pearson of a Royal Commission to study the status of women (RCSW). Royal Commissions are one of the instruments available to governments to address major issues through research, study, and recommendations, which report to Parliament but are not part of parliamentary business.

In the United States, President John F. Kennedy had formed a Presidential Commission on the Status of Women in 1961 to 1963. In Canada, the major women's organizations rallied to apply pressure on the prime minister to establish a Commission here, and this goal was finally achieved. The pressure to create the Commission was led by a number of women from across the country who represented different interests and were activists in their own way. The

Commission consisted of five women and two men under the chair, Florence Bird. They held hearings across the country and commissioned various studies. Many of their support and research staff later became leaders in their own right. The hearings, many of which were broadcast on CBC Radio, raised the awareness of women in all walks of life who had not realized how compromised their rights and full citizenship were in Canada and how at risk they were in many ways. The Commission reported in December 1970.[57]

The same women's groups that had forced the establishment of the Commission also knew that reports and recommendations could easily languish in obscurity, so they set out to ensure that the recommendations were taken seriously at the federal and provincial levels. Inspired by the Report of the RCSW, women organized to press for the implementation of its recommendations. Among the recommendations were many addressed to governments at federal, provincial, and local levels, while others concerned non-governmental organizations and institutions such as schools and universities and private corporations. However, it was clear that representation to governments would be the most effective action for pressure groups. Such groups were quickly formed in the provinces, various cities and regions, and eventually, at the national level. So provincial groups would focus on the recommendations addressed to provincial governments, and the national status of women group put its efforts into the recommendations directed to the federal government. There was a ferment of activity. The timing was propitious with the rise in the number of active women in communities, universities, the labour force, and unions. Status of women

---

57. The Report of the RCSW was made public in December 1970. It contained 167 recommendations on a broad range of topics and was accompanied by separately published background research documents of great interest. So widely used was the Report and the accompanying research reports that the demands for copies outstripped supply.

associations, councils, and committees formed across the country, drawing on both the well-established and newly active women's organizations. With a clear agenda drawn from the RCSW recommendations, there were actionable goals to tackle and meet.

A well-known example of the revival of the widespread women's movement in Canada is the Abortion Caravan that started in Vancouver in 1969 and moved on Ottawa in 1970.[58] It was a brave idea that arose shortly after the hearings of the RCSW and as the baby boom women were entering adulthood. As the women who organized it explained, the abortion issue affected all women, in every social, cultural, and economic setting, and in that sense was of widespread interest. While probably the majority of women opposed abortion or at least opposed talking about it publicly, every woman was vulnerable to the possibility and many women had undergone illegal abortions—illegal because abortion was considered a crime in the Criminal Code. The Caravan estimated that 2,000 women died every year as a result of illegal abortions. The radicalism of the women leaders in Vancouver and across the country arose from the treatment of women in the anti-Vietnam and anti-capitalist movements in North America (and elsewhere). The late 1960s and 1970s were filled with protests against the war in Vietnam, other wars, and the actions of governments across the Western world. Economic equality may have been the goal, but abortion was the timely issue to carry forward the sense of inequality. Furthermore, the door had been slightly opened by Prime Minister Pierre Elliott Trudeau's amendments to the Criminal Code when he was Minister of Justice in 1967–68. These amendments

---

58. The story was best told by Karen Wells on CBC Radio in a documentary called "The Women Are Coming." Rebroadcast on *The Sunday Edition*, CBC Radio, March 2011.

had made abortion legally possible under some very limited circumstances. "Not good enough" was the reaction of
many women, and the Vancouver women were prepared
to act—and did so most effectively. They drove in many
vehicles to Ottawa, gaining supporters along the way; some
of whom joined the Caravan. Their arrival in Ottawa got
widespread media and political attention across the country and showcased some new leaders on a powerful subject.

Perhaps it is not surprising that it was the women of
Vancouver who took up the issue of abortion in such a
dramatic and public way. It was, after all, the women of
Vancouver who during the 1920s sponsored a visit by the
American birth control advocate Margaret Sanger. They did
so after feminists in other cities turned down the opportunity to organize a tour for her. Even in Vancouver, it was the
women in trade unions and the left political movements who
welcomed her, to the great benefit of many women.[59] The
Abortion Caravan was situated in this tradition of support
for causes thought to be highly sensitive or "not respectable"
by other women's and feminist groups while very much
wanted by women from all social groups.

This dramatic public action that caught media attention is
a good example of the many such actions employed in the
second wave of feminism. The widespread influence of television and the increased number of women journalists made
this particularly effective.

Women Lawyers and Constitutional Success

The entry of women into the study of law and then, province
by province, entry to the bar of the provinces is another important case. They led a type of social change different from
the others. It is change brought about by a group of experts

---

59. McLaren and McLaren, *The Bedroom and the State*, 59–67.

from a powerful occupational group educating and mobilizing women and men to create a broad social movement. Furthermore, the women lawyers, because of their occupation and membership in law firms, did not disperse after some of their activist goals were achieved. (Most groups did disband because they were either voluntary associations with changing membership or groups formed with a particular goal in mind—for example, the women groups formed in the wake of the RCSW dispersed after the completion of their original agenda.)[60] In effect, this movement has demographic elements because it could not have happened without the dramatic increase in the number of women lawyers. Those women lawyers came face to face with opportunity in the form of proposed constitutional change in Canada. The coincidence of a large number of women lawyers and a government bent on entrenching rights in the Constitution is not dissimilar to the circumstances for the winning of suffrage. Briefly put, for other reasons entirely, government opened the way to the women who wanted change. Those women in both cases seized the day. It led eventually to the inclusion of sections that redefined the status of women in the law and courts in the Canadian Charter of Human Rights and Freedoms.

The story of the admission of Clara Brett Martin to the practice of law in 1897 in Canada is important and well known. Mabel French's struggle for admission to the bars of New Brunswick and British Columbia was also significant.[61] There were many such struggles. Life was not

---

60. To learn how one feminist group formed to press for the recommendations of the RCSW slowly dissolved, see the forthcoming account of the work of the Ontario Committee on the Status of Women edited by M. Elizabeth Atcheson and Lorna Marsden to be published by the Feminist History Society.

61. See Mary Jane Mossman, *The First Women Lawyers: A Comparative Study of Gender, Law and the Legal Professions* (Oxford: Hart Publishing, 2006), especially 82ff.

pleasant or easy for women in law for many generations. The important issue in this exploration of social change, however, is the way in which women lawyers played a crucial role in securing gains for women's equality much later built on the basis of the work of Clara Brett Martin, Mabel French, and other pioneers.

As consciousness of women's inequality in Canada rose during the late 1960s and 1970s, so did the number of women enrolling in law schools in Canada. It was a remarkable and dramatic increase. Between 1931 and 1986, the number of lawyers and notaries in Canada rose about fivefold—from roughly 8,000 to 43,000—while the number of women lawyers rose from 3 to 22 percent of lawyers in the same period. However, between 1971 and 1981, the growth in the number of women lawyers (over 500 percent) far outstripped the growth in men lawyers (less than 100 percent).[62] In 1931, there were only 54 women lawyers in Canada; in 1941, there were only 129. By 1961, still there were only 309. Twenty years later, there were 5,175.

That growth in numbers in the law schools and professions provided the basis for a particular type of social change in Canada, change created by a significant mass of knowledgeable people in a professional network with available resources. Those resources included the meetings among the women lawyers in various associations, including national meetings; the communication across the country; and the common awareness both of the struggle of women who had preceded them in the practice of law and of the way the laws of the land and the actions of the courts had failed women in some highly significant ways.

The National Action Committee on the Status of Women (NAC), with its provincial status of women committees,

---

62. David A. Stager and Harry W. Arthurs, *Lawyers in Canada* (Toronto: University of Toronto Press with Statistics Canada, 1990), Chapter 6.

formed in 1972 as an umbrella organization of women's groups. Only two years later the National Association of Women and the Law (NAWL) formed. They were both responding to the Report of the RCSW (1970). While the NAC pressed for the implementation of the recommendations of the RCSW that dealt with a wide range of issues, NAWL focused on where those issues could and would be addressed in law.

Both groups created networks of individuals from a generation of women who were largely found outside the more established women's organizations such as the National Council of Women, the Business and Professional Women's associations, the University Women's clubs, the peace organizations, and many other similar groups. They were a younger group of women but connected in many ways to the slightly older and more experienced women who had membership in both the established and the new "radical" feminist groups. They formed bonds across the country and shared ideas, experiences, and data. Both groups and the membership of both organizations were extremely broadly defined, and they worked hard to make changes to influence governments at all levels, including school boards and local bodies. Both worked with unions and employer groups, with Aboriginal women's organizations, with immigrant groups, with victims of family breakdowns and violence, and with what came to be known as equality-seeking groups to address the vital barriers facing women. There were countless local and regional women's rights and feminist organizations with vibrant memberships in this period. The full range of political and economic views was reflected, from time to time, in these organizations.

The women lawyers played a crucial role in these years by educating women about the opportunities and limitations of the laws in Canada. The processes of law in the legislatures, both provincial and federal, and in the courts are very complex. The logic of law is not intuitive to the thinking of most citizens. Many activists, focused on their own particular issues, did not weigh the balances of the law or take into account the subtleties of precedent.

The numbers of women and the lack of concern with the law as it affected women became the impetus for these law students and some of their professors to open up new ideas about law and women. As Mossman describes it, questions were asked during law school years and the number of legal practitioners who were women changed the nature of the conversations.[63] Many were activists. Elizabeth Atcheson's account of her activities while a law student trying to act on women's health issues is illustrative.[64]

Although at the time the women lawyers seemed but one part of the social change process, the big break came when the Government of Canada began its process of constitutional change in the late 1970s. A series of conferences on constitutional issues took place with the provinces, and it was the women lawyers who sounded the alarm in 1978 over the proposal to transfer jurisdiction over divorce to the provinces. This issue had resonance with women's groups across the country. When Prime Minister Trudeau opened the debate on patriation of the Constitution from Westminster, an inviting subject for all lawyers and law students, the door was opened for the now large number of women lawyers to practise their art.[65] While many supported patriation, their particular interests were very diverse, from ambitions of the provinces for more power and/or a different relationship to

---

63. Mossman, *The First Women Lawyers.*
64. M. Elizabeth Atcheson, "Change Is Never Given," in *Feminist Journeys,* ed. Marguerite Anderson (Toronto: The Feminist History Society, 2010).
65. While the Statute of Westminster in 1931 had achieved independence, the Canadian Constitution could be amended only by an act of the British Parliament. It was this that Trudeau and his allies wanted to change.

Ottawa, to the ambitions of Aboriginal peoples, to women's desire for equality rights.

There were more young lawyers by 1981 than ever before in Canadian history. They had networks of contact, ideas about equality, a depth of knowledge, political skills, and leadership potential. The women lawyers not only moved forward on the proposed Charter and constitutional change, but also educated, through the networks of women and their organizations across the country, many thousands of women whose knowledge of the Constitution before this was negligible. They opened a new front for making change. Fortunately, they succeeded. The story of the struggle over the Charter of Human Rights and Freedoms and the eventual establishment of the Women's Legal Education and Action Fund (LEAF) is well known and well told elsewhere.[66] Women's equality rights were considerably improved and secured through this struggle. Knowledgeable women knew that the order in which cases went to the Courts, and how those cases were interpreted, was of great importance. After all, they had lived through the problems of cases being decided under the Bill of Rights. As a consequence, LEAF was set up to promote and defend a careful process.

This chapter has provided examples of the main ways in which women have changed Canada through seizing opportunities to improve women's rights through organization and effective tactics not in one way, or in one era, but throughout Canadian history. Women have used all the resources at their disposal. They have participated in all the major institutions to which they won access, including all political parties, religious organizations, and community groups. They formed and maintained large, complex organizations

---

66. See Sherene Razack, *Canadian Feminism and the Law: The Women's Legal Education and Action Fund and the Pursuit of Equality* (Toronto: Second Story Press, 1991).

of women. They have persisted over generations in pursuit of some rights and programs. They have held an immense variety of political and social opinions but still managed to co-operate on issues they agreed on. They also formed quick, responsive, and short-lived organizations on particular projects to seize the day. They have used their social networks to pressure decision-makers. They have enlisted men who share their views. They have used their education; in particular, the sheer numbers of highly educated women have changed thinking about our society because of their access to journalism, the professions, and key resources. Law is only one example of this but is an important one. Women have won full citizenship before the law and protection in the Constitution, which are major accomplishments. They have also won improvements in every community in the country, for individuals as well as for entire segments of the population. In each generation, they have seen a large agenda ahead of them of rights yet to be won.

There have been endless setbacks, and it is clear these will continue. A sociological look at the struggle for equality in the post-Confederation period shows us that a few main issues have gained ground and several have not. The rights of most women have improved in education, economic areas, politics, representation, health and reproductive health, and safety. The economic status of women in general continues to be inferior to that of men in general, which is especially evident in old age. Women in their status as mothers suffer in most jurisdictions by a lack of licensed child care.[67] This situation is in contrast to women in numerous European countries. Many women still struggle for relief from poverty,

---

67. Some will argue that child care is a parents' issue, not a mothers' issue, but it can be considered a mothers' issue on the grounds that it is most often the mothers' careers that suffer for the lack of good quality licensed and reliable child care for their young children and after-school care for their older children.

domestic violence, marriage breakdown, stereotyping, and racism, especially among recent immigrants. The remedies for these inequalities are still the subject of feminist and other social reformist campaigns. The rights of Aboriginal women have improved only in some regards; despite ongoing legal and social action, Aboriginal women must be regarded as highly disadvantaged in laws and within the major social institutions.

>─┤◆>─O─<◆─┤─<

Women's Rights Organizations
A Chronology

1870   First Canadian YWCA formed in Saint John, New Brunswick.

1874   Women's Christian Temperance Union founded in Picton, Ontario, and becomes a national organization in 1885.

1876   Toronto Women's Literary Club founded by Dr. Emily Howard Stowe, later the Canadian Women's Suffrage Association.

1893   National Council of Women of Canada founded in Toronto; incorporated in 1914 as an Act of Parliament.

1897   Victorian Order of Nurses founded and, in the same year, Clara Brett Martin is first woman admitted to the practice of law in Canada.

1903   The first University Women's Club is founded in Toronto followed closely by clubs in other cities.

1919   The Canadian Federation of University Women is founded in Canada by the University Women's Clubs and became a founding member of the International Federation of University Women.

1972   National Action Committee on the Status of Women formed to press for the Recommendations of the Royal

Commission on the Status of Women. Laura Sabia becomes the founding President at the Strategy for Change Conference, King Edward Hotel, Toronto.

1974   The National Association of Women and the Law is formed.

1985   The Women's Legal Education Action Fund is founded to support cases brought under the equality provisions of the Charter.

>—!—<>—●—<◆—!—<

Women Winning the Vote and Right to Stand for Legislative Office

The Provincial and Territorial Level

1916   Manitoba gives voting and office-holding rights in January.

1916   Alberta gives voting and office-holding rights in February.

1916   Saskatchewan gives voting and office-holding rights in March.

1917   British Columbia gives voting and office-holding rights.

1917   Ontario gives voting rights but office holding only in 1918.

1918   Nova Scotia gives voting rights and later in the year office-holding rights (until 1851 women could vote in Nova Scotia).

1919   New Brunswick gives voting rights and not until 1934 can women sit in the legislature (until 1848 women could vote in New Brunswick).

1919   Yukon gives women voting and office-holding rights.

1922   Prince Edward Island women have right to vote and hold office (women could vote until 1836).

1925   (Newfoundland was a separate dominion until 1949). In 1925 women 25 and older can vote (men only have to be 21 and older); in 1946, age reduced to 21.

1940   Quebec women win both rights provincially although they have been able to vote in federal elections since 1918 (until 1834 women could vote in Quebec).

1951   Women in the Northwest Territories can vote for territorial government.

1999   Nunavut's founding Commission includes equity proposals in legislative composition, but they are defeated in a referendum. Like the rest of the country, women are equal with men in voting and office-holding rights.

>—⟨◆⟩—O—⟨◆⟩—⟨

The Federal Level

1917   The Federal Wartime Elections Act is passed 30 September with limited suffrage for certain women who have a close relative overseas; the Military Voters Act gives women serving in the military the right to vote in this federal election.

1918   A Bill passes expanding the right of women to vote federally whether or not they are associated with the military by service or by family members.

1919   The By-elections Act allows women to stand for federal office.

1920   Dominion Elections Act permits all who are 21 and older and British citizens to vote.

1921   The federal election is the first in which most women are eligible to vote.

1947   Asian and Indo-Canadians win the right to vote.

1960   Status Indians win the vote.

1993   Prisoners have the right to vote.

VI

Making a Living: A Perpetual Frontier for Women

Canada's economy may not be massive on the world scale, but all Canadians who live here must shape their lives within it. Because Canada has a semi-peripheral economy, when there is an economic crisis or a war in the Western world, our economy is shaken.[1] When that happens, we all feel it. It has happened many times since Confederation, and women have been pulled into and pushed out of the paid labour force, changing their world views as they changed their status.

Because of the constant change in our economy—both the national economy and the local and regional economies— the key issues of making a living are constantly changing. The important matter of compensation and all of its components fluctuates. Consider the many aspects of compensation: wages, pensions, and benefits; changing hours of work; shifting skill requirements, trends from farming to manufacturing to service work to computing; and moving household labour, from fireplace cooking to microwaves.

---

1. For a discussion of why we are semi-peripheral, see Marsden and Harvey, *The Fragile Federation*, especially 215–22.

Nothing in women's work lives is settled for long, except the need to find a way to make a living. Finding ways to equality in making a living is a perpetual frontier.

Our relationships in the economy shape our citizenship and our civic engagement. When women could not run their own bank accounts, buy property without the signature of a spouse or a father, or generally be part of the national economy, it constituted a public announcement of their secondary status in society. When women could not vote despite paying taxes and owning property, the democracy was far from complete in Canada. The recognition of women's contributions to the economy (whether for wages or not) is still underway.[2] The integration of women into all jobs and parts of the economy has been one of the greatest transformations of the past century. It has been a long and slow process, and there are many miles to go yet. Nonetheless, looking back on this transformation since Confederation, we can see when major changes were won and which institutions had to be shaken up for women to enter them.

There are five major concepts that emerge from a reading of that history: first, the gradual separation of work and family; second, the changing of the economy from rural to urban, from farming to industrial to service work; third, the treatment and experiences of women in the paid labour force; fourth, the continuous influx of women with different experiences and expectations to the economy by means of immigration; and fifth, based on the workplace, the interaction of women's economic and civic lives in social movements and in political actions and struggles to gain a greater citizenship.

In short, this chapter is concerned less with showing changes in detail, given that they have been so well documented

---

2. For an interesting discussion, see Heidi Macdonald, "Who Counts? Nuns, Work, and the Census of Canada," *Histoire Sociale/Social History* 43, no. 86 (2010): 369–91.

elsewhere, than it is in considering how people's values and cultures with respect to economic institutions determine to a large extent the possibilities available to women.[3]

Women and the Family

In post-Confederation Canada and for most of the period toward the end of the twentieth century, the majority of women made their livelihood as wives and mothers. They might have both paid and unpaid jobs between the end of schooling and marriage, as became the norm following World War I. Married women might shift that balance, taking on some part-time work for pay or full-time work if they were widowed, very poor, or their children grown. As young daughters, they would have prepared for their roles with household duties by assisting their mothers and, at the same time, learning the household arts. Boys undertook different tasks, learning the role of "household head." Women worked, and worked hard, but usually their access to cash income was allocated through the male "head of household," the husband or father. Exceptions might be the "pin money" some could make through some domestic production, such as raising and selling chickens or eggs, taking in laundry, dressmaking, or caring for other people's children.[4] The occasional fortunate woman inherited an income of her own.

Unmarried women had to find their own livelihoods as housekeepers, shopkeepers, telephone operators, and by the 1900s, employees in office or professional jobs. Some

---

3. In addition to the accounts in all three editions of *Canadian Women: A History* (1988, 2004, and 2011), there are studies of most occupations, reports from Statistics Canada, the Report of the RCSW, and numerous analyses by economists, sociologists, and occupational associations.

4. This is why the family allowance provided to mothers after World War II, modest as the amounts were, was such a step to independence for so many women in Canada.

unmarried daughters would "help" their mothers at home. Marriage was the main form of economic attachment for the majority of women and the expectation of most parents and young women.

The key point is that all women have always had to make their livelihood. Families in Canada were most unlikely to have the income to keep their daughters at home between school and marriage, and even those who did might find their daughters reluctant to stay at home. Every economic downturn, and there were several, made it more difficult. In the post-Confederation period and up to the end of World War I, women from all backgrounds would be aware that the ways of earning their livelihood were changing. They needed more qualifications to get good jobs, and they needed more education to get professional qualifications. They needed to live in urban areas for access to industrial and white-collar jobs. While many young women were filling the time between school and their marriage with paid work, some women had long-term goals to serve as artists, lawyers, journalists, or doctors, and many were already teachers in schools. Universities and medical colleges admitted women, and women had been called to the lawyers' bar in some instances in parts of Canada. But that was a very small number of young women.

Preparation for Employment

For a very long time prior to Confederation there was a struggle to gain education for women, but by 1867 the access of schooling to girls and teaching to women was widespread in Canada. It took different forms in different provinces but the idea that girls should learn the three Rs was certainly well established. Whether women should then complete secondary schooling and go on to any form of higher learning was not so well accepted. It depended to a great extent on the values and resources of the family and the community. There are always exceptions, but for the majority of women—and not simply for financial reasons—higher education was not on the agenda. One of those reasons was because women were neither expected nor permitted to occupy a status or occupation similar to that of the men in her life.

Education, as a provincial jurisdiction, remains complex and cannot be reduced to a simple description, then or now. This is one of the problems created by the division of powers at Confederation. This division of powers has been a barrier to Canadians in the labour market and nowhere more so than in post-secondary education and with respect to occupational qualifications.

Each province has created its own standards and its own systems of schooling. Some employers and universities will not accept the qualifications from other provinces. Each school district within a province may show variations even within provincial guidelines. Some have religious school systems that may be privately or publicly supported. It is difficult now for parents moving to a different province to arrange a smooth transition for their children, but it was even more so before World War II. In the period leading up to World War I, secondary school and preparation for employment was a scarce commodity.

Provincial jurisdictions regulate professional occupations. Some are self-regulating, with their own governing structures, such as in law and medicine. Others are regulated but under the provincial government, as in teaching. Some have a restricted title, such as chartered accountants. Legislation governing the professions has been introduced and amended at different times in each province.[5] Some

---

5.   Tracey L. Adams, "The Changing Nature of Professional Regulation in Canada, 1867–1961," *Social Science History* 33, no. 2 (2009): 217–43.

closed occupations or their unions will not accept members who have become licensed in another province.[6]

There have always been women school teachers among Canada's professionals. By 1860, there was some limited access to formal teacher training. The practice of law, however, moved more slowly. Between 1897 and 1923, all provinces except Quebec permitted women to practise law. In Quebec, it was not until 1941 that a woman was admitted to the bar. Similarly, while it was 1930 before a woman was accepted to practise medicine in Quebec, women doctors appeared elsewhere in Canada by the end of the nineteenth century.

Given these circumstances how have women made their livelihoods?

Many made their livelihood through *unpaid* domestic work in their parental or marital home. Religious women in convents who worked in various professions, mainly teaching and nursing, were not paid, in the sense that their earnings if any went to the church.[7] Many others made a living through work outside the family for room and board or in-kind goods rather than for cash or salary.

Just after Confederation, based on data from the Canada Department of Labour, one in eight *paid* workers was a woman working mostly as servants, dressmakers, teachers, farmers, seamstresses, tailors, saleswomen, housekeepers, laundresses, and milliners. This was a period of rising industrialization, and many of those workers were married women.

6. The 21 March 2011 edition of Thomson's *World Insurance News* reports that on 1 July 2011, under the "most recent amendments to the Interprovincial Agreement on Internal Trade," all provinces but Quebec will implement full labour mobility of insurance agents and adjusters, among others. "That means individuals qualified in one province can be licensed in another without additional training, examinations or assessments." Insurance has been sold and adjusting carried out since well before 1867, and this barrier is being formally removed only in 2011.
7. Macdonald, "Who Counts?," documents the lack of recognition for thousands of religious women workers because they were not paid wages.

One account, written about 1890, reports that married women did not generally work outside the home if their husbands were able to support them. But some married women worked in canning factories in summer, and others in laundries and factories during the entire year. In one factory reported upon, most of the women workers were married.[8]

However they did it, women and often girls found a way to eat and dress themselves, a place to sleep, a way to establish their own status in society, and a way to be productive. It has been very rare in the 150 years I am addressing for women to have done this on a basis of equality with men.

At the very low end of the livelihood structure, girls and women would be domestic servants essentially kept by the household,[9] entertainers living off nightly earnings, or even beggars living and eating where charity was found. They might have been in casual labour such as agricultural seasonal work of some kind. Although it might be quite profitable in some periods and for some age groups, it could also be subsistence labour.

Between school and marriage, many women worked as governesses or companions, and many more in the family businesses. Family business has been an important category in Canadian history and I will call it, following Philipps, "non-market labour."[10] For example, these women were on the farms working hard but not for wages, although they perhaps kept the money made from selling produce in the markets.

---

8. Report of the RCSW, 53, paragraphs 175–76.
9. But see Eric W. Sager on the comparatively good wages for live-in servants despite the problems of living and working in a household: "The Transformation of the Canadian Domestic Servant, 1871–1931," *Social Science History* 31, no. 4 (2007): 518.
10. Lisa Philipps uses the term to refer to spouses who work to support their spouse in a non-paid form of labour, which includes farm wives, other family businesses, hostesses, and similar situations: "Income Splitting and Gender Equality: The Case of Incentivizing Intra-Household Wealth Transfers," in *Challenging Gender Inequality in Tax Policy Making: Comparative Perspectives*, eds. Kim Brooks et al. (Oxford: Hart Publishing, 2011), Chapter 13.

At the very high end of the socio-economic structure, women might have been essentially managers of their household staff who carried out the work, had nurses to care for their babies, and served as hostesses for their fathers, husbands, or brothers.[11] They may have been extremely well cared for, but they had to behave in certain constrained ways to maintain this method of livelihood. They were as bound to the timetable, the appropriate relationships, and the forms of labour as any other worker. Livelihood, however, revolved around the household to which they were attached in some way.

Religious women might enter a convent in a few of the Christian churches, but the numbers of women and how they were recorded is a matter for discussion. For Roman Catholic nuns, Heidi Macdonald reports the census data that indicates a number ranging from fewer than 2,000 to almost 12,000 between 1871 and 1991. Her own calculations range from about 10,000 in 1901 to 53,000 in 1971.[12]

The "wheat boom" at the turn of the nineteenth century led to demands for immigrants to develop the West. Men and women were recruited from the United States, Britain, and parts of Europe to farm, work on the railways,[13] and provide the services needed in the West. Between 1896 and 1913, nearly 3 million immigrants swelled Canada's population, and the labour force grew by nearly 1 million.[14] For

11. This was an important point in Canadian society because in Britain or other parts of Europe that work would be done by a full-time housekeeper and/or a butler. In Canada those tasks were seldom done by anyone but the "mistress of the house," that is, the wife or daughter of the male head. Eric Sager, "The Transformation of the Canadian Domestic Servant, 1871–1931", 2007.

12. Macdonald, "Who Counts?," 382. Macdonald points out that the numbers could include members of an order working outside Canada.

13. The use of labourers from China to build the Canadian Pacific Railway is well known. Equally well known is the refusal of the Canadian Government to admit women from China until 1947. See Brandt et al., *Canadian Women*, 341–42.

14. Susan Crompton and Michael Vickers, "One Hundred Years of Labour Force," *Canadian Social Trends* 57 (Summer 2000).

many immigrant women, domestic service was their first job, and by 1901, 38 percent of all women with occupations in the paid labour force were servants. But as Sager points out, domestic service was a declining occupation even by then, and the majority of domestic servants were Canadian born. "If you hired a live-in domestic servant in Canada in 1901, the probability was very high that you were hiring a Canadian-born woman of British, especially English, or French Canadian ethnicity."[15] Women emigrants from areas of "surplus women" moved to the colonies where there were large numbers of single men. A great many of them had finished schooling and even prepared for a variety of occupations. Marriage may not have been the declared intention of emigration but it was often the outcome. Many women had no choice but to marry for livelihood.[16]

This was also a period of attracting women immigrants to Canada from Britain. Especially from the 1880s to the 1930s, opportunities were not extensive in the "old world" for single women with education. Women's groups in England encouraged the independent and career woman to immigrate to the "pioneering new world." The reports of the censuses around the period referred to the "surplus" women. Emigration societies worked to encourage "respectable" young women to come to Canada and the other colonies.[17] The National Council of Women of Canada and other Canadian groups worked to encourage single women to come and be "home help" or "companions." They might have come as single, educated women to occupy "respectable" jobs, but as Chilton says,

15. Sager, "The Transformation," 522.
16. See Prentice et al., *Canadian Women*, 2nd ed., 197.
17. See, for example, Lisa Chilton, *Agents of Empire: British Female Migration to Canada and Australia, 1860–1930s* (Toronto: University of Toronto Press, 2007), 88–89.

> Although the topic of heterosexual love and marriage was purposely avoided by many of the women who wrote promotional literature for the female emigration societies, it was clearly in the back of most emigration promoters' minds as a powerful incentive for single women to emigrate. . . . Marriage predominated in published lists of the emigration societies' enumerated "successes."[18]

In some areas, marriage was an explicit objective of emigration.[19] However, many of these women brought with them the robust attitudes toward women's independence and women's rights that prevailed in Britain in that period. They and the daughters they brought up in Canada contributed to the rebellion of the post–World War I period as described later in this chapter in the discussion about the Winnipeg General Strike, an event only illustrative of strong feelings and actions across the country. Their spirit lived on in their daughters and granddaughters who took part in the women's movements of the 1970s and 1980s.

By the beginning of the twentieth century, the number of large corporations was increasing and clerical jobs became more numerous. The 1921 census found that the number of women in clerical occupations was not far from the number of men, and by 1941, women exceeded men. This period of the transformation of "white-collar" work has been documented in detail.[20] The *white-collar ghetto* is the term connoting the sex segregation that has been characteristic of clerical work to a large extent from its beginning to now; in many cases, these jobs are accompanied by low pay, low security, and few benefits. Until the end of the war, most of the white-collar

---

18. Chilton, *Agents of Empire*, 88–89.
19. See the advertisement shown in Prentice et al., *Canadian Women*, 2nd ed., 197, which reads in part "Thousands of nice girls are wanted in The Canadian West. Over 20,000 Men are sighing for what they cannot get—WIVES! Don't hesitate— COME AT ONCE."
20. See Graham Lowe, *Women in the Administrative Revolution: The Feminization of Clerical Work* (Toronto: University of Toronto Press, 1987).

women were single because it was expected that married women would be at home supported by their husbands and that they would marry men capable of providing that support. White-collar work was considered a "middle-class" and very respectable occupation. As government bureaucracies grew, so did the employment of white-collar women—but only unmarried women. Widows and divorced women were not employed in the civil service until after the 1950s.

However, as we have already seen, there were many married women among those in the paid labour force, as the family wage was quite insufficient in all too many cases. By the end of World War II, a third of married women were in the paid labour force in addition to their household work. As the 1970 Report of the RCSW put it, "Both women and men have always produced some goods and services without pay. But for women, the unpaid production of goods and services has been, and continues to be, a major economic activity."[21]

The domestic roles of women were very practical. Without them, either domestic labour would have to be purchased through servants or other family members, including children, would be required to carry it out. Cooking, cleaning, child rearing, and care of domestic animals were often a woman's basic duties—which were often referred to as "*light* duties"—and to these were usually added care of the elderly in the family or community and many forms of "voluntary" work. Home help was widespread for any family that could afford it. Women "kept an eye" on other women's children at play. Women also maintained family rituals and connections through birthday, religious, and other celebrations. Often their grown or gathered food was vital to the household. They preserved food for the winter,

---

21. Report of the RCSW, 30, paragraph 56.

a labour-intensive activity. They occupied most of the volunteer roles in the community, although seldom the elected role.[22] After all this, they would be alone and without much of an income when their children left home and their husbands had died; in these cases, they would go, often of necessity, into the household of a relative or rely on the charity of the church or community. If the husband had provided adequately for his wife's widowhood, the woman was fortunate. It was not until 1946 that a universal old-age pension was paid.[23]

While over the decades household work was becoming less labour intensive because of the arrival of indoor plumbing, electricity, and therefore household equipment, and while public transportation and telephone communications improved the running of the urban household, in all households there was still a considerable amount of heavy and unremitting work to be done. Even in the late twentieth century, it was not customary for husbands to share the burden.

Those of us who remember our mothers as housewives in the 1940s and 1950s realize that the household labour for the ordinary family was such that a woman working outside the household had an intolerable double burden. Washing clothes even with electrical washing machines with wringers and hot water heaters was a slow process and drying the washed clothes in the Canadian winters was very difficult. The RCSW reports that, in 1958, 84 percent of households

---

22. Long after the majority of women were in the paid labour force, it was still women giving their time to voluntary associations in their churches, communities, and political parties.

23. It should be noted, however, that widows' pensions and mothers' pensions were part of the welfare system in some provinces to help single women with child rearing. See Margaret Hillyard Little, "Claiming a Unique Place: The Introduction of Mothers' Pensions in British Columbia," in *Rethinking Canada*, 5th ed., eds. Mona Gleason and Adele Perry (Toronto: Oxford University Press, 2006), 163–78.

had electrical washing machines. They were not today's machines of automatic washing cycles. The water had to be changed manually from wash to rinse, and the wet clothes had to be put through the wringer. Even in 1963, only 22 percent of households had clothes dryers. Clothes were hung on an outside line or put on a drying rack in the kitchen or a warm room; the rack was then hoisted to the ceiling. The drying clothes froze on the clotheslines in the winter, and drying racks in the kitchens were cumbersome and in some cases a fire hazard. If a wife/mother was out to work or unwell, the children, and sometimes the husband/father, would be called upon to do laundry, and there was a lot of it. Prior to electric irons, irons were heated on the stove. The difficulties of washing, drying, and ironing clothes meant that doing the laundry required two or three days a week, depending on family size. Those who could afford it sent their clothes out to a laundry, but most families could send only selected items, such as dress shirts, that required much starching and careful ironing. Dishes were washed by hand and with the help of as many family members as could safely use a towel to wipe the dishes. Even in 1968, only 5 percent of households owned an automatic dishwasher. Furthermore, the statistics quoted on household equipment excluded households in the Yukon, the Northwest Territories, and Indian reservations, where electricity and running water were often unavailable. In those conditions, the amount and conditions of domestic work were infinitely more difficult. While the new machines in some households made it possible for the ordinary woman to manage without household help, it still did not give her "free" time nor connect her more intensively with the community.

One of the great contributions of the 1970 Report of the RCSW was to raise the unanswered question of the contribution of domestic and household labour to the national economy and the gross national product. The Report made another highly significant contribution in the area of unpaid work—that of farm wives. In addition to the greatly expanded range of work tasks on the farm, the Report notes that women had no access to the assets. This was before the Murdoch decision in 1973 (see Chapter 2), which so dramatically illustrated the results of that problem upon marriage breakdown. In addition, for farm wives and those in family businesses where unpaid family labour accounted for thousands of jobs, the tax legislation made it impossible for a wage to be deducted as a business expense, thus binding women to greater dependence. This was changed only after a further Supreme Court of Canada decision in the Rathwell case in 1978,[24] when a change was legislated in 1979 and enacted in 1980.[25]

This division of household labour need not have been based on gender, of course, but it had been for centuries in ordinary families. In those exceptional cases where it was reversed for some reason, this was a source of embarrassment for many. Men who were unable to work for pay, because they had been wounded in industry or the wars or suffered from poor health, and who remained in the household, would tend to the house and cooking—usually keeping very quiet about doing so. The definition of *manliness* included being the pre-eminent earner for the family, the counterpart of women being at home with children as chief household manager. In families in which the husbands stayed home, the wives would be the breadwinners and this was thought most unusual. Officially, the census did not report men as homemakers, but as Thomas notes, the census enumerators did collect these data, and recorded the men as "unpaid family workers." When the original enumerator

---

24. See Payne and Payne, *Canadian Family Law*, 9–10.
25. See Philipps, "Income Splitting and Gender Equality."

forms were recounted recently in the Canadian Century Research Infrastructure Project (CCRI), they showed that in 1941 there were 2,450,000 women and 12,600 men home-makers.[26] These male homemakers, always described as exceptions, served to reinforce the status quo. In fact, one must conclude that despite the cultural norms and expectations, it was not at all unusual for married women to be in the paid labour force; the statistics show that a very large number of married women with or without children have always worked, out of economic necessity if nothing else. The public conventions about gender roles had not kept up with the realities of family life.

Thomas's study of census enumeration forms in the CCRI describes the situation in the first half of the twentieth century and included a review of the 1921, 1931, and 1941 manuals for enumerators.

> Enumerators were explicitly instructed to treat with skepticism any suggestion that a woman had any "unusual" occupation. Further inquiry and correction was deemed necessary in such cases. For example, according to the 1931 enumeration manual, "there are many occupations such as carpenter and blacksmith which women usually do not follow. Therefore, if you are told that a woman follows an occupation which is peculiar or unusual for a woman, verify the statement."[27]

Thomas goes on to note that despite these instructions enumerators coded "hundreds of women" working as blacksmiths and carpenters, but these responses were changed for the official tabulations.[28]

---

26. Thomas, "The Census and the Evolution," 44.
27. Thomas, "The Census and the Evolution," 44.
28. Thomas, "The Census and the Evolution," 44. Bruce Curtis has also examined the construction of the census in *The Politics of Population: State Formation, Statistics, and the Census of Canada, 1840–1875* (Toronto: University of Toronto Press, 2001).

Sex Segregation and Conditions in the Labour Markets of Canada

Sex segregation in work was institutionalized everywhere and, although there were plenty of exceptions, the society was set up to maintain this form of livelihood. As Thomas points out, the census enumerators were instructed to treat the father/husband as the head of the household (unless there was no adult male present), and define all others in the household in relation to him. This practice did not change until the 1970s when either sex could be defined as the household head. The term *household head* was finally dropped in 1981. If the roles of men and women in the household were highly differentiated, the same divisions were seen in the paid labour force.

By the end of the nineteenth century, many women had to leave the household to earn a living in the paid labour force. Much of the production of goods and services had moved out of the household to shops, factories, hospitals, schools, and offices. In most sectors, work was divided by gender, and the regulations, contracts, and laws were written to maintain this division of labour by sex. Furthermore, the lower value ascribed to women's labour led to openly discriminatory wages and benefits, worker protection, and hours of work until into the last quarter of the twentieth century. Not only were discriminatory laws and practices in place but, with some exceptions, the majority of those affected and the rest of the society did not find this offensive.

In joining the paid labour force, the inevitable issue of women's gender behaviour clashed with the socially ascribed labour force behaviour. Women did not look the same as men nor behave in the same ways as men.[29] This violated

---

29. In her study of women lawyers, Mary Jane Mossman makes the important point that women barrister's robes were designed to make them appear similar to men. See Mossman, *The First Women Lawyers*, 6.

the employer's sense of propriety. Physical segregation or social-status segregation relieved the anxieties raised by mixed-sex workplaces. It also relieved the fears of fathers and husbands anxious about their daughters and wives mixing with men at work. Although for some employers this also allowed them "cheaper" labour, no doubt many were genuinely concerned with what they regarded as the impropriety of the situation.[30]

World War I changed the lives of women and men. Industrialization on a large scale absorbed a very large labour force of both sexes. Despite this experience, many decades passed before the idea took hold that men and women could mix in the workplace on a basis of respect and equality. One of the reasons why the women's movement of the 1970s had considerable success in getting some of those discriminatory laws and practices changed was because many more people had accepted the justice of equality at work. Social conditions and social ideas had evolved. In addition to those employers who changed their practices in accordance with law and regulation, many employers had simply not thought of the issue as a matter of equality until their assumptions were challenged. But this change came almost a century after the first demands for fairness were made by women and by others on their behalf to the employers and supervisors of Canada in the late nineteenth century.

Equal pay for women and men was an issue even in the nineteenth century, and it remains an issue. Trade unions took up the cause of women's pay and working conditions. The famous telegraphers' strike in 1883 was nation-wide, and the demand was for equal wages by occupation and

---

30. That this concern with the subjugation of women is universal and not linked to a particular religion or culture has been explored for a long time, even recently in the Toronto *Globe and Mail* by columnist Doug Saunders, "The Subjection of Women Is Its Own Religion," June 18, 2011, F9.

for men and women.[31] It was only one of the many calls for equal pay for women and men by locals of the international unions and the Knights of Labour across the country. They were joined by the National Council of Women and other women's organizations. The concept was "equal pay for equal work." While this seemed to be progress, the problem was, of course, that men and women seldom did the same work, although the differences might be trivial. Job descriptions would be changed to ensure that men—with "families to support"—were in jobs that paid a higher hourly wage.

Winning the nine-hour day and then the eight-hour day were major struggles between the unions and employers. Given their double burden at home and in the labour force, women would benefit most from shorter hours of work. Innumerable women were in some form of collective labour action, and in the major cities union locals were made up of household workers (e.g., in Ottawa in 1901), and were formed in the textile industries (particularly in Montreal and Toronto). There were craft unions, such as the corset stitchers, industrial unions in the textile industry, and white-collar unions. The stenographers formed a union in Saint John in 1895. There were comprehensive unions such as the Knights of Labour and the One Big Union. Throughout the nineteenth century, union locals affiliated with regional, national, and international unions formed, some of them composed entirely of women and some mixed. But at the next level up from the locals in the organization, it was men who occupied the leadership positions and not all of them were convinced of equality issues.

Acquiring access to jobs normally held by men was a long struggle for women. Forsey reports on the work done by the Trades and Labour Congress in the 1890s to allow female

---

31. Eugene Forsey, *Trade Unions in Canada, 1812–1902* (Toronto: University of Toronto Press, 1982), 7ff.

factory inspectors, a position won in 1901 with the help of Lady Aberdeen. The "lady" factory inspectors earned only half the wages of men inspectors, however.

For those with factory, shop, or white-collar jobs, the wages and benefits were different according to job classification, and since job classification was segregated, women were paid less than men for virtually the same work in many instances.[32] The climb to pay equity is still ongoing, although the gap has closed considerably as a result of regulatory requirements.[33] For most of our history, labour conditions have been worse for visible minorities such as Aboriginal and Asian women, and women with disabilities were virtually excluded. When the employment equity laws were implemented in the 1980s, a long historical wrong was being addressed and those employers subject to employment equity legislation were required to incorporate women, visible minorities, Aboriginal people, and people with disabilities into employment. Employment equity was an important step but not a final one, as wage discrimination, occupational segregation, and new forms of contingent work continue to defeat the search for economic equality between the sexes.[34]

The movements for women's rights, such as suffrage and decent working conditions, resonated through the end of the nineteenth and beginning of the twentieth century. As industrialization intensified, more and more women were drawn into the paid labour force. But as the universities opened up

---

32. See, for example, Marjorie Griffin Cohen, "Paid Work", in *Canadian Women's Issues*, vol. II, *Bold Visions*, eds. Ruth Roach Pierson and Marjorie Griffin Cohen (Toronto: James Lorimer, 1995), Chapter 2 for a short history and documents.

33. See Bradley Brooks, Jennifer Jarman, and R.M. Blackburn, "Occupational Gender Segregation in Canada, 1981–1996: Overall, Vertical and Horizontal Segregation" in *Canadian Review of Sociology and Anthropology* 40, no. 2 (2003): 197–213.

34. See, for example, Leah F. Vosko, *Temporary Work: The Gendered Rise of a Precarious Employment Relationship* (Toronto: University of Toronto Press, 2000).

to women and women had access to the professions, women were spread across the labour market spectrum. Many positions in so-called men's jobs were still closed to women, but women were found in a wider variety of occupations than previously.[35] But then in 1913 and 1914 came an economic depression, with unemployment falling heavily on working people, followed in the same year by World War I. Reaction was swift. Because Britain had declared war, Canada was at war and Britain looked to us for supplies. The economy expanded, unemployment decreased, and slowly women regained paid jobs.

The period from 1918 to 1939, between the two world wars, resulted in suffrage for most women. Strong-Boag notes, "In the years between the two world wars, Canadians tested the promise of equality between the sexes symbolized by federal and provincial woman suffrage victories."[36] This victory for human rights was not duplicated in the workplace. For one thing, the composition of the economy was changing considerably. For example, we saw above that between 1911 and 1921 the number of women clerical workers had nearly doubled; by 1941, men and women occupied almost equal proportions of the clerical labour force.[37] Women were also about 20 percent of the overall labour force—an important part of the workforce. However, they were paid less than men and were in job ghettos. In contract negotiations in industrial workplaces, women's equality was often still traded off for other gains. Or, a percentage wage increase raised everyone's earnings but kept the relative distance of wages between the sexes unchanged. More likely, "improvements"

---

35. Adams ("The Changing Nature," 227, Table 1) notes that between the two world wars nursing, among other occupations, was regulated in the four provinces she studied: Nova Scotia in 1917, British Columbia in 1918, and Ontario and Saskatchewan in 1922.

36. Strong-Boag, "Janey Canuck," 1.

37. Lowe, Women in the Administrative Revolution, 49.

were protective clauses for women workers. A typical example would be safe transportation for women working a night shift, the result of which was often to make it hard for women to get on the better-paid night shift at all because it was an additional expense for the employer. When the first step toward old-age pensions was taken in 1927, while welcomed, it by no means meant a comfortable old age for those who had to apply for it through means-testing.

In 1927, a means-tested old-age pension was introduced at the federal level. While necessary for survival, it was a humiliating experience for many people who had worked all their lives to have to apply for what was seen in the community as charity. The pension was also limited to certain groups of citizens—for example, Status Indians and people who were not British subjects were excluded—and there were provincial residency requirements. The parliamentary committee that had studied the issue estimated that 40 percent of Canadians aged 70 or older would qualify for this support. Clearly, the wages earned at work did not support people in their old age for nearly half the population.

While many young women had always been in the labour force, it was in this period that, among all socio-economic groups, it became the norm for young women to work prior to marriage. This norm represented not only the change in the economy, but also the changing attitudes toward the role of women. But the large proportion of people who saw women's "real" occupation as being in the household strongly resisted seeing women's labour-force participation as permanent, especially for women with children. After World War I, they continued to define men as the breadwinners, for whom women should give up their jobs. This belief was fought by the leading feminists across the country and in many workplaces and households. After all, it was women who were bringing income to the family when the men lost their jobs. The feminists did not prevail. People lost their jobs abruptly after the crash of 1929 and unemployment rose to between nearly 20 and 30 percent, not including all those unpaid workers in family businesses, many of which were forced to close. Katrina Srigley's study of Toronto women in the Depression begins with a sketch of the social context:

> As the streetcar rumbled across the city to Dominion Silk Mills, Norma Vineham bravely faced her first day of work. When her father's small business faltered in the early thirties he put "every bit of insurance money" that the family had into it, but this strategy proved futile in the face of the Great Depression. By 1932, savings were depleted, including money set aside for schooling. As the labour market offered few options for Vineham's father, she and her sisters became the sole wage earners in the household. Someone had to put food on the table, and the family's best options rested with their young daughters.[38]

Based on interviews with women from a variety of backgrounds who lived through the period as "breadwinning daughters," this book describes not only the material, but also the social and psychological shocks and changes of that period. Srigley shows us the importance of those years in both opening up new vistas for women while also crushing many of their hopes. Women in the 1920s expected to complete more education than their mothers; to work until marriage; and then, ideally, to fulfill their ambitions as mothers, wives, and homemakers. They would marry men able to bring in a family wage, they thought. These values had been part of defining the "successful man" and the "happy woman," no matter how unhappy either of them might feel in these roles. A happy ending was always described as a heterosexual couple with children. For many caught in the

38. Katrina Srigley, *Breadwinning Daughters: Young Working Women in a Depression-Era City, 1929–1939* (Toronto: University of Toronto Press, 2010).

Depression, those dreams were on hold, sometimes forever. The already low wages were cut and then many women were told they had been replaced by male workers.[39]

The Great Depression is a lasting moment for Canadians. People lost their jobs, businesses, homes, property, and savings, but they also lost health, dignity, and hope. Those who had an income had much greater buying power than previously as wages and prices fell. Inequalities rose and animosities rose with them. As a historical crisis, the Depression is a guidepost to policy-makers, economists, and union leaders. It created a psychological scar that was passed on for generations.

By this time, the industrial job market was deeply sex-segregated; there were "women's jobs" and "men's jobs" in all sectors of the labour force, including the professions. Few men served as nurses after the war, few women as doctors, and the gender divisions were just as stark in industry. In the factories, jobs were divided into skill levels to maximize the production of repeated actions in the deskilling that had been going on for decades, and it was this division of labour that gave rise to the white-collar jobs for women—women could be paid less and supervised by male managers. So while many women lost their jobs, in some occupations replacement by men was out of the question.

Since there was no unemployment insurance system, relief for women workers was also out of the question for most. The Great Depression saw desperate times. For large numbers of people, there was little available employment, even low-wage or part-time, and many went hungry. Families were torn apart, and the birth rate dropped. The entire Western world was in the grip of the Depression, so there was no relief from emigration. The cities were in bad

---

39. For a more detailed description, read Brandt et al., *Canadian Women*, which discusses the Great Depression at various points.

shape but, on the Prairies, the drought added to the misery. People (largely men) abandoned their families, and children were given away or at least sent away to live with other relatives. Women had to summon all their ingenuity to create the domestic environment, menus with substitute foods, and clothes for their children. The toll on health, both physical and mental, was considerable.

But women workers resisted in many ways, through politics, workers' associations and unions, and community associations. The optimism of socialist politics after World War I dissolved as communal-living ideas gave way to the pressures of long-standing traditional values about gender roles. Consumer associations were formed across the country whose members protested unfair price rises and other matters linked to the cost of living in the new highly urbanized environment. The pressure for better laws, more services such as birth control, and more community supports continued among many who had the time to be involved in women's groups or church groups. In Quebec, the fight for suffrage continued as did the fight for improvements in education and access to the professions. The war had left a devastating mark on the country for both women and men, and the peace movement grew out of it as another version of maternal feminism, a view that women would be more likely to prevent war and vote for peace.

Following the war, the vote for women was won in Canada and several of the provinces—a major victory after a long struggle. But at a broader level, the struggle for women's equality was overwhelmed by the need for economic improvements, and any national movement was made difficult by the divisions caused by the Depression. Nonetheless, it was in the 1920s that the pressure group to gain women seats in the Senate, now known as the Famous Five, was finally successful. With the successful appeal to the British

Privy Council, the case clarified in the minds of many both the weakness of the Canadian Parliament and Courts with respect to women's equality and the weakness of Canada in relation to the British Parliament.[40]

When Canada declared war on Germany in September 1939, the country geared up for war production in industrial and agricultural workplaces as well as the armed forces. Throughout the war, women were drawn into paid and voluntary service of a wide variety of kinds from planning to production. Single women were in the labour force, of course, but in 1942 the Canadian Government and some provinces set up and funded child care centres to facilitate the entry of married women with children. This acknowledgement of the needs of families for child care was a first, and temporary, step toward a crucial service that has yet to be nationally implemented.

Furthermore, because of the wartime contingency, women entered jobs that had higher skill levels and better pay than many of them had experienced before—not equal pay, of course, but better pay. Between 1941 and 1943, women's participation in industry jumped from 19 to 28 percent and in trade and finance from 30 to 50 percent. This employment was never viewed as long term, and the training for such occupations as welding and electronics was brief and insufficient for long-term career purposes.[41]

Working Conditions and Civic Engagement

The period from the late nineteenth century up to the end of World War I was a time of organization and activism by

---

40. Sharpe and McMahon, *The Persons Case*, Chapter 7, reveals how this effort was less a popular movement than it was an effective group of well-connected women using the law to test the issue that created the Persons Case.

41. Prentice et al., *Canadian Women*, 2nd ed., 345; Crompton and Vickers, "One Hundred Years."

workers, and the crisis following the war was widespread. Women were key to the activism before the Great Depression, as shown in the following two examples. At the then dominant T. Eaton Company in 1912, women and men went on strike because of threats to men's wages and women's jobs as management tried to change the allocation of work.[42] This action was by no means the only one by women in that period. A few years later, the Winnipeg General Strike of 1919 was sparked by women telephone workers unplugging their lines and leaving in support of the metal and building trades workers already on strike. Women were involved deeply in those events in Manitoba and in debates and unrest across the country.[43] Dramatic though the Winnipeg General Strike was—with 30,000 workers out on strike, less than half of them unionized—it represented political unrest as much as it did a focus on wages and benefits, working conditions, and access to jobs. Helen Armstrong was a supporter of the cause, although not a worker on strike, when she led the provision of food services for the strikers. She did so out of her socialist convictions.[44] The right to collective bargaining, the need for a living wage, and the cause of equality of men and women was high on the agenda of the women workers.

All the Winnipeg General Strike leaders who were arrested and charged were men, despite the highly visible role of women in setting off the strike. The legal processes during and after the strike reveal the class tensions existing

---

42. Ruth Frager, "Sewing Solidarity: The Eaton's Strike of 1912," in *A Nation of Immigrants: Women, Workers and Communities in Canadian History, 1840s–1960s*, eds. Franca Iacovetta, Paula Draper, and Robert Ventresca (Toronto: University of Toronto Press, 1998), 316–21.
43. Mary Horodyski, "Women and the Winnipeg General Strike of 1919," *Manitoba History* 11, Spring (1986), http://www.mhs.mb.ca/docs/mb_history/11/women-1919strike.shtml. See also Reinhold Kramer and Tom Mitchell, *When the State Trembled* (Toronto: University of Toronto Press, 2010).
44. Manitoba Federation of Labour, Women Who Lead the Way: Helen Armstrong, 2009, http://www.mfl.mb.ca/9/armstrong.shtml (accessed 1 December 2011).

in Manitoba at the time and the fear of insurrection felt by the federal government. For example, some employers—the Canadian Pacific Railway being one—threatened to deny pensions if workers joined the strike.[45] It should be noted that this was the same province in which suffrage for women had been first won only three years before. Manitobans were in the lead in success on behalf of women's rights, but their authorities still seemed to focus on the men activists, rather than the women, among the strikers.

World War II

Bad as the conditions were for many women workers across the country until the 1920s, worse was yet to come in the Great Depression, which began in 1929 and started to ebb only late in the 1930s. Then, in 1939, another world war began, a massive war proceeded by a massive depression. Again Canadians switched into war production and women were pulled into this work in large numbers. Once again it was the crisis and not any desire to reshape the work of women that led to this recruitment. Women might be in the armed forces in a wide variety of ways, but both government and industry based their plans on the retreat of women into the household at the end of the war.[46] In the postwar life of the late 1940s and 1950s, one can see those dreams of a family wage with mothers at home revived. This time and with all that experience of recent memory, the dreams faded

---

45. For a detailed account of the railway workers at the Canadian Pacific Railway, see Mary MacKinnon, "Providing for Faithful Servants: Pensions at the Canadian Pacific Railway, 1903–39," *Social Science History* 21 (1997): 68.

46. Jeff Keshen, "Revisiting Canada's Civilian Women during World War II," *Social History* 30, no. 60 (1997): 256–59. See also Jennifer A. Stephen, *Pick One Intelligent Girl: Employability, Domesticity, and the Gendering of Canada's Welfare State, 1939–1947* (Toronto: University of Toronto Press, 2007).

more quickly as relationships crumbled, divorce rates rose, and their children became the rebels of the 1960s.

But many women did not retreat at the end of the war, at least not permanently. Not only did women struggle to keep jobs and to improve wages through postwar strikes in the textile industry in Quebec and other industries across the country,[47] but married women stayed in the labour force in a far higher proportion in Canada than did those in the United States.[48] The end of World War I had brought women worker militancy, suffrage, and an expansion of the types of paid work for women, and the end of World War II did much the same. Although the opportunities for women in post-secondary education and in careers was by no means equal to that of men, nonetheless, the general expansion of post-secondary education and the postwar industrial prosperity created more opportunities. The involvement of women in government committees and planning during World War II was a form of activism that penetrated into economic institutions. Now women were on the inside of government as well as activists in women's organizations with clearly defined goals about women's economic and social rights.[49]

The Canadian Labour Force Survey was created in 1945. This change was one of many that occurred during and after World War II. Many of the changes reflected the determination of Canadians and their governments not to fall back into the conditions of the Great Depression that preceded the war; many of the reforms emerged from the planning structures such as the Wages and Prices Board created during the war, the planning of industrial production, and other proposals that emerged on the social planning side. The Labour Force Survey gave first quarterly and then monthly

47. See, for example, Prentice et al., *Canadian* Women, 2nd ed., 353.
48. Pierson, *Canadian Women and the Second World War.*
49. Stephen, *Pick One Intelligent Girl.*

information on the labour supply, as Canadians made the transition to a peacetime economy. Through it, Canadians have been able to track the gender composition of those working or looking for work since that period.

These events—industrialization, depression, war, economic boom, Depression, war mobilization, and demobilization—eventually loosened that structure of inequality and sex segregation in the Canadian economy. Nothing changed it as much as those organizations and individuals who negotiated to make improvements for women. It was unions and employers, individual workers with supervisors, women's organizations with governments, and researchers publishing the evidence that brought change. It was in those struggles that large social movements and small local movements changed contracts, regulations and laws, and attitudes about the economic importance of women relative to men in Canada.

Babies, Immigrants, and Employment after World War II

As we saw earlier, while many women did leave the labour force to start families in the late 1940s, far fewer Canadian women left than women in the United States. A great deal is made in Canada of the baby boom, the postwar fertility. While it is true that in the late 1940s the number of marriages and babies born increased, it is also true that these wives and mothers stayed in or re-entered the labour force in the 1950s and thereafter. In 1941, only 4 percent of married women were in the paid labour force, but by 1951, it was 11 percent and, by 1961, 22 percent. By the 1980s, more than half of married women were working for pay as well as in the household.[50]

While the baby boom is an important cultural and policy feature of Canada, it did not end the expansion of women's economic opportunities. There was a pull into paid

---

50. See Crompton and Vickers, "One Hundred Years."

employment by the expansion of so-called women's jobs in the white-collar and service sectors and in health and education. Women were pushed into the labour force by the consumer desires for a family car and household goods such as new machines to reduce domestic labour. For married women to work when their children started school first became desirable and then the norm rather than the exception in the 1960s and 1970s. No longer frowned upon by the community, women's labour force preparation in terms of education and their labour force attachment to full-time or part-time paid work were both rising. Furthermore, by the end of the war, Canada's industry had diversified and expanded. Consumer spending rose and continued to rise in household goods and services.

While during the Depression more people left Canada than immigrated to the country, by 1941 the situation was reversed. The flow of refugees from Europe just before and after World War II, when the average education of Canadians was much lower, contributed many highly educated people to the Canadian workforce. More than 1 million immigrants arrived before 1961, and a great many of these people were skilled and professional workers. The predominance of men in the immigrant flow to Canada changed in this period toward a more balanced ratio from many sources of immigration.[51] By and large, the refugees of these decades, both women and men, were highly qualified and most found employment. Their education and training was absorbed into the Canadian workforce. The postwar immigrants also brought skills that were rapidly incorporated into the growing economy. Many personal

---

51. Warren Kalbach and Wayne McVey, *The Demographic Bases of Canadian Society*, 2nd ed. (Toronto: McGraw-Hill Ryerson, 1979), 180, Table 7.4. See also Nicholas De Maria Harney, ed., *From the Shores of Hardship: Italians in Canada. Essays by Robert F. Harney* (Toronto: Centro Canadese Scuola e Cultura, 1993).

and scholarly accounts of postwar immigrant lives analyze the experiences of women.[52] After this period, immigrants arrived from a much more diverse range of countries and had more varied experience and education levels; from the 1970s forward, the jobs, incomes, and work experiences of immigrants have been much more diverse and complex.[53]

Governments in Canada had been interested in women in the economy for a long time, collecting statistics about the subject, especially during wartime. Under pressure from groups, including the NCWC, the federal government established the Women's Bureau in the Department of Labour in 1954. The Bureau published a number of well-researched reports and distributed booklets on topics such as employment law, part-time work, maternity leave, and equal pay. After the Report of the RCSW in 1970, a department called Status of Women Canada was established, which reported to a minister responsible for the status of women.[54] Its mandate was to oversee the implementation of the recommendations of the RCSW at the federal level. It also commissioned a great many studies, which were published and distributed, and was active in many programs. These and other activities on behalf of women were important and helpful but were more in the "side-stream" than the mainstream. The phrase *women and minorities* was used frequently, implying the existence of a different population of importance—that is, men. But the economic situation of women changed, and there was a major demand for their paid and unpaid labour; attitudes had changed.

---

52. See, for example, the essays in Jean Burnet, ed., *Looking into My Sister's Eyes: An Exploration in Women's History* (Toronto: Multicultural History Society of Ontario, 1986).
53. Detailed analyses are found in the CERIS studies found at http://www.ceris.metropolis.net, including a bibliographic review of the experiences of women from the 1970s to the end of the century.
54. Status of Women Canada experienced sharp cuts in offices and programs in 2006.

Some people who had not expected women to be increasingly attached to the labour force developed an extraordinary interest in the subject. For example, economists started to study wage rates and try to explain the differences in wages, salaries, and lifetime earnings of women. Statistics Canada and the monthly Labour Force Survey tracked the changes; by the time of the 1981 census, when 50 percent of women aged 15 and older were in the labour force, this became a matter for public policy focus.[55] Statistics Canada put out a series of monographs. In the 1980s, the Economic Council of Canada became engaged with the topic. Chair of the Council, David Slater, wrote in a foreword to one of its monographs:

> Perhaps the most remarkable change affecting Canadian labour markets over the last three decades has been the steady increase in the number of women in the workforce. . . . Unlike some other disciplines, the Canadian economic profession has paid little attention to the issues raised by the increased participation of women in the economy.

The Council set about what Slater called "a modest research program on the role of women in the economy."[56] Indeed, economists had paid little attention to the importance of women's paid work since World War II. It is telling, however, that the first of their monographs—written by the distinguished economist Albert Breton—is on "marriage markets" in an attempt to explain the differences in male/female labour-market behaviour in a way that went beyond the explanations given by previous studies. Those studies, Breton argues, had focused too much on labour markets and

55. See for example, Statistics Canada, *Women in the Work World*, Statistics Canada Catalogue no. 99-940 (Ottawa: Minister of Supply and Services, 1984).
56. David Slater, "Foreword," in *Marriage, Population, and the Labour Force Participation of Women*, ed. Albert Breton (Ottawa: Economic Council of Canada, 1984), vii–viii.

had attitudinal, informational, and emotional variables bundled into the residual term *discrimination*. He points to the inadequacies of those residual variables and the weakness of the American economist Gary Becker's "conjectures" about the inequalities of women and men. He looked at the intersections of marriage and the labour force for both men and women in an expansion of the traditional economic approach. Many other studies were undertaken and regular reports on the "wage gap" between the sexes by education, occupation, and other variables were published.[57] However, the inequalities have resisted all attempts by economists to get to a solution up to the present time. Even so, the inequalities have been extensively described and analyzed.[58]

It was in the 1970s that women's permanence in the labour force became accepted as the social norm and the major push to equality in pay and access reached all parts of Canada and all industry sectors.[59] It was not that the issues were different, but the shift in public opinion was now toward getting government regulation to implement equality. The labour movement and the women's movement were at their peak of membership, and pressure was on governments at all levels to take action. As mentioned in Chapter 1, the Abella Commission on equality in employment was an important expression of this change.

By the end of the twentieth century and in the first decade of the twenty-first century, women became "main" wage

---

57. See, for example, the work of Morley Gunderson, whose numerous books and articles have focused on pay and benefits policy and discrimination and who has provided deep analysis of inequities from an economist's viewpoint. For example, *Comparable Worth and Gender Discrimination: An International Perspective* (Geneva: International Labour Office, 1994), and more recent general works.

58. Nicole M. Fortin and Michael Huberman, "Occupational Gender Segregation and Women's Wages in Canada: An Historical Perspective," Supplement, *Canadian Public Policy* 28 (2002): S11–S39.

59. Francine Roy, "From She to She: Changing Patterns of Women in the Canadian Labour Force," *Canadian Economic Observer* 19, no. 63 (2006): 3.1–3.10.

earners in an increasing number of families. The majority
of couples were dual-earner families, and in many families,
wives were the primary wage earners. In the economic
downturns since the late 1980s, because the manufacturing sector has been hit by closures and unemployment, men
have been the most affected.[60] In the sharp recession of
2008, more families than ever depended on the income of
the wife, although her income was almost always smaller
than her husband's. The point, though, was that not only
did women keep their employment in larger numbers, but
also that no one, least of all governments, were arguing that
women should give up their jobs for men. The roles and importance of women in the economy had been so institutionalized that the roles of men and husbands were undergoing
significant change.

>⊷⊶O⊷⊷⊰

In the large scope of things, the economic issues facing
women in 1867 were not very different from those facing
women today. Women needed a livelihood. They needed to
make a living; to avoid or be protected from abuse and ex-
ploitation of a mental, physical, or financial nature; to have
opportunities commensurate with their skills and abilities;
and to be able to follow a career line, whatever form that
might take. The economy, having shifted to services both in
the public and private sectors, has absorbed women workers
in virtually all occupations. The ongoing division of labour
and of jobs into more specialized or more segregated units
has led to both opportunities and obstacles for women, but
the impact on wages has resulted in the norm of the dual-
earner family. Since the late nineteenth century, women's

60. Susan Crompton and Leslie Geran, "Women as Main Wage-Earners,"
    Perspectives (Winter 1995): Statistics Canada Catalogue 75-001E.

organizations have pressured governments into implementing concepts of equality for workers, forcing regulation on employers to end job segregation, enhance pay and benefits, and improve working conditions. Despite this, campaigns to recognize the work of child rearing have not achieved subsidized child care nor reduced the double burden of women.[61]

>─┼─◆>─○─<◆─┼─<

Women and Work
A Chronology

1883	Telegraphers strike; demand for equal wages for men and women a key issue.
1893	Stenographers in Saint John form a union.
1901	Ottawa household works for a union local, and the first "lady" factory inspector is appointed—at only half the wages of men in the same job.
1912	Strike at the T. Eaton Company to protect women's jobs and men's wages.
1919	The Winnipeg General Strike, a crisis of the post–World War I economic recession.
1927	Old age pensions available but only through means testing.
1942	Wartime and child-care centres are established to permit mothers to work for the war effort. They are disbanded when the war ends.
1945	The Labour Force Survey created that gives national data on employment.
1954	Women's Bureau created in the federal government.

---

61. Canadian Labour Congress, *Women in the Workforce: Still a Long Way from Equality* (Ottawa: Canadian Labour Congress, 2008).

1971   Minister for the Status of Women created in the Federal
              Government with a coordinator appointed in the Privy
              Council Office. In 1976, Status of Women Canada be-
              came the department serving the minister headed by a
              coordinator. The first minister was Robert Andras and
              the first coordinator was Frieda Paltiel.

VII

The Continuation:
Patterns of Change

A young woman at the beginning of the twenty-first century is unlikely to either know or care much about her predecessors in Canada. This may not be a bad thing at all. If she realized how many decades of struggle and pain women before her had undergone, she might become too discouraged. For that matter, our young woman probably sees many obstacles to her equality right now, and she would not be wrong.

At the start of this analysis, we identified two major obstacles set in place at the time of Confederation: first, the silence on women's rights, such as the right to vote and be independent citizens, and second, the division of powers between the federal and provincial levels of government. That decision left most of the issues of daily life in the power of the provinces—matters such as education, professional qualifications, family laws, child custody, and property rights.

This book has focused on the social forces and dynamics in Canadian society that made possible significant social changes. Change happened, but how? What does this book tell us about recurring forms of social action in Canada?

There is another major obstacle to equality that did not have its origins in the Constitution: the secondary social status of women. Some of this status was the result of male control over women, fathers' rights over children, husbands over wives, and male-dominated institutions over all women. Underlying these relationships was a patriarchal understanding of society, shared to a large extent by both sexes. That sense of the innate rights of men has not been overcome entirely, even by the multiple changes in laws and customs, but those changes indicate that the power of patriarchal ideas is diminished.[1] The conceptualization of women's roles in society as "separate spheres" and of women as being in need of protection or moral guidance was paramount in the nineteenth century. Indeed, maternal feminism took the reciprocal position, arguing that the presence of women's moral values in public decisions would improve society. The ability to imagine women as being equal to men in citizenship, the economy, education, and learning was confined to the few in the early days of Confederation, although it was not unknown. Conceptualizing the idea of "different but equal" came only very late in the twentieth century and benefited not only women, but also anyone who was "different" from the healthy white male (e.g., those with disabilities and visible minorities). But this concept, which may go well beyond that now defined in certain labour laws, is by no means universally accepted. Despite

---

1. While scholars have written on patriarchy for generations, it is significant when a journalist such as Doug Saunders describes it in the *Globe and Mail* (18 June 2011) as a "faith in itself": "The subjection of women is its own religion; it is a cause, not an effect" found in all social classes, religions, and cultures at some points in time. For earlier discussions, see Gerda Lerner, *The Creation of Patriarchy* (Toronto: Oxford University Press, 1986), and Pierson and Cohen, *Canadian Women's Issues*, vol. II, *Bold Visions*.

laws and regulations, many women—and others—continue to struggle with poor treatment in daily life. Issues of workplace harassment and unequal compensation and opportunity are still serious problems. Some minorities, whether ethnic or racial (or socially categorized as different in other ways), struggle much harder to be accepted with equal treatment in Canadian society. Prejudice, racism, and patriarchy are not absent now, nor have they been at any point in our history.[2]

However, one of the major obstacles that faced our young woman's predecessor in 1867 has been diminished. Thanks to the women, organizations, and events described in the preceding chapters, our modern woman is living through a period when her *constitutional* rights are greater than they have ever been. Once she meets age requirements, she may vote at all levels of government and she is entitled to hold public office. She is a citizen in her own right. She may sit as a senator in the upper chamber, and she can be called for jury duty. Should she choose to do so, and if she can afford to, she can challenge the denial of her rights through various powerful commissions and the courts.

She can own and sell property and manage her own finances without her father's or husband's signature. She is entitled to some direct benefits from the State, including education, a pension, health care, and if necessary, some sort of welfare. She may own, control, and develop property privately and commercially. She is entitled to privacy. She can control her own body. Her decisions are her own.

---

2. This history can be traced in many ways, but one striking example is found in Griffiths' analysis of the annual meeting debates and resolutions of the National Council of Women. Similar issues were apparent in accounts of the labour organizations and religious groups. While the fact that there were debates indicates a range of opinion, the idea of ethnic hierarchy in the social structure does not disappear. In the early twentieth century, Italians were seen as "visible minorities" as had been the Irish before them.

In law, she can expect to be protected from domestic violence in her family and the community by the authorities. In the case of marital breakdown, she can expect financial support in the division of property between the spouses. Her husband does not have total control over the children of a marriage, as he would have had in most of the twentieth century. If widowed, she has financial entitlements and while she may be very poor, she is unlikely to be destitute.

Equally, she must accept the responsibilities of this life. She must decide how she will vote; she must make her own decisions about her future and her financial situation. She is responsible for her own actions and her own debts. She is responsible for her own property. She must insure it and she must pay taxes. Her public benefits are limited. She must look after her own health, contribute to her retirement income, and work toward her own educational completion.

She will not be thought of as a member of the "tender" sex and live in a separate sphere. She can be charged in the case of domestic violence and be subject to the laws just as any other citizen is subject. If a marriage breaks down, the woman's spouse may be entitled to her property. She must be prepared to share custody and care of the children. Most often, she will need to be a contributor to the family income through work in the paid labour force. Her husband, if she has one, will not bear the sole responsibility as the breadwinner, and indeed, most women regard their occupations as a crucial part of their identity.

Canadian women aspire to and hold many of the highest offices in the country.[3] For a long time, women were denied access to many of the thousands of occupations in Canada,

---

3. Women are on the Supreme Court of Canada, including as chief justice; in high military command; and in government positions, such as provincial premiers, Cabinet ministers, and deputy ministers at both the federal and provincial level. In general, women are entrenched in the running of the State.

not only high offices. Women are astronauts and military personnel and chefs in the finest restaurants; they are entrepreneurs and professors. It is easier to list the occupations in which women are not able to be present. The only *legal* constraint lies in what are called those jobs requiring "bona fide" occupational requirements—such as some religious positions, actors playing certain roles, or of course, sports in which teams or individuals compete on the basis of sex.

To a significant extent, the rights of women and men overlap in the public sphere and therefore their statuses are far less differentiated than ever before. Earlier chapters have described how the private sphere also shows less differentiation between the roles of wife and husband/mother and father in many families.

Of course, the existence of those rights does not mean that women can access them equally or that most women and men respect the spirit of Charter rights. Much of the work of women's organizations, unions, and human rights organizations throughout Canadian history has been, and still is, directed to helping women realize the benefits of whatever rights were and are in existence. Some groups are equally determined to ensure that traditional sex and gender differences are maintained and reinforced.[4]

The second major obstacle, the division of powers between federal and provincial governments, has been modified only over the past century. Just as each colony was anxious to protect its powers, language, customs, and economy when joining Confederation, so they have continued to guard their rights vigorously. Even after Confederation, Joseph Howe in

---

4. Groups that lobby for support for mothers to stay home to raise the children and for wives to be submissive to their husbands for reasons of tradition, religion, or plain patriarchy are found throughout Canada. R.E.A.L. Women are active lobbyists for such ideas. See http://www.realwomenca.com.

Nova Scotia tried to take that province out of the agreement, and the same threat comes from other provinces from time to time.

At the Charlottetown Conference, it was George Brown who spoke to the division of powers. Some months later in the recorded debates in the legislature of the Province of Canada, we have the arguments as they relate to Upper and Lower Canada where "our fiercest contests were about local matters that stirred up sectional jealousies and indignation to its deepest depth."[5] The differences were of language, religion, money, and a myriad of local matters in which history was important in the laws and customs of the colonies. However, even the matters left to local control were clouded over in the words of some debaters.

George Brown, in the same speech to the Province of Canada, said, "But the proposal now before us is to throw down all barriers between the provinces—to make a citizen of one, citizen of the whole . . . the law courts, and the schools, and the professional and industrial walks of life, throughout all the provinces, shall be thrown equally open to us all."[6] That may have been the ambition in 1865, but it was not the outcome, as we have seen in previous chapters.[7]

So the patchwork of laws at the provincial level continued to prevail; this affected then, as it does now, the lives of anyone who moves from province to province or, in other matters, has to cope with the varying laws, regulations, and barriers between the provinces.

---

5. See P.B. Waite, ed., *The Confederation Debates in the Province of Canada, 1865*, 2nd ed. (Montreal and Kingston: McGill-Queen's University Press, 2006), 35–54.
6. Waite, *The Confederation Debates*, 46.
7. As Ged Martin and others have shown, there was little trade among the provinces both before and after Confederation. Exports went to Britain or the United States. Perhaps that is another part of the explanation for the failure to coordinate certain laws and regulations at Confederation.

Between 1 July 1867 and today there have been an extraordinary, almost continuous, number of federal–provincial
negotiations and conferences. First were the conferences created to bring other colonies and territories into Confederation.
Then there have been conferences and meetings to iron out
misunderstandings and difficulties on a long list of concerns.
There have been constitutional conferences that succeeded;
conferences that ended in stalemate; conferences that never
really got started; and bilateral, multilateral, regional, and
every other type of conference one can imagine. There have
been meetings in railway cars and old railway stations; in
the west, the north, and the east; on Parliament Hill and in
mountain resorts. No premier escapes the federal–provincial
negotiations and issues. Professional and occupational associations try to harmonize qualifications, unions try to win mobility across provincial boundaries, students seek recognition
for their academic standing in other provinces, and new immigrants and foreigners are bewildered by all this complexity.

Some problems have been solved. For example, when the
federal government passed legislation to give women the
vote, it was on the condition that women met their provincial
voting requirements. These were different in each province,
and the voter and electoral offices were equally confused.
We have seen how this was rectified. Federal legislation has
resolved some of these provincial variations, as have constitutional amendments.

Since the federal government has the power to spend in
support of individuals, it could and did create the family
allowance program after World War II. The family allowance cheque was sent to mothers. Old-age pension benefits
are sent to seniors. In the 1960s, loans programs for college
and university students were created in a field—education—
where otherwise the federal government has no jurisdiction. Education belongs to the provinces.

Provinces now have departments of federal–provincial relations with offices in Ottawa and officials who spend their days working on such issues. Senators are appointed still according to the original agreements to represent provincial and regional interests, although premiers and provincial authorities work diligently to ensure that senators do not become important representatives of their provinces at the expense of provincial politicians. Caucuses of all federal parliamentarians are held regularly to discuss provincial interests. But still problems remain.

Justice is divided by jurisdictions, although the system of courts can lead, eventually, to the Supreme Court of Canada, where the buck stops. But if a couple thinks of divorce in Canada they—or one of the spouses—may well establish residence in the jurisdiction in which the division of martial property will benefit them the most since even now it is slightly different in each province. He or she might look for the province in which custody of the children is most beneficial to the interests of one of the parents.

Health care minimums at present are likely to be very similar under the conditions of the 1984 Canada Health Act. Beyond the minimums, provisions can vary widely. A woman wanting an abortion, for example, cannot get that service in Prince Edward Island. While not illegal, as described in Chapter 5, the service is not provided. In provinces where it is provided, access can be highly uneven among small towns and rural areas or where hospitals run by religious organizations that oppose abortion may force women to travel to other centres. Care for women's health, from reproductive health to cancers and any other gender-specific condition, also varies widely. There may be empty beds and a good supply of cancer surgeons in one province, while in another overcrowding and a lack of cancer surgeons becomes a crisis. Drug plans and other health benefits vary widely.

The labour laws are different in each province and territory and in the federal jurisdiction. While reducing the barriers to workers has been successful in some ways, even so some professionals moving across provincial boundaries may have to wait for a licence to practise, tradespeople may not be able to join the local union, and some workers may not have their educational qualifications recognized (or fully recognized). Indeed, technical standards and systems differ in each province and territory, causing endless problems.

A woman running a business must come to grips with meeting different provincial standards if she wants to expand beyond her province, and a woman moving her family to another province must cope with all the changes in schools, health care, taxes, and other requirements.[8]

So while much has changed since Confederation, and much about the first two obstacles placed in the way of Canadians has been removed, there are struggles still ahead. One hundred and fifty years is only the start of the changes required for gender equality. So much remains that erodes the rights won, undermines the idea of equality, and discourages the aspiration to equality in girls and women. With the increasing mobility of people, and especially workers, the federal–provincial jurisdictional issues have intensified. Provincial differences in the laws governing everyday life as well as the systems of education, the labour force, and so much more remain as barriers.

We cannot then say that women have achieved equality with men in Canada. It is especially not true in some cultures and communities where custom does not allow the freedoms given to women in the society as a whole and

---

8. Refer to the notice in *Thompson's World Insurance News* of 21 March 2011 that financial sector occupations will have "full labour mobility" by 1 July 2011—excluding the province of Quebec.

where women are still considered inferior to men. It is also true where Canadian law is anachronistic, as it is among First Nations people living on reservations.[9]

All of these changes and all the incomplete efforts for change are signs of a dynamic society in which the people are able to advance their standing in the society through joint and individual efforts. This progress may not be easy, but it is possible and known to be possible. As women today face struggles to expand rights and opportunities, how might we expect such changes to be won? Is there any reason to believe that in contemporary Canada with our modern communications and transportation systems and with many victories behind us that social change will be any different? Several aspects of the situation of women stand out when one tries to understand the changes that occur.

First, women's role in the economy has been essential at all periods. Whether women made their livelihood in the household or the paid labour force, or both, their work was essential. It was also unacknowledged, underpaid, or undervalued for most of our history. Equality seekers who understood this fundamental issue have been crucial at all times. They have recognized that while women's labour has been considered dispensable at times, it is essential and that employers in all sectors must be pressured to both recognize the value of women's work and the requirement to provide equality in working conditions, pay, benefits, and opportunities. This is a never-ending struggle. It is an area where persistence through generations is crucial.

Second, to gain access to full citizenship, women had to find ways and means in crises such as war, in the willingness

---

9. For a view of the fraught situation of Aboriginal feminists, see Joyce Green, ed., *Making Space for Indigenous Feminism* (Black Point, NS: Fernwood Publishing, 2007), and Cora Voyageur, *Firekeepers of the Twenty-First Century: First Nations Women Chiefs* (Montreal and Kingston: McGill-Queen's University Press, 2008).

of men to help them in legislatures or in law, and in unexpected opportunities such as the decision of a prime minister to pursue constitutional change.[10] Because these were
the paths open to them, those people wanting to improve
the status of women had to be continually prepared to seize
such opportunities; that is, they had to have a set of goals
ready and enough support in the community to pursue those
goals. When pressing for social, legal, and economic changes, women—initially through their organizations and more
recently through their networks—have been very well prepared. Throughout our history, one finds many Canadian
women who read deeply and developed sophisticated views
about public issues of the day. They had thought through the
interests of the wider population and developed an under-
standable case that could be spoken to in many settings and
at short notice. In the example of mobilizing the suffrage
movement, the leadership had for years linked temperance
to suffrage as a way of expanding the understanding of the
need for the vote—that was a more palatable approach in the
era of "separate spheres." Making the straight case for equality would not have drawn the support that they achieved by
making the case for the moral superiority of women and,
therefore, the need for women's influence on politics. The
public absorbed that case and, when the opportunity arose
in Manitoba, women sprang into action. In the case of abortion, women from many walks of life and belief systems had
been affected for generations. Sensing the public readiness
to face the issue, they focused on the case for protecting

10. Prime Minister Trudeau's determination to patriate the Constitution and Prime
   Minister Mulroney's Meech Lake proposals stand out as these "unexpected opportunities." In both cases, feminist constitutional lawyers and their supporters
   worked to shape the outcome. For the reaction in some women's organizations,
   see Jill Vickers, Pauline Rankin, and Christine Appelle, *Politics as if Women
   Mattered: A Political Analysis of the National Action Committee on the Status of
   Women* (Toronto: University of Toronto Press, 1993).

health and preventing death rather than matters of equality. When the Vancouver group began the Abortion Caravan to Ottawa, the press and the public had been prepared, and the issues were framed in a way that drew the widest range of support among Canadians.

In other cases, there was no possibility of gaining popular support. In the run-up to the constitutional changes of the late 1970s and 1980s, the work done by women lawyers was based on shared professional knowledge and training. The membership base of women lawyers was either familiar with the case for change or was ready to learn about it. In such instances, supporters in the general population trust the leadership in areas where they have no specialized knowledge. This same is true in many of the victories for women's health, where highly specialized knowledge is required. Trust in expert knowledge forms the basis of lobbies in reproductive health and treatments of many kinds. Increasingly, leading experts are women in economics, medicine, law, and many other fields. When these experts work with and brief journalists, the ideas are spread through the popular understanding of complex issues. No gain or equality right has been won without great preparedness and persistence.

The successful leadership on issues of concern has always been pragmatic and opportunistic. True women equality seekers may also have been idealists and philosophers, or moralists and theorists, but they were ready to seize the day. It has been suggested, for example, that the rise of maternal feminism stressing the moral superiority of women as mothers was seized upon as the vehicle to gain rights of women over a role in decisions about children, since the law at the time granted virtually all the authority to fathers/husbands.[11]

---

11. See Arnup, *Close Personal Relationships*, Chapter 4, footnote 9.

Looking for such opportunities in times of national stress is a learned activity and it is here that organizations with continuity and training of the leadership provide great benefits. This dynamic is unlikely to change. While organizations may change in purpose and structure, their role in preparing women to take action remains essential.

Third, it may have been the research and thinking of a few individuals who created the objectives and agendas of the women's movements, but their work was modified and spread throughout women's organizations. Such organizations were sometimes of occupational or worker groups, and sometimes of groups linked to equality issues that were not particularly focused on the rights of women, such as religious or political associations, but often these organizations were made up of women seeking women's rights. Such groups produce leaders and provide backup for them. They often have international networks and gatherings through which they can take a comparative approach to how to make gains for women. They are important for communicating with governments and the media and for recruiting like-minded people. They can organize social action. They keep records and are self-funded for the most part. Their membership may rise and fall, but it is their continuity, their reach, and their ability to gather and share information that has been the backbone of women's activism in Canada.

Broadly speaking, organizations pressing for the rights and status of women have been of two major types. They were either *project*-focused, with a particular short-term goal, or broadly based *umbrella* organizations, with a continuing and changing agenda for action.

Several organizations that formed not long after Confederation were powerful voices for women in the nation-building debates. Some, such as the Women's Christian

Temperance Union, were focused on a particular issue (in that case, temperance), but later developed a broad rights agenda. The Girls' Friendly Society and the subsequent Young Women's Christian Association were representative of organizations committed to service to those with need. Others, such as the National Council of Women, provided a debating place for a wide range of interests and views from local councils in all parts of the country.

Project groups form to achieve a particular goal and then disband or slowly fade away. Suffrage groups disappeared as the vote was won. Their successors were found in the women's groups within the political parties or the non-partisan groups, such as the Association of Women Electors in Toronto (begun in the late 1930s) or the contemporary Equal Voice. Such groups have the somewhat different aim of involving women in elected office and protecting the interests of women in legislative bodies. The many groups formed after the Report of the RCSW in 1970 have disappeared, as that work was mostly completed or taken over by other groups. Groups, such as the Organizational Society of Spouses of Military Members (OSSOMM), have a particular group of women to protect and advance (in that case, the spouses of members of the military). Many groups are advancing the cause of specific groups of women, such as immigrant and cultural communities, occupational groups, and age groups. The thousands of community projects carried out by women's societies of all kinds respond to the needs of local communities. Project groups thrive on particular goals and timetables for their work. When they reach their goals, they either change their purpose and set new goals or disappear.

Broadly based women's organizations, whether of business and professional groups or large debating societies, such as the National Council of Women of Canada, usually

remain in existence much longer.[12] As these structured national organizations developed in the nineteenth century,
they built a powerful voice in public affairs. The maintenance of a constantly renewed agenda for women's interests
required a structure of positions that allowed women to be
represented at regional and national meetings where ideas
were exchanged and trusted relationships were formed
by groups across the country. The hierarchy of president,
vice-presidents, and other offices had two major functions:
communications and succession planning. A structured
hierarchy arose in part from the costs and difficulties of
holding meetings across our huge country. Without easily
accessible communications and transportation, it would be
the lucky person who had the means to attend a national
meeting, or even a regional meeting. For most women, transportation to a legislature to present a petition or witness the
presentation of a bill was well beyond their resources of
time or money. It was only after World War II that more than
a scant few women could attend national meetings. So it is
not surprising that issues were won either on a provincial or
local basis, or among a small group whose members must
be described as either social elites or adherents to powerful
networks and ideas. Nurses who had served together in a
war, for example, would keep in touch. Journalists who travelled for business gathered and spread information. Wives
of men whose business took them across the country could

---

12. The case of the Federation of Women Teachers' Associations of Ontario is exceptional and telling. For 80 years, it was a powerful presence in the struggle both
for women's rights and for feminism. After existing since 1918, it was challenged
on the basis of inequality: all women teachers had to join the Federation and pay
dues to it, while the men were in a different organization. There was a very long
struggle in the Associations and the Courts based on differing views of equality and on the future of teachers' unions. In August 1998, the two organizations
merged. See Mario Spagnuolo and Larry A. Glassford, "Feminism in Transition:
The Margaret Tomen Membership Case and the Formation of the Elementary
Teachers Federation of Ontario," *Historical Studies in Education* 20 (2008): 55–72.

keep in touch personally with others. That might include the wives of ministers, members of Parliament, senators, or businessmen. However, as noted earlier, in the late 1930s, as women learned about the situation in Europe, women's paramilitary groups were organized across the country and linked together, forcing the national government to respond. Some of these women had known each other in World War I, one way or another, and they had found like-minded women demonstrating their capacity to communicate and their power to influence government decisions.

In the late twentieth century, with the emergence of women business travellers who could meet their counterparts on a regular basis and especially with the arrival of fast electronic communication and less expensive telephone services, women have been able to quickly form powerful and broad working bonds on issues of importance to them. These women may be volunteers, but they bring with them their occupational skills as organizers and communicators. Women inside and outside government, unions, all workplaces, the media, and the professions are linked at many levels and in many ways. The women who fought the Persons Case in the late 1920s were very well connected politically and used those links to bring pressure. But now, many thousands of women are well connected with members of Parliament and the media. In a matter of a few days, women and their supporters can raise concerns that legislators cannot ignore. The transition is one sociologists are familiar with—from formal, hierarchical organization to social networks. In our era, networks are more powerful—faster, deeper, and wider—than formal organizations alone.

But in the nineteenth and twentieth centuries, the word would come down to the local group from the regional, provincial, or national meetings by letter or visits. The word would go up to the regional and national level from the locals in the same way. The hierarchical structure also arose because it was widely understood in a country of representative democracy and responsible government. It provided a framework for orderly decision-making and succession from one generation to the next.

Fourth, equality-seeking women have been a numerical minority. Even when such important issues as suffrage,[13] legal birth control, and legal rights were at the top of the agenda and being considered by governments, the majority of women did not speak out in favour of these changes. While the great majority of women benefited, and in retrospect may have supported these rights, it was the leaders of the organizations who carried the torch for the cause.[14] Even the strong ambition for workplace equity may be expressed through outside friendly groups or unions if the workers fear for their jobs or are otherwise unwilling to make their own case. Many women, from all social classes and regions, may deny an ambition to expand their human rights. It is important to realize that securing women's rights to full citizenship and equality in education and the economy was not a popular cause.[15] In the Second Wave,

---

13. In her study of English-Canadian suffragists, Bacchi concludes, "The suffragists were predominantly members of an Anglo-Saxon, Protestant social elite, dominated by professionals and the wives of professionals, who endorsed woman suffrage as part of a large reform programme designed to reinstate Puritan morality, Christianity, the family, and the rule of the professional. The identification with women as a separate collectivity was secondary" (*Liberation Deferred?*, 149). This statement is rather harsh; but it is an accurate description of the majority of the leadership. Furthermore, in Quebec then and until 1940, a similar sort of group was taking into account the Roman Catholic, francophone elites.

14. This period was not an era of survey research. We do not know who really hoped for the vote, nor the characteristics of these men and women. We know the people and events reported on by journalists, who are included in the category of professionals.

15. It is astonishing for women who were around in the 1960s to read Barbara Freeman's study of the media coverage of the RCSW and to realize how much media attitudes have changed, not only about white middle-class women but also about minorities and Aboriginal women. Outspoken sexism and racism, sexist jokes, and assumptions about male superiority among reporters and cartoonists were not universal but were widespread. Freeman, *The Satellite Sex*.

the "consciousness raising" of informal groups of women and girls was an attempt to rouse support for activism, but that approach soon faded. As leaders over several generations have concluded, large membership numbers are nice but not essential if the agenda is clear and the timing is right; communicating to the right people at the right time, applying pressure at the right time, mobilizing the media at strategic moments, and using social networks well has been more effective than waiting for large numbers of people to appear on the streets.[16]

What is impressive in our history is the continuously strong sense of efficacy among women activists. There were always women organizing and publicly representing the need for change. Such women were found in all areas of society. They were fearless and determined to win wars, not only battles.

Some would argue that the pioneer culture gave women that confidence and desire to assert their independence and rights. Others argue and document much more complexity in economic relations.[17] Some would say that the lack of an aristocracy and the patterns of immigration and emigration contributed to a constantly changing elite structure that provided opportunities for women to become active.[18] Except for a long period in Quebec when the discipline of the Roman Catholic church was strong, there were few points of traditional authority in the social structure of the country, and that traditional authority changed rapidly during and

---

16. We look at the timing of gaining suffrage both in Manitoba and federally; at Laura Sabia's threat to bring masses of women to Parliament Hill if the prime minister did not set up the RCSW, a threat she subsequently said she could not have done; at the timing of the constitutional interventions by women lawyers; and at the use of networks in the Persons Case. We look at the many strikes, work stoppages, and legislative interventions that came in time to turn opinion and votes.

17. See Kathryn McPherson, "Was the 'Frontier' Good for Women? Historical Approaches to Women and Agricultural Settlement in the Prairie West, 1870–1925," *Atlantis* 25, Fall/Winter (2000): 75–86.

18. R. Ogmundson, "Good News and Canadian Sociology," *Canadian Journal of Sociology* 7, no. 1 (1982): 73–78.

after World War II—everywhere, but especially in Quebec. Even under that traditional church authority women enjoyed good opportunities as teachers and nurses.[19]

The sense of efficacy could not have been universal. Throughout the nineteenth and twentieth centuries, Aboriginal women and minority women were actively seeking rights but were for the most part sidelined by the ruling culture. The rights and efficacy of Aboriginal women were diminished under the post-Confederation Indian Acts. The majority of women's organizations were not insisting on the vote for Aboriginal or visible minority women in 1918.[20]

Fifth, this book has emphasized the importance of basic life chances such as length of life, marriage rates, widowhood, child-bearing and its control, and the influence of these patterns on the expectations of young women for their future. It was changes in these social-demographic patterns, sometimes described as "the historical moment," that helped women emerge into the public sphere. They were not the cause of the change in women's activism, but they created the opportunity for it. When women's livelihood was not dominated exclusively by marriage, when birth control allowed couples to plan the number and spacing of their children, and when women's expectations of a long life became firm, then their sense of what they could achieve in their lifetimes changed.

Other features of these social movements on behalf of women have also been important. Building alliances has been and remains crucial. Women's organizations have always called on their networks of contact with sympathizers

---

19. See Macdonald, "Who Counts?"
20. Voyageur, *Firekeepers*, 9; and Joan Sangster, "Criminalizing the Colonized: Ontario Native Women Confront the Criminal Justice System, 1920–60," in *Nation and Society: Readings in Post-Confederation Canadian History*, eds., Margaret Conrad and Alvin Finkel, 374–90 (Toronto: Pearson Education Canada, 2004), 374–90. See especially footnote 9.

in unions and professional associations as well as powerful institutions such as religious organizations, the legislatures, and the public service. Two groups in our society stand out as essential to the successes of women activists: Canadian men and women journalists.

In some Canadian men, women found stalwart supporters.[21] Throughout the 150 years since Confederation, women have worked through and with men on most objectives. It is important to emphasize that sex segregation has never been the case in the general movements of women for greater equality. For example, until women could practise law in the courts, any cases concerning divorce, property, and domestic violence in the criminal or civil courts involved the representation of women by men. It was male-led and male-dominated organizations such as the Manitoba and Saskatchewan Grain Growers Associations that made a major difference to the victory for suffrage in those provinces. It was also men who introduced the dozens of suffrage petitions and bills into the provincial legislatures until women were elected, and even afterwards; men who directly or indirectly financed much of the work of suffrage; men who took up the issues of women workers in unions and in negotiations; and a male lawyer, Newton Wesley Rowell, who took the case for Emily Murphy and her colleagues to the Judicial Committee of Privy Council of Britain. It was a male doctor, Henry Morgenthaler, who took up the fight for abortion rights for women and a man, Elijah Harper, who stopped the progress of the Meech Lake Accord in 1990 when those constitutional proposals threatened the rights of women recently won in the constitutional reforms. In labour

21. See studies of attitudes in Angus Reid Associates, "Canadians' View of the Role of Women in Society," News Poll, 24 January 1987; and Monica Boyd, Canadian Attitudes toward Women: Thirty Years of Change (Ottawa: Women's Bureau, Labour Canada, 1984).

movements, such as the Canadian Labour Congress and its predecessors, the elected leaders have most often been men, but those men have taken up the concerns of women throughout our history—not always but often.[22] One might argue that working with men in such organizations has sometimes delayed or diverted the aims of women equality-seekers. This was true in the case of teachers in Ontario.[23] In the case of First Nations women dealing with their rights to housing on reserves, for example, loyalties can be divided between their loyalty to First Nations goals and their loyalty to the rights of women.[24] This division of allegiance can be true in religious or ethnic organizations as well.

The other group—journalists and primarily women journalists—was even more essential to women's success. It is difficult to overemphasize the work of women journalists, as they were a key to solving equality issues. Several became important politicians,[25] such as Nancy Hodges from Victoria, who became the first woman Speaker in the British Columbia legislature, and Florence Bird, who was chair of the RCSW and then a senator. From Mrs. Willoughby Cummings and the other women journalists who helped found and advance the National Council of Women, to Doris Anderson and the *Chatelaine* writers in the beginning of the Second Wave of feminism, journalists played key roles.

---

22. For a review of the complexity and changes in union work and leadership, see Julie White, *Sisters and Solidarity: Women and Unions in Canada* (Toronto: Thompson Educational Publishing, 1993); Frager, "Sewing Solidarity," 316–21; and Susan Crean, *Grace Hartman: A Woman for Her Time* (Vancouver: New Star Books, 1995). In addition to being a key labour leader, Grace Hartman had served as president of NACSW in 1974–75.
23. See Spagnuolo and Glassford, "Feminism in Transition."
24. See Native Women's Association of Canada, "Aboriginal Women and the Constitutional Debates, Continuing Discrimination," *Canadian Woman Studies*, 12, no. 3 (1992).
25. Emily Murphy, the prime mover who made it possible for women to be appointed to the senate, was a journalist, as were several of the earliest female appointments to the senate (e.g., Nancy Hodges and Josie Quart). Marsden and Busby, "Feminist Influence through the Senate."

They not only reported on women's activities, they also interpreted them for the general public. They were "embedded" in women's equality-seeking organizations from an early date. Their interests were often synonymous with those of women in general.[26]

One wonders if the outcome of the BNA Act would have been better in terms of women's rights if a woman journalist had been among those at the conferences on Confederation in Charlottetown, Quebec City, and London. Certainly, the public would have been given a better understanding of the issues had particular women journalists been writing about the various proposals.

Another characteristic of the women's movements in Canada is the remarkable lack of violence. There have been incidents of great violence in Canada's history by those seeking equality and justice. The Métis leader Louis Riel, with his battle against Canadian soldiers in Manitoba in 1885 and his death by hanging, and the kidnapping and death of Pierre Laporte in the Quebec FLQ crisis in 1970, are two of the incidents of violence since Confederation in which citizens were killed for political reasons. It has been different in the women's movements. Women have marched, protested, picketed, and participated in many types of social action in Canada but seldom with violence. There have been arrests, imprisonment, and other legal and social sanctions along the way but, compared to the suffrage movements in England and even the United States, our movement has been peaceful. Canadian women did not have to resort to throwing bricks through windows or tying themselves to

---

26. See, for example, the case of Mrs. Willoughby Cummings described by French (*Ishbel and the Empire*) and others. She was a founder of the NCWC, worked a journalist, and was involved in Lady Aberdeen's political affairs. For more recent instances, see the role of journalists in the work of the NACSW in Vickers et al., *Politics as if Women Mattered*. For an account of the influence, see Lang, *Women Who Made the News*, Chapter 8.

railings.[27] Rather, they have used humour in clever ways to make others, including men, laugh at those opposed to their equality. The most famous example is that of the mock Parliaments used during the suffrage movements and imitated many times since for other causes. The famous suffragist Nellie McClung, playing the premier of Manitoba to a large crowd in the Walker Theatre of Winnipeg on 28 January 1914, brought down the house with laughter and raised consciousness and enough money to keep the suffrage movement going.[28] The "Raging Grannies," a group of older women emerging in the Second Wave and appearing on women's and peace causes, often completely disarm their opponents by singing their satirical lyrics, presenting their grandmotherly looking selves and making themselves at one and the same time vulnerable and resolute. It is not that Canadian women were not passionate and intense in their desire to improve conditions for women. Violent thoughts and words have been uttered about the persistent unfairness in women's group meetings, in private conversations, and elsewhere, but at the end of day, getting change meant using the means available, and violence was not seriously considered as one of those means.

Furthermore, it is clear that Canadian men in general have been more reasonable about women's concerns than the men in some other countries, more willing to hear the case, and sometimes more willing to act on women's behalf. While some men have been serious opponents to some equality issues, men as a category have not been united against equality.

---

27. The suffragettes in England were particularly violent at certain stages of their movement and some died in the cause. American women, such as Alice Paul, took some of those tactics into the US movement. See Walton, *A Woman's Crusade*, or Martin Pugh, *The March of the Women: A Revisionist Analysis of the Campaign for Women's Suffrage, 1866–1914* (Toronto: Oxford University Press, 2000).
28. Cleverdon, *The Woman Suffrage Movement*, 59.

The Impermanence of Victory

Women leaders challenged governments, judges, the military leadership, business leaders, religious leaders, and anyone with the power to hold back equality. Sometimes they won, but often they lost—in the short term. Sometimes they won and then lost later on the same issue. Women had the vote before Confederation on the same basis as men because there was no negative legislation on the female vote until the deliberate exclusion of women was passed in the legislatures. Most women appear not to have exercised their vote, but they might have. Suffrage had to be won again. Other rights can be removed by changes in legislation, or the cancellation of programs or funding. An ideological shift in the country could change access to health care, pensions, or equality opportunity in education or the workplace through government decisions.[29] Diligent monitoring of the environment remains crucial.

A challenge to legislation can reverse apparent gains for women. The Bill of Rights passed in 1960 was designed to protect rights, including women's rights, but when tested in the Courts, it was found to be wanting. It could not protect the rights of women in the Lavell and the Bedard cases in 1973 because of the logic of the law.[30] An Indian woman who married a non-Indian man lost her Indian status.

The Bill of Rights failed in a different instance as well. Stella Bliss, a pregnant woman, left her employment four days before giving birth and applied for unemployment insurance under the regulations then existing. On a technicality, she

---

29. See, for example, "The Assault on Reproductive Rights," *The Lancet* 378, no. 9786 (2011), 100, for a reversal in the area of reproductive health and sexual rights.
30. See the technical discussions in Wikipedia, *Attorney General of Canada v. Lavell* and *Bedard v. Issac*. See also Lilianne E. Krosenbrink-Gelissen, "The Canadian Constitution, The Charter, and Aboriginal Women's Rights: Conflicts and Dilemmas," *International Journal of Canadian Studies* 7–8 (1993): 207–24.

was told that the regulations were that she could not have these benefits for six weeks after giving birth. She appealed through the courts on the grounds that she was denied equality with men in access to unemployment insurance. The case went to the Supreme Court where in a 1978 decision she lost on the argument that the law did not discriminate against women but only pregnant people. This absurdity was overturned in a subsequent case in 1989 when the courts ruled that discrimination against pregnant people is equal to discrimination against women. The lessons learned from these cases linked to the Canadian Bill of Rights were important when women were challenging the first wording of section 15 of the Canadian Charter of Human Rights and Freedoms.

The Murdoch case, described in Chapter 2, brought home to women that assumptions about protection of the rights of women can be dangerously wrong. The law is complex and, despite the Charter, sex discrimination continues to push back gains in some cases.[31] The women teachers' associations in Ontario won the right to organize on the basis of sex in 1918 and lost that right in 1998. Some would interpret that as a gain for equality, while others regard it as a defeat in the struggle for equal rights.

The influx of populations with new assumptions about behaviour, morality, and social arrangements is not unfamiliar in Canada. The history of French–English and Aboriginal relations in North America is rich with examples of attempts to replace laws, language, and customs and the serious long-term consequences of this. After Confederation, at the end of the nineteenth century, white and European settlements in Manitoba and the West forced the end of the Métis and Aboriginal laws and customs. Many of the Aboriginal cultures were matriarchal and open to greater

---

31. See, for example, Lorna Turnbull, "How Does the Law Recognize Work?," *Journal of the Association for Research on Mothering* 6, no. 2 (2004): 58–67.

equality for women than the settlers were. We have a culture of accommodation, but there are limits to accommodation, and as the land was taken over and settled by Europeans, accommodation by the Métis did not prevail.[32] The problems of accommodation are raised in Canada with each wave of immigration from cultures with quite different values.

We have seen the ebb and flow of feminism in many manifestations with many renewals of ideas and issues. We have seen important strategic gains and setbacks in the struggle for equality. From the first group of leaders in Confederation to the current day, we find the full range of human behaviours and beliefs among both women and men set into a society of "peace, order, and good government." By and large, the "women's movements" can be described as rational and legal in their approaches to social change. Women wanted suffrage before Confederation and afterwards. They talked, they petitioned, they formed coalitions, they persuaded men to introduce legislation, they organized, they published articles—the work never stopped. Women still want high-quality care for their children and are still petitioning, organizing, educating, writing, and continuing that quest. The same is true for all the perennial issues of domestic violence, workplace discrimination, pay equity, health care, and the myriad of concerns and problems that never disappear. The National Council of Women, like other groups, continues to prepare briefs for legislators and meet with governments, as it has since 1924.

Very often these continuing issues have been carried from generation to generation. The equal-pay issue was of concern to women in 1867. Again and again, women tried and

---

32. Cynthia C. Wesley-Esquimaux, "Trauma to Resilience: Notes on Decolonization," in *Restoring the Balance*, eds. Valaskakis et al., 13–34, for a specifically women-oriented discussion. See J.R. Miller, *Skyscrapers Hide the Heavens*, for a longer discussion.

were defeated in attempts to get laws changed and social benefits won. Their great-granddaughters are edging closer to it. Persistence has paid off before and will again.

Bibliography

Abella, Irving, and Harold Troper. *None Is Too Many: Canada and the Jews of Europe, 1933–1948*. Toronto: L&O Denny, 1983.

Abella, Rosalie Silberman. *Equality in Employment: A Royal Commission Report*. Ottawa: Canadian Government Publishing Centre, Supply and Services Canada, 1984.

Acadiensis Reader. 3rd ed. Vol. 1, *Atlantic Canada Before Confederation*. Fredericton: Acadiensis Press, 1998.

———. Vol. 2, *Atlantic Canada After Confederation*. Fredericton: Acadiensis Press, 1999.

Acton, Janice, Penny Goldsmith, and Bonnie Shepard, eds. *Women at Work: Ontario, 1850–1930*. Toronto: Canadian Women's Education Press, 1974.

Adams, Tracey L. "The Changing Nature of Professional Regulation in Canada, 1867–1961." *Social Science History* 33, no. 2 (2009): 217–43.

Aisenberg, Nadya, and Mona Harrington. *Women of Academe: Outsiders in the Sacred Grove*. Amherst, MA: University of Massachusetts Press, 1988.

Ajzenstat, Janet. *The Once and Future Canadian Democracy: An Essay in Political Thought*. Montreal and Kingston: McGill-Queen's University Press, 2003.

Ajzenstat, Janet, Paul Romney, Ian Gentles, and William D. Gairdner, eds. *Canada's Founding Debates*. Toronto: University of Toronto Press, 2003.

Anderson, Marguerite, ed. *Feminist Journeys*. Toronto: The Feminist History Society, 2010.

Andrew, Caroline. "Women as Citizens in Canada." In *From Subjects to Citizens: A Hundred Years of Citizenship in Australia and Canada*, edited by Pierre Boyer, Linda Cardinal, and David Headon, 95–106. Ottawa: University of Ottawa Press, 2004.

Angus Reid Associates. "Canadians' View of the Role of Women in Society," *News Poll*, 24 January 1987.

Armour, Moira, and Pat Staton. *Canadian Women in History: A Chronology*. Toronto: Green Dragon Press, 1990.

Armstrong, Pat. "Missing Women: A Feminist Perspective on *The Vertical Mosaic*." In *The Vertical Mosaic*, edited by Rick Helmes-Hayes and James Curtis. Toronto: University of Toronto Press, 1998.

Arnup, Katherine. "Close Personal Relationships between Adults: 100

Years of Marriage in Canada." Paper prepared for the Law Commission of Canada, 21 March 2001. http://epe.lac-bac.gc.ca/100/200/301/lcc-cdc/close_personal-relation-e/html.

Atcheson, M. Elizabeth. "Change Is Never Given." In *Feminist Journeys*, edited by Marguerite Anderson. Toronto: The Feminist History Society, 2010.

Atcheson, M. Elizabeth, Mary Eberts, and Beth Symes, with Jennifer Stoddart. *Women and Legal Action: Precedents, Resources and Strategies for the Future.* Ottawa: Canadian Advisory Council on the Status of Women, 1984.

Axelrod, Paul. *Making a Middle Class: Student Life in English Canada during the Thirties.* Montreal and Kingston: McGill-Queen's University Press, 1990.

Bacchi, Carol Lee. *Liberation Deferred? The Ideas of the English-Canadian Suffragists, 1877–1918.* Toronto: University of Toronto Press, 1983.

Backhouse, Constance B. "Married Women's Property Law in Nineteenth-Century Canada." *Law and History Review* 6, no. 2 (1988): 211–57.

———. *Petticoats and Prejudice: Women and Law in Nineteenth-Century Canada.* Toronto: Women's Press, 1991.

———. "Women and the Law in Nineteenth Century Canada." Canadian Legal History Project, Faculty of Law, University of Manitoba, 1991.

Bala, Nick. *Family Law in Canada and the United States: Different Views of Similar Realities.* Toronto: Oxford University Press, 1987.

Banks, Margaret A. *Dictionary of Canadian Biography Online*: Bourinot, Sir John George. 2000. http://www.biographi.ca/009004-119.01-e.php?&id_nbr=6573 (accessed 12 December 2011).

Barman, Jean. *The West Beyond the West.* Toronto: University of Toronto Press, 1991.

Baskerville, Peter, and Eric Sager. *Unwilling Idlers: The Urban Unemployed and Their Families in Late Victorian Canada.* Toronto: University of Toronto Press, 1998.

Beard, Mary. *Women as a Force in History.* New York: Macmillan, 1946.

Beaujot, Roderick, and Don Kerr. *Population Change in Canada.* 2nd ed. Toronto: Oxford University Press, 2004.

Belanger, Alain, and Genevieve Ouellet. "A Comparative Study of Recent Trends in Canadian and American Fertility, 1980–1999." *Report on the Demographic Situation in Canada 2001.* Ottawa: Statistics Canada, 2002.

Big Eagle, Cleo, and Eric Guimond. "Contributions that Count: First Nations Women and Demography." In *Restoring the Balance: First Nations Women, Community, and Culture,* edited by Gail Guthrie Valaskakis, Madeleine Dion Stout, and Eric Guimond, 46–60. Winnipeg: University of Manitoba Press, 2009.

Bourbeau, Robert, Jacques Légaré, and Valerie Emond. *New Birth Cohort Life Tables for Canada and Quebec, 1801–1991.* Statistics Canada Catalogue no. 91-F0015-MPE, no. 3. Ottawa: Demography Division, 1997.

Boutilier, Beverly, and Alison Prentice, eds. *Creating Historical Memory: English-Canadian Women and the Work of History.* Vancouver: UBC Press, 1997.

Boyd, Monica. *Canadian Attitudes toward Women: Thirty Years of Change.* Ottawa: Women's Bureau, Labour Canada, 1984.

Boyd, Monica, and Michael Vickers. "100 Years of Immigration in Canada." *Canadian Social Trends* 58 (Autumn, 2000): 2–12.

Boyd, Susan B. *Child Custody, Law and Women's Work.* Toronto: Oxford University Press, 2003.

Bradbury, Bettina. "Women at the Hustings: Gender, Citizenship, and the Montreal By-Elections of 1832." In *Rethinking Canada: The Promise of Women's History.* 5th ed., edited by Mona Gleason and Adele Perry, 73–94. Toronto: Oxford University Press, 2006.

Bradbury, Bettina, and Tamara Myers, eds. *Negotiating Identities in 19th and 20th Century Montreal.* Vancouver: UBC Press, 2005.

Brady, Alexander, "Canada and the Model of Westminster." In *The Transfer of Institutions*, edited by W.B. Hamilton, 59–80. Durham, NC: Duke University Press, 1964.

Bramham, Daphne. *The Secret Lives of Saints.* Toronto: Random House, 2009.

Brandt, Gail Cuthbert, Naomi Black, Paula Bourne, and Magda Fahrni. *Canadian Women: A History.* 3rd ed. Toronto: Nelson, 2011.

Breton, Raymond, and Albert Breton. "Why Disunity? An Analysis of Linguistic and Regional Cleavages in Canada." The Dal Grauer Memorial Lecture, Institute for Research on Public Policy, Montreal, 1980.

Brinton, Mary C., and Victor Nee, eds. *The New Institutionalism in Sociology.* Palo Alto, CA: Stanford UP, 2001.

Briskin, Linda, and Lynda Yanz, eds. *Union Sisters: Women in the Labour Movement.* Toronto: Women's Educational Press, 1983.

Brodie, Janine. *Women and Canadian Public Policy.* Toronto: Harcourt Brace, 1996.

Brookfield, Tarah. "Divided by the Ballot Box: The Montreal Council of Women and the 1917 Election." *Canadian Historical Review* 89, no. 4 (2008): 473–501.

Brooks, Bradley, Jennifer Jarman, and R.M. Blackburn. "Occupational Gender Segregation in Canada, 1981–1996: Overall, Vertical and Horizontal Segregation." *Canadian Review of Sociology and Anthropology* 42, no. 2 (2003): 197–213.

Brown, Robert Craig. *Dictionary of Canadian Biography Online:* Pugsley, William.   2000.   http://www.biographi.ca/009004-119.01-e.php?&id_nbr=8335 (accessed 15 December 2011).

Buckner, P.A., and David Frank, eds. *Atlantic Canada Before Confederation.* In *Acadiensis Reader.* 2nd ed. Vol. 1. Fredericton: Acadiensis Press, 1990.

Bumsted, J.M. *A History of the Canadian Peoples.* 3rd ed. Toronto: Oxford University Press, 2007.

Burke, Sara Z. "New Women and Old Romans: Co-education at the University of Toronto, 1884–95." *Canadian Historical Review* 80, no. 2 (1999): 219–39.

Burnet, Jean, ed. *Looking into My Sister's Eyes: An Exploration in Women's History.* Toronto: Multicultural History Society of Ontario, 1986.

Bye, Christine Georgina. "'I Like to Hoe My Own Row': A Saskatchewan Farm Woman's Notions about Work and Womanhood during the Great Depression." *Frontiers* 26, no. 3 (2008): 135–267.

Canada. *Official Report of the Debates of the House of Commons of the Dominion of Canada, 27 April 1885: The Electoral Franchise,* Sir John A. Macdonald, 1388.

Canadian Labour Congress. *Women in the Workforce: Still a Long Way from Equality.* Ottawa: Canadian Labour Congress, 2008.

Canadiana.org. 1931–1982: Toward Renewal and Patriation. http://www.canadiana.ca/citm/themes/constitution/constitution15_e.html (accessed 15 December 2011).

Careless, J.M.S. *George Brown and the Mother of Confederation, 1864.* Ottawa: Canadian Historical Association, 1960.

Carter, Sarah. "'Complicated and Clouded': The Federal Administration of Marriage and Divorce among the First Nations of Western Canada, 1887–1906." In *Unsettled Pasts: Reconceiving the West through Women's History,* edited by Sarah Carter, Lesley Erickson, Patricia Roome, and Char Smith, 151–78. Calgary: University of Calgary Press, 2005.

Chambers, Lori. *Married Women and Property Law in Victorian Ontario.* Toronto: The Osgoode Society for Canadian Legal History / University of Toronto Press, 1997.

Chilton, Lisa. *Agents of Empire: British Female Migration to Canada and Australia, 1860–1930s.* Toronto: University of Toronto Press, 2007.

Christie, Nancy. *Engendering the State, Family, Work and Welfare in Canada.* Toronto: University of Toronto Press, 2000.

Clapton, Mysty S. "Murdoch vs Murdoch: The Organizing Narrative of Matrimonial Property Law Reform." *Canadian Journal of Women and the Law* 20, no. 2 (2008): 197–230.

Clark, Howard C. *Growth & Governance of Canadian Universities, An Insider's View.* Vancouver: UBC Press, 2003.

Clark, Samuel, Paul Grayson, and Linda Grayson, eds. *Prophecy and Protest: Social Movements in Twentieth-Century Canada.* Toronto: Gage, 1975.

Clement, Dominique. *Canada's Rights Revolution, Social Movements and Social Change, 1937–82.* Vancouver: UBC Press, 2008.

Cleverdon, Catherine L. *The Woman Suffrage Movement in Canada: The Start of Liberation 1900–1920.* 2nd ed. Toronto: University of Toronto Press, 1974.

Clio Collective. *Quebec Women: A History* (translation). Toronto: Women's Press, 1987.

Coale, Ansley, and Susan Cotts Watkins. *The Decline of Fertility in Europe,*

Princeton, NJ: Princeton University Press, 1986.

Cohen, Andrew. *Lester B. Pearson*. Extraordinary Canadians. Toronto: Penguin Books, 2008.

Cohen, Marjorie Griffin. "Paid Work." In *Canadian Women's Issues*. Vol. II, *Bold Visions*, edited by Ruth Roach Pierson and Marjorie Griffin Cohen. Toronto: James Lorimer, 1995.

Conrad, Margaret. "'Sundays Always Make Me Think of Home': Time and Place in Canadian Women's History." In *Not Just Pin Money*, edited by Barbara K. Latham and Roberta J. Pazdro, 1–16. Victoria: Camosun College, 1984.

Conrad, Margaret R., and James K. Hiller. *Atlantic Canada: A History*. 2nd ed. Toronto: Oxford University Press, 2010.

Cooke, Katie, et al. *Report of the Task Force on Child Care*. Ottawa: Status of Women Canada, 1986.

Coomber, Jan, and Rosemary Evans. *Women: Changing Canada*. Toronto: Oxford University Press, 1997.

Crean, Susan. *Grace Hartman: A Woman for Her Time*. Vancouver: New Star Books, 1995.

Creighton, Donald. *John A Macdonald: The Young Politician. The Old Chieftain*. Toronto: Macmillan, 1965.

———. *The Road to Confederation: The Emergence of Canada, 1863–1867*. Toronto: Macmillan, 1964.

Crompton, Susan, and Leslie Geran. "Women as Main Wage-Earners." *Perspectives* Winter (1995): Statistics Canada Catalogue no. 75-001E.

Crompton, Susan, and Michael Vickers. "One Hundred Years of Labour Force." *Canadian Social Trends* 57 (Summer 2000).

Cuneo, Carl J. *Pay Equity, The Labour-Feminist Challenge*. Toronto: Oxford University Press, 1990.

Curtis, Bruce. *The Politics of Population: State Formation, Statistics, and the Census of Canada, 1840–1875*. Toronto: University of Toronto Press, 2001.

Curtis, James, and Lorne Tepperman, eds. *Images of Canada: The Sociological Tradition*. Toronto: Prentice-Hall, 1990.

———, eds. *Understanding Canadian Society*. Toronto: McGraw-Hill, 1988.

Denton, Margaret, and Isik Urla Zeytinoglu. "Perceived Participation in Decision-Making in a University Setting: The Impact of Gender (Canada)." *Industrial and Labor Relations Review* 46, no. 2 (1993): 320–31.

Dickinson, John A. "Law in New France." Canadian Legal History Project, Faculty of Law, University of Manitoba, 1992.

D-Johnson, Micheline, "History of the Status of Women in the Province of Quebec." *Cultural Tradition and Political History of Women in Canada*. Studies of the Royal Commission on the Status of Women in Canada, Vol. 8. Ottawa: Information Canada, 1971.

Dobrowolsky, Alexandra. *The Politics of Pragmatism: Women, Representation, and Constitutionalism in Canada*. Toronto: Oxford University Press, 2000.

Douglas, Kristen. *Divorce Law in Canada*. Ottawa: Parliamentary Information and Research Service, Library of Parliament, 2006.

Douglas, Stacey. "Readiness and Rights: Developments in Canadian Military Family Politics and Policy." *Proceedings of the Fifth Annual Society of Military and Strategic Studies Student Conference* , Calgary, February 2003: 28–41.

Dranoff, Linda Silver. *Every Canadian's Guide to the Law*. Toronto: Harper Collins, 2011.

———. *Every Woman's Guide to the Law*. Markham, ON: Fitzhenry and Whiteside, 1985.

Duhaime, Lloyd. *Women Suffrage - Act I*. 11 September 2007. http://www. duhaime.org/LawMuseum/LawArticle-158/1885-Women-Suffrage--Act-I.aspx (accessed 15 December 2011).

Duley, Margot. *Where Once Our Mothers Stood We Stand: Women's Suffrage in Newfoundland, 1890–1925*. Charlottetown: Gynergy Press, 1993.

Dumont, Micheline. *The Women's Movement Then and Now*. Ottawa: Canadian Research Institute for the Advancement of Women, 1986.

Dundas, Barbara. *A History of Women in the Canadian Military*. Ottawa: Art Global and Department of National Defense, 2000.

Eberts, Mary. "Women and Constitutional Renewal." In *Women and the Constitution in Canada*, edited by Audrey Doerr and Micheline Carrier. Ottawa: Canadian Advisory Council on the Status of Women, 1980.

Eichler, Margrit. "Social Policy Concerning Women." In *Canadian Social Policy*, edited by Shankar A. Yelaga, 139–56. Waterloo: WLU Press, 1987.

Emery, George. "Age-Parity and Marital Status Compositional Influences on the Maternal Mortality Rate in Canada, 1930–1969: A Regional Comparison." *Social History* XXV, no. 50 (1992): 229–56.

English, John. "Conscription." In *Readings in Canadian History Post-Confederation*. 2nd ed., edited by R. Douglas Francis and Donald D. Smith, 337–47. Orlando, FL: Holt, Rinehart and Winston, 1986.

Errington, Elizabeth Jan. *Wives and Mothers, Schoolmistresses and Scullery Maids: Working Women in Upper Canada, 1790–1840*. Montreal and Kingston: McGill-Queen's University Press, 1995.

Fabian, Katalin. *Contemporary Women's Movements in Hungary: Globalization, Democracy and Gender Equality*. Baltimore: John Hopkins University Press, 2009.

Faraday, Fay, Margaret Denike, and M. Kate Stephenson, eds. *Making Equality Rights Real: Securing Substantive Equality Under the Charter*. Toronto: Irwin Law, 2009.

Fiamengo, Janice. *The Woman's Page: Journalism and Rhetoric in Early Canada*. Toronto: University of Toronto Press, 2008.

Fingard, Judith. "The Prevention of Cruelty, Marriage Breakdown and the Rights of Wives in Nova Scotia, 1880–1900." *Acadiensis* XXXII, no. 2 (1993): 84–101.

Forsey, Eugene. *Trade Unions in Canada, 1812–1902*. Toronto: University of Toronto Press, 1982.

Fortin, Nicole M., and Michael Huberman. "Occupational Gender Segregation and Women's Wages in Canada: An Historical Perspective." Supplement, *Canadian Public Policy* 28 (2002): S11–S39.

Foster, Hamar. "English Law, British Columbia: Establishing Legal Institutions West of the Rockies" Working paper series, University of Manitoba. Canadian Legal History Project, 1992.

Frager, Ruth. "Sewing Solidarity: The Eaton's Strike of 1912." In *A Nation of Immigrants: Women, Workers and Communities in Canadian History, 1840s–1960s*, edited by Franca Iacovetta, Paula Draper, and Robert Ventresca, 316–21. Toronto: University of Toronto Press, 1998.

Francis, D. Douglas, and Donald B. Smith. *Readings in Canadian History: Post Confederation*. Toronto: Holt, Rinehart and Winston, 1986.

Freeman, Barbara M. *The Satellite Sex: The Media and Women's Issues in English Canada, 1966–1970*. Waterloo: WLU Press, 2001.

French, Doris. *Ishbel and the Empire: A Biography of Lady Aberdeen*. Toronto: Dundurn Press, 1988.

Friedland, Martin. *The University of Toronto: A History*. Toronto: University of Toronto Press, 2002.

Garner, John. *The Franchise and Politics in British North America, 1755–1867*. Toronto: University of Toronto Press 1969.

Gaskell, Jane, and Arlene McLaren. *Women and Education: A Canadian Perspective*. 2nd ed. Calgary: Detselig Enterprises, 1991.

———. "Unequal Access of Knowledge." In *Women and Education: A Canadian Perspective*," edited by Jane Gaskell and Arlene McLaren, 151–70. Calgary: Detselig, 1987.

Gee, Ellen M. "The Life Course of Canadian Women: An Historical and Demographic Analysis." *Social Indicators Research* 18 (1986): 265.

Gidney, R.D., and W.P.J. Millar. *From Hope to Harris: The Reshaping of Ontario's Schools*. Toronto: University of Toronto Press, 1999.

———. *Inventing Secondary Education: The Rise of the High School in Nineteenth-Century Ontario*. Montreal and Kingston: McGill-Queen's University Press, 1990.

Gleason, Mona, and Adele Perry. *Rethinking Canada: The Promise of Women's History*. Toronto: Oxford University Press, 2006.

Godfrey, C.M. "The Origins of Medical Education of Women in Ontario." *Medical History* 17, no. 1 (1973): 89–94.

Gorham, Deborah. "Flora MacDonald Denison: Canadian Feminist." In *A Not Unreasonable Claim: Women and Reform in Canada, 1880s–1920s*, edited by Linda Kealey. Toronto: Women's Press, 1979.

Gray, Charlotte. *Canada: A Portrait in Letters, 1800–2000*. Toronto: Doubleday, 2003.

———. *Nellie McClung*. Toronto: Penguin, 2008.

Green, Joyce, ed. *Making Space for Indigenous Feminism*. Black Point, NS: Fernwood Publishing, 2007.

Griffiths, N.E.S. *The Splendid Vision: Centennial History of the National Council of Women of Canada, 1893–1993*. Ottawa: Carleton University Press, 1993.

Guildford, Janet, and Suzanne Morton, eds. *Separate Spheres, Women's Worlds in the 19th Century Maritimes*. Fredericton: Acadiensis Press, 1994.

Gunderson, Morley. *Women and the Canadian Labour Market: Transitions toward the Future*. Toronto: Statistics Canada and Nelson, 1998.

Guppy, Neil, Doug Balson, and Susan Vellutini. "Women and Higher Education in Canadian Society." In *Women and Education: A Canadian Perspective*," edited by Jane Gaskell and Arlene McLaren, 171–92. Calgary: Detselig, 1987.

Gwyn, Richard. *The Man Who Made Us: The Life and Times of John A. Macdonald*. Vol. 1, *1815–1867*. Toronto: Random House, 2007.

———. *Nation Maker, Sir John A. Macdonald: His Life, Our Times*. Toronto: Random House, 2011.

Hamilton, Roberta. *Setting the Agenda: Jean Royce and the Shaping of Queen's University*. Toronto: University of Toronto Press, 2002.

Harney, Nicholas De Maria, ed. *From the Shores of Hardship: Italians in Canada. Essays by Robert F. Harney*. Toronto: Centro Canadese Scuola e Cultura, 1993.

Harney, Robert F. *From the Shores of Hardship: Italians in Canada*. Welland, ON: Canadian Society for Italian Studies, 1993.

Harris, Robin S. *A History of Higher Education in Canada, 1663–1960*. Toronto: University of Toronto Press, 1976.

Harrison, Deborah, and Lucie Laliberté. "Gender, the Military, and Military Family Support." In *Wives and Warriors*, edited by Laurie Weinstein and Christie Whites. Westport, CT: Bergin and Garvey, 1997.

Harzig, Christiane. "MacNamara's DP Domestics: Immigration Policy Makers Negotiate Class, Race, and Gender in the Aftermath of World War II." *Social Politics* (Spring 2003): 23–48.

Heap, Ruby, and Alison Prentice, eds. *Gender and Education in Ontario*. Toronto: Canadian Scholar's Press, 1991.

Henchey, Norman, and Donald Burgess. *Between Past and Future: Quebec Education in Transition*. Calgary: Detselig Enterprises, 1987.

Henripin, Jacques. *Trends and Factors of Fertility in Canada*. Ottawa: Statistics Canada, 1972.

Hiller, Harry H. *Canadian Society: A Sociological Analysis*. Toronto: Prentice Hall, 1976.

Historica-Dominion Institute. *Canadian Encyclopedia*: Indian Act. http://www.thecanadianencyclopedia.com/index.cfm?PgNm=TCE&Params=A1ARTA0003975 (accessed 6 December 2011).

Horodyski, Mary. "Women and the Winnipeg General Strike of 1919." *Manitoba History* 11, Spring (1986). http://www.mhs.mb.ca/docs/mb-history/11/women1919strike.shtml

Houston, Susan E., and Alison Prentice. *Schooling and Scholars in Nineteenth-Century Ontario*. Toronto: University of Toronto Press, 1988.

Hunter, Alfred A. *Class Tells: On Social Inequality in Canada*. Toronto: Butterworth, 1981.

Hutchison, Ann. "100 Years on . . . Women at University College." *University College Alumni Magazine* 8, no. 2 (1984): 8–11.

———. "Co-op Education is Cheap." *University College Alumni Magazine* 9, no. 1 (1985): 9–11.

Iacovetta, Franca, ed., with Paula Draper and Robert Ventresca. *A Nation of Immigrants: Women, Workers, and Communities in Canadian History, 1840s–1960s.* Toronto: University of Toronto Press, 1998.

Ignatieff, Michael. *The Rights Revolution.* CBC Massey Lecture 2000. Toronto: House of Anansi, 2007.

James, Jacquelyn B. "What Are the Social Issues Involved in Focusing on Difference in the Study of Gender?" *Journal of Social Issues* 53, no. 2 (1997): 213–20.

Jean, Dominique. "Family Allowances and Family Autonomy: Quebec Families Encounter the Welfare State, 1945–1955." In *Canadian Family History, Selected Readings*, edited by Bettina Bradbury, 401–37. Toronto: Copp Clark Pitman, 1992.

Jhappan, Radha, ed. *Women's Legal Strategies in Canada.* Toronto: University of Toronto Press, 2002.

Johnson, Terence J. *Professions and Power.* London: Macmillan, 1972.

Jones, Charles, Lorna Marsden, and Lorne Tepperman. *Lives of Their Own: The Individualization of Women's Lives.* Toronto: Oxford University Press, 1990.

Kalbach, Warren, and Wayne McVey. *The Demographic Bases of Canadian Society.* 2nd ed. Toronto: McGraw-Hill-Ryerson, 1979.

Katz, Michael B., and Paul H. Mattingly. *Education and Social Change: Themes from Ontario's Past.* New York: NYU Press, 1973.

Kealey, Linda, ed. *A Not Unreasonable Claim: Women and Reform in Canada, 1880s–1920s.* Toronto: Women's Press, 1979.

———. *Pursuing Equality, Historical Perspectives on Women in Newfoundland and Labrador.* St. John's: Institute of Social and Economic Research, MUN, 1993.

Kelly, John Joseph. "Der Deutsche Kriegsgefangener auf Alberta: Alberta and the Keeping of German Prisoners of War, 1939–1947." In *For King and Country: Alberta in the Second World War*, edited by K.W. Tingley, 285–302. Edmonton: Reidmore Books, 1995.

Keshen, Jeff. "Revisiting Canada's Civilian Women during World War II." *Social History* 30, no. 60 (1997): 239–66.

Kramer, Reinhold, and Tom Mitchell. *When the State Trembled.* Toronto: University of Toronto Press, 2010.

Kroeger, Arthur. *Hard Passage, A Mennonite Family's Long Journey from Russia to Canada.* Edmonton: University of Alberta Press, 2007.

Krosenbrink-Gelissen, Lilianne E. "The Canadian Constitution, The Charter, and Aboriginal Women's Rights: Conflicts and Dilemmas." *International Journal of Canadian Studies* 7–8 (1993): 207–24.

Labarge, Margaret Wade. "The Cultural Tradition of Canadian Women: The Historical Background." Vol. 8. Ottawa: Studies of the Royal Commission on the Status of Women in Canada, 1971.

Lang, Marjory. *Women Who Made the News: Female Journalists in Canada, 1880–1945*. Montreal and Kingston: McGill-Queen's University Press, 1999.

Langlois, Simon, Jean-Paul Baillargeon, Gary Caldwell, Guy Frechet, Madeleine Gauthier, and Jean-Pierre Simard. *Recent Social Trends in Quebec, 1960–1990*. Montreal and Kingston: McGill-Queen's University Press, 1992.

Lerner, Gerda. *The Creation of Patriarchy*. Toronto: Oxford University Press, 1986.

Lévesque, Andrée. *Making and Breaking the Rules: Women in Quebec, 1919–1939*. Translated by Yvonne M. Klein. Toronto: University of Toronto Press, 2010. First published 1994 by McClelland & Stewart.

Light, Beth, and Joy Parr. *Canadian Women on the Move, 1867–1920*. Toronto: New Hogtown Press and the Ontario Institute for Studies in Education, 1983.

Light, Beth, and Ruth Roach Pierson. *No Easy Road: Women in Canada, 1920s to 1960s*. Toronto: New Hogtown Press, 1990.

Light, Beth, and Alison Prentice, eds. *Pioneer and Gentlewomen of British North America, 1713–1867*. Toronto: New Hogtown Press, 1980.

Little, Margaret Hillyard. "Claiming a Unique Place: The Introduction of Mothers' Pensions in British Columbia." In *Rethinking Canada: The Promise of Women's History*. 5th ed., edited by Mona Gleason and Adele Perry, 163–78. Toronto: Oxford University Press, 2006.

Logan, H.A. *Trade Unions in Canada*. Toronto: Macmillan, 1948.

Lowe, Graham. *Women in the Administrative Revolution: The Feminization of Clerical Work*. Toronto: University of Toronto Press, 1987.

Luffman, Jacqueline, and Deborah Sussman. "The Aboriginal Labour Force in Western Canada. *Perspectives*, January (2007): Statistics Canada Catalogue no. 75-001-XIE.

Macdonald, Heidi. "Who Counts? Nuns, Work, and the Census of Canada." *Social History* 43, no. 86 (2010): 369–91.

MacGill, Elsie Gregory. *My Mother the Judge*. Toronto: Ryerson Press, 1955. Reprinted with new introduction, especially Chapter 7. Toronto: PMA Books, 1981.

Mackinnon, Alison, Inga Elgqvist-Saltzman, and Alison Prentice, eds. *Education into the 21st Century: Dangerous Terrain for Women?* London, ON: Falmer Press, 1998.

MacKinnon, Mary. "Providing for Faithful Servants: Pensions at the Canadian Pacific Railway, 1903–39." *Social Science History* 21 (1997): 59–83.

MacLellan, Margaret E. *History of Women's Rights in Canada*. Ottawa: Royal Commission on the Status of Women, 1970.

MacMurchy, Marjory. "Women and the Nation." In *The New Era in Canada: Essays Dealing with the Upbuilding of the Canadian Commonwealth*, edited by J.O. Miller. Toronto: J.M. Dent, 1917.

Magnuson, Roger P. *The Two Worlds of Quebec Education during the Traditional Era, 1760–1940*. London, ON: Althouse Press, 2005.

Majury, Diana. "The Charter, Equality Rights, and Women: Equivocation and Celebration." *Osgoode Hall Law Journal* 40, nos. 3 and 4 (2002): 297–334.

——. "Women's (In)equality before and after the Charter." In *Women's Legal Strategies in Canada*, edited by Radja Jhappan. Toronto: University of Toronto Press, 1992.

Manitoba Federation of Labour. Women Who Lead the Way: Helen Armstrong. 2009. http://www.mfl.mb.ca/9/armstrong.shtml (accessed 1 December 2011).

Mann, Susan. *Margaret Macdonald: Imperial Daughter.* Montreal and Kingston: McGill-Queen's University Press, 2005.

Mann Trofimenkoff, Susan. *The Dream of Nation: A Social and Intellectual History of Quebec.* Toronto: Gage, 1983.

Marcus, Sharon. *Between Women: Friendship, Desire, and Marriage in Victorian England.* Princeton, NJ: Princeton University Press, 2007.

Marsden, Lorna. "The Role of the National Action Committee on the Status of Women in Facilitating Equal Pay Policy in Canada." In *Equal Employment Policy for Women*, edited by Ronnie Steinberg Ratner. Philadelphia: Temple University Press, 1980.

——. "The Senate and the Death Benefit." Paper presented at the meeting of the Canadian Sociology and Anthropology Association, Queen's University, Kingston, ON, June 1991.

Marsden, Lorna, and Joan Busby. "Feminist Influence through the Senate: The Case of Divorce 1967." *Atlantis* 14, no. 2 (1989): 71–81.

Marsden, Lorna, and Edward Harvey. *The Fragile Federation: Social Change in Canada.* Toronto: McGraw-Hill Ryerson, 1979.

Marsh, Leonard. *Report on Social Security of Canada.* 1943. Reprint, Toronto: University of Toronto Press, 1975.

Marshall, Debbie. *Give Your Other Vote to the Sister: A Woman's Journey into the Great War.* Calgary: University of Calgary Press, 2007.

Marshall, Dominique. *The Social Origins of the Welfare State: Quebec Families, Compulsory Education, and Family Allowances, 1940–1955.* Waterloo: WLU Press, 2006.

Matheson, Gwen, ed. *Women in the Canadian Mosaic.* Toronto: Peter Martin, 1976.

McCallum, Margaret. "Prairie Women and the Struggle for a Dower Law, 1905–1920." Canadian Legal History Project Working Paper series, 92, no. 2. Faculty of Law, University of Manitoba, 1992.

McClean, Sylvie. *A Woman of Influence: Evlyn Fenwick Farris.* Victoria: Sono Nis Press, 1997.

McDonald, Lynn. "Canada's Population in the Twentieth Century." In *A Population History of North America*, edited by Michael R. Haines and Richard H. Steckel, Chapter 12. New York: Cambridge University Press, 2000.

——. *Women Founders of the Social Sciences.* Ottawa: Carleton University Press, 1994.

McInnis, Marvin. "The Population of Canada in the Nineteenth Century."

In *A Population History of North America*, edited by Michael Haines and Richard H. Steckel, Chapter 9. Cambridge, MA: Cambridge University Press, 2000.

McKenzie, Judith. *Pauline Jewett: A Passion for Canada*. Montreal and Kingston: McGill-Queen's University Press, 1999.

McKillop, A.B. *Matters of Mind: The University in Ontario, 1791–1951*. Toronto: University of Toronto Press, 1994.

McLaren, Angus, and Arlene Tigar McLaren. *The Bedroom and the State: The Changing Practices and Politics of Contraception and Abortion in Canada, 1880–1980*. Toronto: McClelland & Stewart, 1986.

McPherson, Kathryn. "Was the 'Frontier' Good for Women? Historical Approaches to Women and Agricultural Settlement in the Prairie West, 1870–1925." *Atlantis* 25, Fall/Winter (2000): 75–86.

Milan, Anne. "One Hundred Years of Families." *Canadian Social Trends* 57 (Spring 2000): 2–12.

Miller, J.O., ed. *The New Era in Canada: Essays Dealing with the Upbuilding of the Canadian Commonwealth*. London: J.M. Dent, 1917.

Miller, J.R. *Skyscrapers Hide the Heavens: A History of Indian-White Relations in Canada*. Rev. ed. Toronto: University of Toronto Press, 1989.

Mitchison, Wendy, et al. *Canadian Women: A Reader*. Toronto: Harcourt Brace, 1996.

Mossman, Mary Jane. *The First Women Lawyers: A Comparative Study of Gender, Law and the Legal Professions*. Oxford: Hart Publishing, 2006.

National Council of Women. *Women of Canada: Their Life and Work*. Montreal: n.p., 1900. Reprinted 1975.

Native Women's Association of Canada. "Aboriginal Women and the Constitutional Debates, Continuing Discrimination." *Canadian Woman Studies* 12, no. 3 (1992): 14–17.

Nett, Emily M. "Canadian Families in Social Historical Perspective." *Canadian Journal of Sociology* 6, no. 3 (Summer, 1981): 239–360.

Nicholson, Virginia. *Singled Out: How Two Million Women Survived without Men after the First World War*. London: Viking, 2007.

Nidiffer, Jana, and Carolyn Terry Bashaw, eds. *Women Administrators in Higher Education: Historical and Contemporary Perspectives*. Albany: State University of New York Press, 2001.

Nies, Judith. *The Girl I Left Behind: A Personal History of the 1960s*. New York: Harper, 2008.

Nyland, Chris. "John Locke and the Social Position of Women." *History of Political Economy* 25, no. 1 (1993): 39–63.

Ogmundson, R. "Good News and Canadian Sociology." *Canadian Journal of Sociology* 7, no. 1 (1982): 73–78.

Ornstein, Michael. *Lawyers in Ontario: Evidence from the 1996 Census*. A Report for the Law Society of Upper Canada, January 2001.

Owen, Wendy, and J.M. Bumsted. "Divorce in a Small Province: A History of Divorce on Prince Edward Island from 1833." *Acadiensis* XX, no. 2, (1991): 86–104.

Park, Rosemary. "Overview of the Social/Behavioral Science Evaluation of the 1979–1985 Canadian Forces Trial Employment of Servicewomen in Non-Traditional Environments and Roles." Research Report 86-2. Willowdale, ON: Canadian Forces Personnel Applied Research Unit, 1986.

Parliament of Canada. The Constitution since Patriation: Chronology. 19 November 2010. http://www.parl.gc.ca/Parlinfo/Compilations/Constitu tion/ConstitutionSincePatriation.aspx (accessed 22 November 2011).

Parr, Joy. The Gender of Breadwinners: Women, Men and Change in Two Industrial Towns, 1880–1950. Toronto: University of Toronto Press, 1990.

———, ed. A Diversity of Women. Toronto: University of Toronto Press, 1995.

Payne, Julien D., and Marilyn A. Payne. Canadian Family Law. 2nd ed. Toronto: Irwin Law, 2006.

Philipps, Lisa. "Income Splitting and Gender Equality: The Case of Incentivizing Intra-Household Wealth Transfers." In Challenging Gender Inequality in Tax Policy Making: Comparative Perspectives, edited by Kim Brooks et al., 235–54. Oxford: Hart Publishing, 2011.

Pickles, Kate. Female Imperialism and National Identity: Imperial Order of the Daughters of the Empire. Manchester, UK: Manchester University Press, 2002.

Pierson, Ruth Roach. Canadian Women and the Second World War. Booklet No. 37. Ottawa: Canadian Historical Association, 1983.

———. "Two Marys and a Virginia: Historical Moments in the Development of a Feminist Perspective on Education." In Women and Education: A Canadian Perspective. 2nd ed., edited by Jane Gaskell and Arlene McLaren, Chapter 8. Calgary: Detselig Enterprises, 1987.

Pierson, Ruth Roach, and Marjorie Griffin Cohen. Canadian Women's Issues. Vol. II, Bold Visions. Toronto: James Lorimer, 1995.

Pierson, Ruth Roach, Marjorie Griffin Cohen, Paula Bourne, and Philinda Masters. Canadian Women's Issues. Vol. I, Strong Voices. Toronto: James Lorimer, 1993.

Prentice, Alison. "Mapping Canadian Women's Teaching Work: Challenging the Stereotypes." In Education into the 21st Century: Dangerous Terrain for Women? edited by Alison Mackinnon, Inga Elgqvist-Saltzman, and Alison L. Prentice, 31–42. New York: Routledge, 1988.

Prentice, Alison, Paula Bourne, Gail Cuthbert Brandt, Beth Light, Wendy Mitchinson, and Naomi Black. Canadian Women: A History. Toronto: Harcourt Brace Jovanovich, 1988.

———. Canadian Women: A History. 2nd ed. Toronto: Nelson, 2004.

Pugh, Martin. The March of the Women: A Revisionist Analysis of the Campaign for Women's Suffrage, 1866–1914. Toronto: Oxford University Press, 2000.

Randolph Higonnet, Margaret, Jane Jenson, Sonya Michel, and Margaret Collins Weitz, eds. Behind the Lines: Gender and the Two World Wars. New Haven, CT: Yale University Press, 1987.

Razack, Sherene. *Canadian Feminism and the Law: The Women's Legal Education and Action Fund and the Pursuit of Equality.* Toronto: Second Story Press, 1991.

Report of the Royal Commission on the Status of Women in Canada. Ottawa: Government of Canada, 1970.

Rex, Kay. *No Daughter of Mine: The Women and History of the Canadian Women's Press Club, 1904–1971.* Toronto: Cedar Cave Books, 1995.

Reynolds, Louise. *Agnes: The Biography of Lady Macdonald.* Toronto: Samuel Stevens, 1979.

Roberts, Lance W., Rodney A. Clifton, Barry Ferguson, Karen Kampen, and Simon Langlois. *Recent Social Trends in Canada, 1960–2000.* Montreal and Kingston: McGill-Queen's University Press, 2005.

Robeson, Virginia E., ed. *Debates about Canada's Future, 1868–1896.* Toronto: Ontario Institute for Studies in Education, 1977.

Robinson, Jane. *Bluestockings: The Remarkable Story of the First Women to Fight for an Education.* London, UK: Penguin Books, 2009.

Romaniuc, Anatole. "Fertility in Canada: Retrospective and Prospective." *Canadian Studies in Population* 18, no. 2 (1991): 56–77.

Romney, Paul. "The Administration of Justice in Ontario, 1784–1900." Faculty of Law, University of Manitoba, 1991.

Ross, Murray G. *The University: The Anatomy of Academe.* Toronto: McGraw-Hill, 1976.

———. *The Way Must Be Tried: Memoirs of a University Man.* Toronto: Stoddart Publishing, 1992.

Roy, Francine. "From She to She: Changing Patterns of Women in the Canadian Labour Force." *Canadian Economic Observer* 19, no. 6 (2006): 3.1–3.10.

Rudy, Willis. *Total War and Twentieth-Century Higher Learning: Universities of the Western World in the First and Second World Wars.* London and Toronto: Associated University Presses, 1991.

Sager, Eric W. "The Transformation of the Canadian Domestic Servant, 1871–1931." *Social Science History* 31, no. 4 (2007): 509–37.

———. "Women Teachers in Canada, 1881–1901: Revisiting the 'Feminization' of an Occupation." *Canadian Historical Review* 88, no. 2 (2007): 201–36.

Sangster, Joan. "Criminalizing the Colonized: Ontario Native Women Confront the Criminal Justice System, 1920–60." In *Nation and Society: Readings in Post-Confederation Canadian History*, edited by Margaret Conrad and Alvin Finkel, 374–90. Toronto: Pearson Education Canada, 2004.

———. *Earning Respect: The Lives of Working Women in Small-Town Ontario, 1920–1960.* Toronto: University of Toronto Press, 1995.

Saul, John Ralston. *Louis-Hippolyte LaFontaine and Robert Baldwin.* Toronto: Penguin, 2010.

Sharpe, Robert J., and Patricia I. McMahon. *The Persons Case: The Origins and Legacy of the Fight for Legal Personhood.* Toronto: University of

Toronto Press / Osgoode Society for Canadian Legal History, 2007.

Sharpe, Robert J., and Kent Roach. "Equality Rights." In *The Charter of Rights and Freedoms*, Chapter 15. 4th ed. Toronto: Irwin Law, 2009.

Slater, David. Foreword to *Marriage, Population, and the Labour Force Participation of Women*, edited by Albert Breton. Ottawa: Economic Council of Canada, 1984.

Smith, Janet. "Equal Opportunity in the Public Service." *Canadian Labour* 20, no. 2 (June 1975): 13–15, 24.

Smith, Jennifer. *Federalism*. Vancouver: UBC Press, 2004.

Smyth, Elizabeth, Sandra Acker, Paula Bourne, and Alison Prentice, eds. *Challenging Professions, Historical and Contemporary Perspectives on Women's Professional Work*. Toronto: University of Toronto Press, 1999.

Snell, James. *In the Shadow of the Law: Divorce in Canada, 1900–1939*. Toronto: University of Toronto Press, 1991.

Sokoloff, Heather. "Am I Doing My Job Well?" *National Post*, 3 December 2003.

Spagnuolo, Mario, and Larry A. Glassford. "Feminism in Transition: The Margaret Tomen Membership Case and the Formation of the Elementary Teachers Federation of Ontario." *Historical Studies in Education* 20 (2008): 55–72.

Srigley, Katrina. *Breadwinning Daughters: Young Working Women in a Depression-Era City, 1929–1939*. Toronto: University of Toronto Press, 2010.

Stager, David A., and Harry W. Arthurs. *Lawyers in Canada*. Toronto: University of Toronto Press and Statistics Canada, 1990.

Stamp, Robert M. *The Schools of Ontario, 1876–1976*. Toronto: University of Toronto Press, 1982.

Statistics Canada. *The Canadian Population in 2011: Population Courts and Growth*. Statistics Canada Catalogue no. 98-310-X2011001. Ottawa: Statistics Canada.

———. *Canadian Social Trends*. Vol. 3. 2000 and 2010.

———. *History of the Census of Canada*. 16 May 2005. http://www12.statcan.ca/english/census01/info/history.cfm (accessed 1 December 2011).

———. *Population Growth in Canada: From 1851 to 2061*. Statistics Canada Catalouge no. 98-310-X2011003. Ottawa: Statistics Canada.

———. *Report on the Demographic Situation in Canada 2003 and 2004*. Statistics Canada Catalogue no. 91-209-XIE. Ottawa: Demography Division and Health Statistics Division, 2006.

———. Summary Table. "Population and Growth Components (1851–2001 Censuses)." Ottawa: Statistics Canada, n.d.

———. *Women in the Work World*. Statistics Canada Catalogue no. 99-940. Ottawa: Minister of Supply and Services, 1984.

Status of Women Canada with Statistics Canada. *Women and Men in Canada: A Statistical Glance*. 2003. 2nd ed. Ottawa: Status of Women Canada.

Stephen, Jennifer A. *Pick One Intelligent Girl: Employability, Domesticity, and the Gendering of Canada's Welfare State, 1939–1947*. Toronto: University of Toronto Press, 2007.

Stobert, Susan, and Anna Kemeny. "Childfree by Choice." *Canadian Social Trends* 69 (Summer 2003): 7–10.

Stott, Anne. "The Second Reform Act, 1867." October 2010. http://nine-teenthcenturybritain.blogspot.com/2009/10/second-reform-act.html (accessed 11 November 2011).

Strong-Boag, Veronica. "'The Citizenship Debates': The 1885 Franchise Act." In *Contesting Canadian Citizenship*, edited by Robert Adomski, Dorothy E. Chunn, and Robert Menzies, 69–94. Peterborough, ON: Broadview Press, 2002.

———. "Creating 'Big Tent' Feminism: The Suffrage Politics of Isbel Marjoribanks Gordon, Lady Aberdeen." Paper presented at the Berkshire Conference of Women Historians, University of Massachusetts, June 2011.

———. *"Janey Canuck": Women in Canada 1919–1939.* Booklet No. 53. Ottawa: Canadian Historical Association, 1994.

———. *The Parliament of Women: The National Council of Women of Canada, 1891–1929.* Ottawa: National Museums of Canada, 1976.

Strong-Boag, Veronica, Mona Gleason, and Adele Perry. *Rethinking Canada: The Promise of Women's History.* 4th ed. Toronto: Oxford University Press, 2002.

Sturnick, Judith A., Jane E. Milley, and Catherine A. Tisinger, eds. *Women at the Helm: Pathfinding Presidents at State Colleges & Universities.* Washington, DC: American Association of State Colleges and Universities, 1991.

Sugiman, Pamela. "Passing Time, Moving Memories: Interpreting Wartime Narratives of Japanese Canadian Women." *Social History* 37, no. 73 (2004): 51–79.

———. *Labour's Dilemma: The Gender Politics of Auto Workers in Canada, 1937–1979.* Toronto: University of Toronto Press, 1994.

Tepperman, Lorne. *The Sense of Sociability: How People Overcome the Forces Pulling Them Apart.* Toronto: Oxford University Press, 2010.

Thomas, Derrick. "The Census and the Evolution of Gender Roles in Early Twentieth Century Canada." *Canadian Social Trends* March (2010): 40–46.

Toman, Cynthia. "Front Lines and Frontiers: War as Legitimate Work for Nurses, 1939–1945." *Social History* 40, no. 79 (2007): 45–75.

———. *An Officer and a Lady: Canadian Military Nursing and the Second World War.* Vancouver: UBC Press, 2007.

Trovato, Frank. "A Macrosociological Analysis of Change in the Marriage Rate: Canadian Women, 1921–25 to 1981–85." *Journal of Marriage and the Family* 50, no. 2 (1988): 507–21.

Turnbull, Lorna. "How Does the Law Recognize Work?" *Journal of the Association for Research on Mothering* 6, no. 2 (2004): 58–67.

Turpel, Mary Ellen. "Aboriginal Women and Matrimonial Property: Feminist Responses." Feminism and Law Workshop Series, Faculty of Law, University of Toronto, 1994.

Valaskakis, Gail Guthrie, Madeleine Dion Stout, and Eric Guimond, eds. *Restoring the Balance: First Nations Women, Community, and Culture.* Winnipeg: University of Manitoba Press, 2009.

Vickers, Jill, Pauline Rankin, and Christine Appelle. *Politics as if Women Mattered: A Political Analysis of the National Action Committee on the Status of Women.* Toronto: University of Toronto Press, 1993.

Vosko, Leah F. *Temporary Work: The Gendered Rise of a Precarious Employment Relationship.* Toronto: University of Toronto Press, 2000.

Voyageur, Cora. *Firekeepers of the Twenty-First Century: First Nations Women Chiefs.* Montreal and Kingston: McGill-Queen's University Press, 2008.

Waite, P.D., ed. *The Confederation Debates in the Province of Canada, 1865.* 2nd ed. Montreal and Kingston: McGill-Queen's University Press, 2006.

———. *Life and Times of Confederation, 1864–1867: Politics, Newspapers and the Union of British North America.* Toronto: University of Toronto Press, 1962.

———. *Macdonald: His Life and World.* Toronto: McGraw-Hill Ryerson, 1975.

Walton, Mary. *A Woman's Crusade: Alice Paul and the Battle for the Ballot.* New York: Palgrave Macmillan, 2010.

Wang, Jason. "Property Rights of Common-Law Spouses in Canadian Provinces." *Money and Family Law* 21, no. 4 (2006): 30–32.

Weinstein, Laurie, and Christie White, eds. *Wives and Warriors.* Westport, CT: Bergin and Garvey, 1997.

Wells, Karen. "The Women Are Coming." Rebroadcast on *The Sunday Edition.* CBC Radio. March 2011.

Wesley-Esquimaux, Cynthia C. "Trauma to Resilience: Notes on Decolonization." In *Restoring the Balance: First Nations Women, Community, and Culture,* edited by Gail Guthrie Valaskakis, Madeleine Dion Stout, and Eric Guimond. Winnipeg: University of Manitoba Press, 2009.

White, Julie. *Sisters and Solidarity: Women and Unions in Canada.* Toronto: Thompson Educational Publishing, 1993.

Wilson, Donald, Robert M. Stamp, and Louis-Philippe Audet. *Canadian Education: A History.* Scarborough, ON: Prentice Hall, 1970.

Winslow, Donna, and Jason Dunn. "Women in the Canadian Forces: Between Legal and Social Integration." *Current Sociology* 50, no. 5 (2002): 641–67.

Yelaja, Shankar A., ed. *Canadian Social Policy.* Rev. ed. Waterloo, ON: WLU Press, 1987.

Zuker, Marvin A., and June Callwood. *The Law Is Not for Women: A Legal Handbook for Women.* Toronto: Pitmans, 1976.

Index

Page numbers in italics refer to figures.

child-rearing, 21–22, 101; children from previous marriages, 94–95

child support and alimony, 97

Chilton, Lisa, 207–8

Chirot, Daniel, 20n21

citizenship, 3, 30

Citizenship Act (1947), 56

civic engagement, 132, 226. *See also* women's organizations

Civil Code (Quebec), 26, 131

Civil Marriage Act, 131

civil servants: death benefit for employees, 182–84; women as, 209

Civil Service Association, 183

clerical occupations, 208–9, 218

Cleverdon, Catherine A., 71, 152, 152n18, 153, 155, 159

co-education, 164, 165, 166, 174, 175, 176

Cohen, Marjorie, 167

Cold War, 84

colleges: technical, 169; for women, 170. *See also* education; universities

colonies, North American, 26–28; schooling in, 162–63

common-law relationships, 26n1

Confederation (1867), 15, 55, 136; flaws of, 30–43

consciousness-raising, 136–37, 252

conscription (World War I), 67–69

Constitution of Canada: 1867 Act, 26n1, 133; 1982 Act and patriation, 2, 57, 73, 85, 137, 179, 193–94, 245n10; amendments, 52–53; chronology of, 55–57; debates of 1864, 29, 30, 36, 39, 241; interpretation of, 181–82; 237–39

consumer associations, 222

contraceptives, 11. *See also* birth control; pill, the

Convention of Forty, 34–35

Crawford, Mary, 159

Criminal Code of Canada: abortion in, 188–89; birth control and

abortion in, 131; birth control in, 93, 125

crude birth rate, 112

Cummings, Mrs. Willoughby, 146n12, 255, 256n26

data sources, 103–5; women and economy, 229–231

daycare. *See* child care

death, 91–92, 111; causes of infant, 116–17; in childbirth, 91–92, 93; probabilities for selected birth cohorts, *118*

"Declaration des droits de la femme et de la citoyenne," 135

demography: chronology of, 131; transitions, 111, 115–16

Denis, Solange, 139n6

Diefenbaker, John, 178

"different but equal," 236

discrimination, 231, 259; in armed forces, 85–86; employment and, 123, 214

diseases, communicable, 5, 8, 92, 99; sexually transmitted, 8–9, 100

displaced persons, 80. *See also* immigrants

Disraeli, Benjamin, 32

division of powers. *See* federal–provincial division of powers

divorce, 10; in 1960s, 96; federal government and, 41, 42, 54; law, 48–49, 54; military families and, 87; provincial legislation and, 54, 242; reform, 182–84

domestic servants, 205, 207

domestic (household) work, 204, 206, 209–13; clothes-washing and drying, 210–11; dishwashing, 211; in Report of RCSW, 211–12

Dominion Elections Act, 69–70, 198

double burden, women's, 79, 210, 216

Douglas, Amelia, 5n6

versus boys, 117–18
influenza epidemic, 63, 119–21
institutions, 22, 24, 38
International Council of Women
(ICW), 146–47, 150
internment policies, 75
Ishbel and the Empire, 148

Jewish refugees, 75
journalists, 255–56
Judicial Committee of the Privy
Council of Great Britain, 41n27,
74, 181, 223, 254

Kaufman, A.R., 124
Keefer, Betsy Starr, 146n12
Kennedy, John F., 186
Khartoum, Siege of, 60, 89
kinship network, 94–95, 97
Knights of Labour, 216
Korean War, 78

labour, division of, 214–15
labour force: acceptance of
women in, 121; attention paid
to women in, 230–31; increase
of women in, 3–4, 90, 129, 218;
married women in, 82, 83, 201,
209, 213, 223, 226, 228; mothers in, 83; post–World War I, 72;
post–World War II, 79, 83, 226,
227–28; single women in, 201–2,
223. *See also* employment
Labour Force Survey, 230, 233
labour laws, 178, 243
labour movement, 65–66, 216,
224–25
language rights: education and,
163–64
Laporte, Pierre, 256
Laurier, Wilfrid, 68
Lavell, Jeannette Corbiere, 57, 178,
258
law, practice of: entry of women
into, 189, 191
laws, 12, 20; attempts to

harmonize, 53–54; British and
French in colonies, 28–29, 37;
Canadian, 25–26, 37, 179–80;
changes to, 48, 101–2, 184; civil
and marital, 53; division of powers and, 37–38; divorce, 48–49,
54, 182–84; employment, 178;
equality rights, 177–84; labour,
243; marital property, 43–55, 97;
in Quebec, 26, 37
lawyers, women, 189–94, 204, 246
leadership, 143
League for Women's Rights, 154,
155
legal rights, 11, 20, 95, 136, 195,
251, 258, 259; Aboriginal women
and, 4, 5, 106, 179, 253, 255, 258;
Confederation and, 30–43; citizenship and, 3, 30; Constitution
and, vii, 30, 35, 235; divorce and,
41–42, 49, 102; dower rights,
49–50; illegitimate children
and, 99, 100, 131; in labour
market, 214–23; marital property and, 43–55; minorities and,
36, 163–4; social change and,
182–84. *See also* equality rights;
suffrage (voting rights)
life expectancy, 90, 99, 110
life experiences: 1860s woman,
5–7, 91–95; 1960s woman, 7–10,
95–99; contemporary woman,
10–11, 99–102
livelihoods, of women and families, 201–2
Llandovery Castle, 63
Local Council of Women (BC), 47
Locke, John, 31, 31n7, 36n19
Lower Canada, 28

MacAdams, Roberta, 70–71
Macdonald, Heidi, 206
Macdonald, John A., 28, 32–33n14,
33–34, 40, 71; first wife Isabella,
33, 94; second wife Agnes, 6–7,
33, 94